JOHN BROWN
The Making of a Revolutionary

JOHN BROWN
The Making of a Revolutionary

THE STORY OF JOHN BROWN
IN HIS OWN WORDS
AND IN THE WORDS OF THOSE
WHO KNEW HIM

(Originally published under the title *A John Brown Reader*)

Edited and with Introductions
and Commentary
by
LOUIS RUCHAMES

The Universal Library
GROSSET & DUNLAP
New York

TO MIRIAM

I would sing how an old man, tall, with white hair,
  mounted the scaffold in Virginia
(I was at hand, silent I stood with teeth shut close, I watch'd,
I stood very near you old man when cool and indifferent,
  but trembling with age and your unheal'd wounds
  you mounted the scaffold)

Walt Whitman
Year of Meteors [*1859-60*]

ACKNOWLEDGMENTS

The following selection is reprinted with the kind permission of the publisher: "John Brown and Sons in Kansas" by Salmon Brown; reprinted by permission of the *Indiana Magazine of History*.

* * *

I wish to express my appreciation to those whose counsel and assistance have been helpful in the preparation of this anthology. Many libraries and historical societies have placed their collections of John Brown letters and manuscripts at my disposal and provided photostats and typescripts of needed materials. They include the Kansas Historical Society, whose staff member, Miss Elsie Beine, and treasurer, Mrs. Lela Barnes, were exceptionally helpful; the Henry E. Huntington Library and Art Gallery, the University of Rochester Library, the Cornell University Library, the Historical Society of Pennsylvania, Yale University Library, the Library of Congress, Boston Public Library, Houghton Library of Harvard University, the Historical Society of Pennsylvania, Storer College, the Maryland Historical Society, Columbia University Library (particularly Miss Alice Bonnell), the Illinois State Historical Library, the Ohio Historical Society, the Massachusetts Historical Society, the Chicago Historical Society, the New York Public Library, the Western Reserve Historical Society, Torrington Public Library, Springfield (Mass.) Public Library, and the Connecticut Valley Historical Society (particularly Miss Juliette Tomlinson).

I am grateful to the Research Council of the University of Massachusetts for generously providing a research grant and to Provost Shannon McCune for his interest and encouragement.

Miss Ada Remington, of Osawatomie, Kansas, was most helpful during the early part of my research. I am deeply indebted to Dr. Clarence S. Gee, of Lockport, New York, who has provided much valuable information out of his wide knowledge of all matters relating to John Brown, and especially genealogy. He has also placed at my disposal copies of original letters and other items out of his fine collection of John Brown materials and has read the entire manuscript and made valuable comments.

To Mr. Boyd B. Stutler, the master of all scholars interested in John Brown, who placed his vast manuscript collection of John Brown materials, his library, and his knowledge at my disposal, no expression of gratitude would be adequate. He provided numerous photostats and typescripts of original letters, diligently answered requests for information, and, after the completion of the manuscript, read it in its entirety. His corrections and suggestions for improvement have been invaluable. His devotion to truth and learning has been an inspiration.

Finally, it was Professor Sidney Kaplan, of the University of Massachusetts, who first suggested the need for a John Brown anthology and provided the encouragement that helped get it under way. He also read the Introduction and offered many helpful suggestions; to him my sincere thanks.

L. R.
1959

This book first appeared in 1959 as *A John Brown Reader*. Its new title is more representative of the true purpose of this collection: to portray John Brown, in life and death, as one of the great revolutionaries in American history. Several selections from Part Three of the original volume have been eliminated and the remainder have been placed at the end of Part Two. There is a new Introduction, "John Brown in the Light of History and Ethics," and a detailed Table of Contents has also been added. Over the past ten years the confrontation of Americans, black and white, with the issue of civil liberties and rights for all has borne out the influence of John Brown's ideas and actions; this book affirms our recognition of his role in our nation's past, present and future.

I wish to express my thanks to Joseph Greene, editor of Grosset & Dunlap, for his interest in reprinting the book, and to Miss Paula Cohn for her editorial assistance.

L. R.
1969

CONTENTS

JOHN BROWN IN THE LIGHT OF HISTORY
AND ETHICS

A Universal Library Introduction

There are three types of revolutionaries: (1) those who spend many years planning and hoping for a revolution which never comes because conditions never seem quite ripe for action; (2) those who initiate revolution and succeed in bringing it to fruition; and (3) those who make the attempt and fail.

It is to this last category that the subject of our book, John Brown, apparently belongs. He spent the better part of his life in preparing for a revolution that was designed, ultimately, to overthrow slavery in the South, yet his efforts came to naught in a matter of two days. In one very important sense, Brown was a failure. Yet in a more profound sense the categories of success and failure are less relevant in evaluating his life than those of ethics and morality. Thus, the most valuable questions concerning Brown's life and his final act at Harpers Ferry are those which ask, first, whether he was justified in doing what he did, and whether his action was what any American with a strong sense of justice and a feeling of identity with the oppressed should have felt impelled to do in the year 1859; and second, what lessons in social and personal ethics are to be learned from a study of his life and death.

The theme of the life and death of John Brown is one man's answer to the question, "Am I my brother's keeper?" To what extent should a man identify with the oppressed, the persecuted, and the impoverished of this world? How far should his efforts in their behalf go? How far, his sacrifices? Is the sacrifice of time and effort and a small part of one's material means sufficient, or, if necessary, should these be followed by the sacrifice of all one's material possessions, and even life itself?

Throughout the ages, in every generation, John Brown's answer of total identification with the oppressed has been given by only a few, the revolutionaries and radicals, themselves despised and frequently hunted. When Brown decided to invade Harpers Ferry and forcefully to liberate the slaves of the South, he was attacking a system which had existed within the borders of the United States for two hundred and forty years, since the first boatload of Negro slaves landed on the shores of Virginia in 1619. Their numbers had increased, through kidnappings from Africa as well as by natural

15

means, to 500,000 or more in 1790; 2,000,000 in 1830; and 4,000,-000 in 1860.

At the time of the Revolution, many of the Founding Fathers, even those who were slaveholders, had qualms about fighting for their own freedom while keeping the Negro enslaved; and it seemed that slavery might be abolished. But, principle gave way to expediency when Georgia and South Carolina demanded protection for slavery as their price for joining the Union and ratifying the Constitution. The result was that the Constitution which provided the guidelines of freedom for a newly created nation forged strengthened chains for the enslaved Negro. It did so covertly, for not once did it mention slavery or the slave; yet it permitted the existence of slavery; it placed power over the institution in the hands of state governments committed to it; it provided for the enforced return of fugitive slaves; and it promised the use of the armed forces of the Federal Government to put down insurrections by slaves or their friends. As the years passed, slavery grew stronger and slaveholders increased in wealth and political power. Most Presidents of the United States were either slaveholders or friends of slavery.

In 1846, the country fought a war with Mexico to wrest territory from it—so anti-slavery men believed—to permit the expansion of slavery. In 1857, the Supreme Court determined to lend its support to the institution by decreeing that Negroes in the United States had no rights which the white man was bound to respect and that the Missouri Compromise, which had limited the expansion of slavery, was unconstitutional. At the time of Brown's assault on Harpers Ferry, the slave system prevailed in fifteen states, with eight million whites ruling over a population of four million Negroes who were treated as chattels, bought and sold at the whim of their owners, without any right of protest. Barred by law from an education, unable to testify in a court of law against any slaveholder, subjected to flogging, torture and even death for insubordination or attempting to escape, slaves lived under a dictatorship as severe and formidable as any in history.

Brown was not the first American to desire freedom for the slave. His predecessors included Benjamin Franklin, Thomas Paine, and John Jay—to name but three of the Founding Fathers—Benjamin Lundy, William Lloyd Garrison, Wendell Phillips, Theodore Weld, and many, many others. These men had one thing in common. Abjuring the use of force, they proposed to free the slave peacefully, through persuasion and the use of public opinion. Although by the

16

1850's public opinion in the North had been educated to the evil of slavery, the institution itself had grown. The anti-slavery men led by Garrison and Phillips saw no possibility of eliminating slavery under the Constitution, and in the 1840's were urging Northern secession from the Union as the one way of helping the slave. In 1859 both major political parties were committed to the maintenance of slavery where it already existed and to the enforcement of the Fugitive Slave Law of 1850. The Republican Party, as the political party of the anti-slavery men of the day, opposed only slavery's expansion, not its continuance in the South.

To John Brown, who had attended many anti-slavery meetings, had read William Lloyd Garrison's *Liberator* and a great deal of other anti-slavery literature, and knew many of the anti-slavery leaders of his day, both personally and through their writings, the failure of peaceful means to liberate the slave was obvious, as it was to many other anti-slavery men. He had met slaveholders and their sympathizers on his way to Kansas and in Kansas in 1855 and 1856. His experience was best exemplified in an encounter he is supposed to have had with a Missourian on the way to Kansas in 1855. The Missourian asked him, "Whar you going?" "To Osawatomie," Brown replied. "Whar you from?" "New York." "You'll never live to git thar," said the Missourian. "We are prepared not to die alone," answered Brown quietly, and the Missourian slouched off.

Brown had learned that slavery was an institution based upon force and terror, with slaveholders willing to use every means, including killing, to keep their property. Slavery was a state of war by the slaveholders against the slaves, and it was for this reason that Victor Hugo once stated that "Certainly, if insurrection be ever a sacred duty, it is against slavery." Brown knew that against men who never hesitated to use force and violence to keep their slaves, whose property in slaves was protected by the Constitution itself, and who would never accept the liberation of their slaves even if, in the very unlikely eventuality, they were liberated by constitutional means, the only recourse left to anyone with a sense of justice and compassion for the slave was forceful liberation.

That the North, in its innermost conscience, was beginning to accept this view is shown by the change in public opinion which occurred between the announcement of Brown's attack and his execution. The earliest public reactions were of amazement and disbelief. The possibilities of success were so slight, the forces raised against him so great, that only a madman would undertake so impossible a task. But as people watched Brown's behavior in court, read his speeches to judge and jury and his letters from prison, more and more came over to his side and many who had condemned began to admire and justify.

Those who in his day best represented the conscience of America in thought and letters regarded him as a saint and a hero. Three examples will suffice. Emerson, in an address in Boston in November, 1859, predicted that Brown's martyrdom "will make the gallows as glorious as the cross," and after the hanging remarked that "all people, in proportion to their sensibility and self-respect, sympathize with him." Thoreau, the first American to speak publicly in defense of Brown, remarked in a eulogy several months after Brown's execution that "I never hear of any particularly brave and earnest man, but my first thought is of John Brown, and what relation he may be to him. I meet him at every turn. He is more alive than ever he was. He has earned immortality. He is not confined to North Elba nor to Kansas. He is no longer working in secret. He works in public, and in the clearest light that shines on this land." And Theodore Parker, the great scholar and Unitarian minister, one of Brown's earliest supporters, wrote in November, 1859: "I think there have been few spirits more pure and devoted than John Brown's, and none that gave up their breath in a nobler cause. Let the American state hang his body, and the American Church damn his soul; still, the blessing of such as are ready to perish will fall on him; and the universal justice of the Infinitely perfect God will take him welcome home. The road to heaven is as short from the gallows as from a throne; perhaps, also, as easy."

On the day of his execution, Brown gave the following message to one of his guards: "I John Brown am now quite *certain* that the crimes of this *guilty, land:* will never be purged *away;* but with Blood. I had *as I now* think: *vainly* flattered myself that without *verry* much bloodshed; it might be done." When the Civil War came, many in the North realized that Brown's prediction had come true, that slavery, which had survived through force and violence, would have to be destroyed by the very same means.

Yet, ultimately, the message of John Brown is a far greater and nobler one. It speaks of man's compassion for man, of identification with the poor and the lowly, of the unity of all men, black, white and yellow, of justice and a love so great that all that one has and is may be given to affirm the brotherhood and equality of all men.

18

JOHN BROWN IN THE AMERICAN TRADITION

An Introduction

IT is a hundred years since John Brown was hanged at Charlestown, Virginia on December 2, 1859, for his attack on Harpers Ferry. Perry Miller, in his study of Jonathan Edwards, refers to Harpers Ferry as a part of "the symbolism of America." As a symbol, Brown's desperate attack upon Harpers Ferry on Sunday night, October 16, 1859, has had different and frequently contradictory meanings for different groups. To the slaveholder and his sympathizers, both North and South, it was a criminal and murderous attack upon an institution sanctioned by law and justified by an ideology which regarded slavery as part of the very nature of things, with the white man born to rule and the Negro to serve. Brown was therefore a murderer and criminal who sought " to incite slaves to murder helpless women and children." His courageous behavior at his trial and execution was no more worthy of veneration than the similar behavior of any criminal. "Pirates have died as resolutely as martyrs," said the Baltimore *American*. "If the firmness displayed by John Brown proves anything, the composure of a Thug, dying by the cord with which he had strangled so many victims, proves just as much."

To many Southerners, the attack was an earnest of what could and would happen, multiplied tenfold, under a government not totally committed to a defense of slavery. The thought of a possible Republican victory in the forthcoming election of November, 1860, when seen by Southerners in the context of Harpers Ferry, caused almost hysterical alarm. In the Senate, during the following January, Robert Toombs counseled his people, "Never permit this Federal government to pass into the hands of the black Republican party. It has already declared war against you and your institutions. It every day commits acts of war against you : it has already compelled you to arm for your defence. . . . Defend yourselves! The enemy is at your door, wait not to meet him at your hearthstone; meet him at the doorsill, and drive him from the Temple of Liberty, or pull down its pillars and involve him in a common ruin."

On the other hand, in Northern anti-slavery circles, Brown represented the highest idealism : the willingness to sacrifice one's life and possessions for the freedom and welfare of one's fellow men. In a lecture on November 8, 1859, in Boston, Emerson referred to Brown as "The Saint, whose fate yet hangs in suspense, but whose martyrdom, if it shall be perfected, will make the gallows as glorious as the Cross." In an address delivered in Concord almost two weeks after Harpers Ferry, Thoreau remarked that "when I think of him, and his six sons, and his son-in-law, not to enumerate the others, enlisted for this fight, proceeding coolly, reverently, humanely to work, for months, if not years . . . without expecting any reward but a good conscience, while almost all America stood ranked on the other side, —I say again, that it affects me as a sublime spectacle." Thoreau indeed anticipated his friend Emerson in comparing Brown to Jesus. "Some eighteen hundred years ago Christ was crucified; this morning, perchance, Captain Brown was hung. These are the two ends of a chain which is not without its links. He is not Old Brown any longer; he is an angel of light." Wendell Phillips, who had devoted the previous twenty-five years to the anti-slavery movement, went so far as to regard Harpers Ferry as the beginning of emancipation. Invoking Brown as "marvellous old man," he said : "History will date Virginia Emancipation from Harper's Ferry. True, the slave is still there. So, when the tempest uproots a pine on your hills, it looks green for months,—a year or two. Still, it is timber, not a tree. John Brown has loosened the roots of the slave system; it only breathes,—it does not live,—hereafter."

Few events in American history provide so vivid an illustration of the thesis that the historian's evaluations of men and events are dependent not upon facts alone but upon the basic premises from which he views those facts. It is his "inarticulate major premises," as Oliver Wendell Holmes aptly put it, that determine his judgments. In the case of Brown, the determining factor in all judgments, whether of the ordinary citizen or the scholar, was one's attitude toward slavery. To those who regarded slavery as "the sum of all villainies," as legalized kidnapping maintained by jails, the lash, and, ultimately, the death penalty for those who sought to secure their freedom or to help others do so, Brown's action was one of great idealism and placed him in the company of the great liberators of mankind. Theodore Parker, the great Unitarian clergyman and Abolitionist, expressed this point of view as ably and frankly as anyone, in a letter to Francis Jackson, an outstanding anti-slavery leader in Boston. "A man held against his will as a slave," he wrote, "has a natural right to kill every one who seeks to prevent his enjoyment of liberty. The freeman has a natural right to help the slaves recover their liberty, and in that enterprise to do for them all which they have a right to do for themselves." After asserting the duty of one man to help another get rid of a wolf or a murderer in case of an attack, he asks: "Suppose it is not a murderer who would kill you, but a kidnapper who would enslave, does that make it less my duty to help you out of the hands of your enemy? Suppose it is not a kidnapper who would make you a bondman, but a slaveholder who would keep you one, does that remove my obligation to help you?" In the light of these opinions one can well appreciate Parker's final judgment that "there have been few spirits more pure and devoted than John Brown's, and none that gave up their breath in a nobler cause. Let the American State hang his body, and the American Church damn his soul; still, the blessing of such as are ready to perish will fall on him, and the universal justice of the Infinitely Perfect God will take him welcome home. The road to heaven is as short from the gallows as from a throne; perhaps, also, as easy." Even men like Garrison, who were non-resistants, and did not themselves wish to use force to achieve freedom for the slave, cheered Brown's effort as a valid alternative to continued slavery. "Rather than see men wearing their chains in a cowardly and servile spirit," he said at a meeting memorializing Brown, "I would, as an advocate of peace, much rather see them breaking the head of the tyrant with their chains. Give me, as a non-resistant, Bunker Hill, and Lexington, and Concord, rather than the cowardice and servility of a Southern slave-plantation."

Those whose opposition to slavery was only lukewarm, whose dislike of the institution led them to oppose its extension but was not sufficiently strong to cause them to strive for its elimination in the South, condemned Brown's attack and accepted his execution as justified. But they too saw a certain element of nobility in his character and behavior. Samuel J. Kirkwood, Governor of Iowa, expressed this point of view, which was shared by many, when he said: "While the mass of our people utterly condemn the act of John Brown, they feel and they express admiration and sympathy for the disinterestedness of purpose by which they believe he was governed, and for the unflinching courage and calm cheerfulness with which he met the consequences of his failure."

The conflict of ideologies has continued to our own day. The grandson of William Lloyd Garrison, Oswald Garrison Villard, a man of broad humanitarian sympathies, who has written the definitive biography of Brown, concludes his study with this observation, "The story of John Brown will ever confront the spirit of despotism, when men are struggling to throw off the shackles of social or political or physical slavery. His own country, while admitting his mistakes without undue palliation or excuse, will forever acknowledge the divine that was in him by the side of what was human and faulty, and blind and wrong. It will cherish the memory of the prisoner of Charlestown in 1859 as at once a sacred, a solemn and an inspiring American heritage."

In opposition to this point of view stands James Malin,[1] the foremost anti-Brown historian, who seems unable to forgive the North for having used force against Southern secession, or the Abolitionists for having taught that the abolition of slavery would be a step forward for American society, or the Negro for having believed that his welfare would be furthered by the forceful elimination of slavery. To Malin, minor errors of date or place committed by writers who have a high regard for Brown are frequently labeled deliberate falsehoods, while the errors of Brown-haters are simply unintentional blunders. Very few anti-slavery leaders and writers emerge unscathed under Malin's furious onslaught. Typical of his method are his comments on Emerson, Thoreau, Parker and the other leaders of New England opinion, whom he contemptuously refers to as the "New England Transcendental Hierarchy, the self-appointed keepers not only of New England culture, but, according to their own estimates, of national civilization." Following in the footsteps of earlier anti-Brown biographers, such as Hill Peebles Wilson and Robert Penn Warren, Malin refers to the sympathetic evaluation of Brown as "the John Brown legend," a "hoax" created largely by the abovementioned "hierarchy." To expose the "hoax," he concludes, would result in breaking "the spell of its authority" and deflating "other fakes and fakers" as well. Malin has accumulated a wealth of facts in his volume and thereby has induced many historians to accept his point of view, but a closer examination of the book reveals many errors of fact,[2] and an approach which, though it claims to be scien-

[1] James C. Malin, *John Brown and the Legend of Fifty-Six* (Philadelphia: American Philosophical Society, 1942), 794 pp.
[2] For example, on pp. 4-5, one finds at least eight errors in the reproduction of a letter from John Brown to his father. In other parts of the book, names are misspelled and key phrases omitted from documents. It is important to note that in the reconstruction of the events leading to the Pottawatomie killings in Kansas, the reminiscences of members of the Brown family are arbitrarily excluded. Furthermore, the book is based almost exclusively on the materials available in the files of the Kansas State Historical Society. The important collections of John Brown material owned by other state historical societies, the Library of Congress, college libraries, and authorities on John Brown such as Boyd B. Stutler and Dr. Clarence S. Gee are either not used at all or only in a very limited way.

tific, is notably lacking in the dispassionate objectivity of the true scientist.

The purpose of this volume is not, however, the examination of all that has been written about John Brown, whether pro or con, or its evaluation from the point of view of historical accuracy. It is intended, rather, to present the positive impact of John Brown upon American thought, viewing his life and death as events which evoked great idealism as well as some of the noblest and most memorable writing in the history of American letters.

We approach this task from the point of view of those who believe that the struggle against slavery and its elimination during the Civil War was one of the great positive achievements in American history; that the Abolitionists and other anti-slavery leaders, who devoted their lives to the achievement of freedom for the slave and equality of opportunity for Negro and white alike, seeking through their writings and lectures to educate the American public to the evils of slavery, were not paranoiacs or narrow-minded fanatics, but men and women who were devoted to the highest ideals of equality and democracy, influenced by the best in the Judaeo-Christian tradition and all that was good and noble in the thoughts and actions of the Founding Fathers. John Brown was one of this company of anti-slavery men. This anthology, by presenting the John Brown tradition, seeks to contribute to a firmer understanding of one of the vital aspects of American history, as well as to help our own generation, in a small way, toward a greater appreciation of those very ideals which motivated Brown and his friends.

HIS LIFE IN BRIEF

JOHN BROWN was born on May 9, 1800, in Torrington, Connecticut, the second son of Owen and Ruth Mills Brown. According to family tradition, the Browns were descended from Peter Brown of the Mayflower through Peter Brown of Windsor, Connecticut, who was presumed to be the former's son.[1] Both of John Brown's grandfathers fought in the American Army during the Revolution. His mother, Ruth Mills Brown, was descended from Dutch settlers who had come to this country during the seventeenth century. His father, Owen, an anti-slavery man even before John Brown's birth, and an agent of the Underground Railroad, was a God-fearing Congregationalist, who earned a livelihood as farmer, shoemaker and tanner.

In 1805, Owen Brown moved his family to Hudson, Ohio. There John received his education, and grew up as a hard-working, pious and disciplined young man. In the spring of 1816, John made a formal profession of religion and was accepted into the Congregational church at Hudson. Deciding to enter the ministry, with the intention of ultimately preparing for it at Amherst college, he went East with his brother, Salmon, and a friend, Orson Oviatt, and enrolled at a school conducted by the Rev. Moses Hallock in Plainfield, Mass. He stayed there only a few months and transferred in the winter of 1816-17, with his brother and friend, to Morris Academy, near Litchfield, Conn. Litchfield was then, according to Boyd B. Stutler, an "abolition and anti-slavery center, birthplace of Harriet Beecher Stowe, and home of many other notables." Because of an inflammation of the eyes and a lack of funds, John was forced to give up his studies and return home, resuming his work at his father's tannery in Hudson.

At the age of twenty he married Dianthe Lusk, the plain-looking, pious and amiable daughter of a widow who lived near the Brown

---

1 Oswald Garrison Villard, in his biography of John Brown, denied that Peter Brown of Windsor was the son of Peter Brown of the Mayflower. His opinion was based on the researches of several genealogists. Donald Lines Jacobus, editor-in-chief of *The American Genealogist*, has recently re-evaluated all the known facts in the case and has come to the same conclusion. (See his " Peter Brown of Windsor, Conn.," in *The American Genealogist*, XXXIII [October, 1957], 214-222.) However, Dr. Clarence S. Gee, of Lockport, New York, probably the foremost living student of the Brown familly genealogy, maintains the validity of the family tradition.

homestead, whose maiden name was Mary Adams[2] and who traced her ancestry back to the renowned Adams family of Massachusetts. Six years later they moved to Randolph (now New Richmond), Pennsylvania, with their three children, John, Jr., Jason and Owen—there were to be four more children, only two of whom, Ruth and Frederick, were to live to maturity.

The years from 1826 to 1835 were filled with business successes and noteworthy achievements in commercial leadership. Ernest A. Miller, in a pamphlet entitled " John Brown, Pennsylvania Citizen,"[3] has dwelt upon the events of those years. Brown cleared twenty-five acres of land; built a tannery, a log house and a barn—which included a carefully concealed room to hide fugitive slaves escaping to Canada and elsewhere; organized a school for his own children and those of a neighbor; formed a church, which he served as clerk; and helped establish a post office in Randolph, which he served as postmaster. His success as a cattle breeder was notable, his tannery prospered, employing at times as many as fifteen men, and he was generally recognized and looked up to as a valuable member of the community.

This period has justifiably been described as "the most peaceful and prosperous period in the nearly sixty years of his turbulent life."[4] But it was not without its sorrows. In March, 1831, Brown's four-year-old son, Frederick, died and in August, 1832, Brown's wife, Dianthe, thirty-one years old, died a few hours after the death of a new-born infant son. About a year later, Brown remarried, taking as his wife Mary Ann Day, the daughter of a blacksmith who lived fifteen miles from New Richmond. Brown's second wife bore him thirteen children, of whom seven died in childhood and two were slain at Harpers Ferry.

In 1835, attracted by new business opportunities, especially the offer of a partnership in tanning with Zenas Kent, a successful businessman, Brown moved his family to Franklin Mills (now Kent), Portage County, Ohio. The partnership did not materialize but Brown involved himself in land speculation, utilizing, for the most part, borrowed funds. With the onset of the depression of 1837, his speculations failed, leaving him deeply in debt for the rest of his life.

From 1837 to 1844, he tried various sources of income—tanning, breeding race horses, raising sheep, and buying and selling cattle.

---

[2] I am indebted to Dr. Clarence S. Gee for this name. Previous biographers do not mention it.
[3] Published by the Pennsylvania State Press, Warren, Pa., 1952. 27 pp.
[4] Boyd B. Stutler in a Radio Broadcast entitled " Old John Brown of Osawatomie," a chapter in *The American Story*, Number: AS-84, 1956.

With none of these did he succeed in recouping his fortune. In fact, so great had his poverty become that, at one point, he turned to his personal use $2800.00 which had been given him for the purchase of wool by the New England Woolen Company, at Rockville, Conn., through its agent, George Kellogg. Fortunately, the company had no desire to prosecute him and it accepted his pledge to pay the amount in installments, as circumstances would permit. (In 1859, in his last will and testament, Brown bequeathed fifty dollars toward payment of the remainder of his debt.)

His fortunes reached their lowest ebb in 1842, when he was forced into bankruptcy and emerged stripped of almost all his possessions. For years afterwards he was plagued with lawsuits by creditors. To cap his misfortunes, he lost four children, aged nine, six, three and one, in an epidemic during the following year.

In spite of his financial reverses, Brown's reputation for industry and integrity remained intact and in 1844 he entered into a business partnership—the last of his career—with Simon Perkins, a wealthy businessman of Akron, Ohio, whose flock of sheep Brown was to manage. He moved his family from Richfield, Ohio, where they had been living since 1842, to Akron, and there they remained for the next two years. In 1846, the two partners opened an office and wool depot in Springfield, Mass., for the purpose of disposing of wool for Western wool-growers. Brown was placed in charge. Although the wool-growers showed their enthusiasm for the new company's plans by sending in large quantities of wool, the resistance of the wool manufacturers and uncertain business conditions placed the firm in difficulties almost from the beginning. Brown was unable to sell the wool at profitable prices, and although he undertook a trip to Europe, from August to October 1849, to sell the wool abroad, his effort failed disastrously and he returned to a business that was in greater difficulties than ever before. In 1850 it had to be abandoned entirely. Brown returned to Akron, partly to continue farming and sheep-raising in partnership with Perkins, and partly to carry the burden of a multiplicity of lawsuits resulting from their business failure.

Whatever may be said of Brown's lack of business ability, his failure as a businessman in Springfield did not prevent him from achieving an enviable reputation for integrity and honesty. In December, 1859, at a public meeting in Northampton, Mass., held several days after Brown's hanging, Thomas Musgrave, a wool manufacturer of Northampton, who had bought heavily from Perkins & Brown, had this to say of Brown: "I never saw a man more upright in all his dealings than he was. I saw him after he had lost every dollar, and he remarked to me that he was thankful to God that he was yet alive. Men were willing to trust everything in his hands. There was not a man that he ever dealt with that could say that he had ever wronged them out of a single penny. I will say to you, ladies and gentlemen, that whatever he said could be depended upon."[5]

During his years in Springfield, Brown had involved himself increasingly in anti-slavery activities. According to Frederick Douglass, the Negro anti-slavery leader, who visited Brown in Springfield in 1847, Brown attributed the meager furnishings of his home and his rather primitive manner of living to his efforts to save money for a project involving the forceful liberation of slaves. Toward the end of 1847 or the first half of 1848, Brown wrote an essay entitled "Sambo's Mistakes," for *The Ram's Horn*, a Negro newspaper published in New York, in which he urged Negroes to show a more vigorous resistance to their oppressors. In 1851, he organized among the Negroes of Springfield a League of Gileadites, whose purpose it was to resist attempts under the recently enacted Fugitive Slave law to capture fugitive slaves and return them to slavery.

Previously, his desire to help the Negroes induced him to move his family in 1849 from Springfield, where they had been living since 1847, to North Elba, New York, for two years. This step resulted from an offer made in 1846 by Gerrit Smith, of Peterboro, New York, an outstanding anti-slavery philanthropist and political figure, to give one hundred and twenty thousand acres of land in northern New York to Negroes for settlement. Brown decided that he wanted to settle with his family among them "to aid them by example and precept." He purchased 244 acres of farmland from Smith and, until such time as he could erect his own house, rented a farmhouse near North Elba, into which he moved his family in 1849. In spite of Brown's assistance, the Negro settlement at North Elba failed. Brown, beset by numerous lawsuits following the failure of his business in Springfield in 1850, and under an obligation to continue the farming and sheep-raising part of his partnership with Simon Perkins, moved back to Akron, Ohio, with his family, in 1851.

The return to Akron was originally conceived by Brown as a temporary measure. He planned to remain there and to continue working with Perkins only as long as it would take to terminate their partnership and to wind up their affairs. This took longer than

5 *The Hampshire Gazette* (Northampton, Mass.), December 6, 1859.

expected, but by 1854 the partnership of Perkins and Brown came amicably to an end. By then Brown had accumulated sufficient funds to enable him to transport his family back to North Elba, where they moved into an unplastered four-room house built for them by Henry Thompson, Ruth Brown's husband, who had previously set up house-keeping with Ruth in North Elba. It was there that the Browns were still living when John Brown was executed in 1859.

The return to North Elba marks a turning point in Brown's life. Thereafter, he gave up all thoughts of business and devoted himself entirely to the struggle against slavery; first, as a guerrilla leader in Kansas and then in preparation for his attack upon Harpers Ferry.

The passage of the Kansas-Nebraska Act in May, 1854, which provided that the issue of slavery in Kansas and Nebraska was to be decided by the residents of those territories, set off a contest between North and South, with both sides making every effort to pour men and money into the Territory to assure control. John Brown's children, Owen, Frederick and Salmon, dissatisfied with their circumstances in Ohio and eager to lend a helping hand to the forces of freedom in Kansas, left Ohio for Kansas in October, 1854, and arrived there the following spring. They were joined in May by Jason and John, Jr., who arrived with their families. They settled eight miles from Osawatomie, where their uncle, Rev. Samuel Lyle Adair, had settled the previous year. Although in 1854 John Brown had no intention of accompanying his children to Kansas, he seems to have changed his mind at the beginning of 1855. When, in May of that year, he received a letter from John, Jr., stressing an urgent need for arms, he decided to leave for Kansas as soon as possible with whatever arms he could secure. He purchased arms with funds raised at a number of anti-slavery meetings, and arrived in Kansas in October, 1855, accompanied by his son-in-law, Henry Thompson, and his son, Oliver.

Kansas was at the time in the grip of a reign of terror unloosed by pro-slavery Missourians and other Southerners determined on making the Territory safe for slavery. The following remarks by one Missourian leader in a speech at St. Joseph, Missouri, in March, 1855, indicate the policy being pursued: "I tell you to mark every scoundrel among you that is the least tainted with free-soilism, or abolitionism, and exterminate him. Neither give nor take quarter from the d—d rascals. . . . To those having qualms of conscience, as to violating laws, state or national, the time has come when such impositions must be disregarded, as your lives and property are in danger,

28

and I advise you one and all to enter every election district in Kansas, in defiance of Reeder and his vile myrmidons, and vote at the point of the bowie-knife and revolver. Neither give nor take quarter, as our cause demands it. It is enough that the slave-holding interest wills it, from which there is no appeal."[6]

Such advice was implemented by a liberal use of tar and feathers, beatings, murders and attacks upon the homes and crops of Free-State men. Periodically, hordes of armed Missourians would invade the Territory at election time, vote for pro-slavery candidates and return to their homes. One invasion took place in November, 1854, when upward of a thousand armed Missourians crossed into Kansas, voted for a pro-slavery delegate to Congress, and returned home. A second occurred in March, 1855, when at least five thousand men in armed companies crossed into Kansas, voted for a pro-slavery legislature, stuffed ballot boxes and terrorized anti-slavery voters and officials. The legislature they helped to elect proceeded to enact a code of laws which Oswald Garrison Villard has called "one of the foremost monuments of legislative tyranny and malevolence in the history of this country,"[7] and which a pro-slavery leader in Kansas praised as being "more efficient to protect slave property than those of any state in the Union."[8] Only pro-slavery men could hold office or serve as jurors; it was a felony punishable by at least two years' imprisonment to deny the legality of slavery in Kansas, or even to discuss whether slavery in Kansas "exists or does not exist," and death was the penalty for creating dissatisfaction among slaves or inciting them to conspire or rebel.

In effect, not only was slavery thenceforth legal in Kansas but no effort could be made, through democratic methods of expression and assembly, to eliminate it. Such efforts were illegal and punishable by imprisonment and even death. To make matters worse, "every sheriff and probate judge, as well as every other county officer in the Territory was an appointee of the bogus Legislature and a Pro-Slavery man. There were no Free-State officers."[9] The panoply of the law constituted a shield for every violent and lawless pro-slavery action, and an additional means of terror against those who refused to surrender their anti-slavery beliefs.

The months following John Brown's arrival in Kansas, in the fall

[6] Quoted in Sara T. Robinson, *Kansas: Its Interior and Exterior Life.* (Boston, 1857), pp. 14-15. Andrew T. Reeder was the first territorial governor of Kansas.
[7] *John Brown: A Biography Fifty Years After* (New York: Alfred A. Knopf, 1943), p. 91.
[8] Quoted in George Martin, "The First Two Years of Kansas," *Kansas State Historical Society Collections*, X, 132.
[9] Address by Honorable T. Dwight Thacher, *Kansas State Historical Society Collections*, III, 443.

of 1855, were spent by Brown and his sons in building homes, contending with illness, battling freezing temperatures, attending meetings of Free-State settlers and defending the anti-slavery cause. Those months were also marked by a resurgence of violence, slayings of three Free-State settlers within three months, an invasion of Kansas and a threatened attack upon Lawrence in December. Brown and four sons joined other Free-State men in going to the defense of Lawrence. Fortunately, warfare was averted through a last-minute agreement between the Free-State leaders of Lawrence and Wilson Shannon, the pro-slavery Governor of Kansas.

The remaining months of winter were quiet, but this period was, in the words of Charles Robinson, a Free-State leader and later Governor of Kansas, " one of preparation." The onset of spring witnessed new invasions by desperadoes from Missouri, Georgia and Alabama, arrests and attempted arrests of Free-State leaders on charges of treason—punishable by imprisonment and even death—and further killings of Free-State men. These culminated in a descent upon Lawrence on May 20 and 21, by a " swearing, whiskey-drinking, ruffianly horde,"[10] under the command of a United States Marshal, I. B. Donaldson, for the ostensible purpose of serving writs of arrest against a number of Free-State leaders who had been indicted for " constructive treason " by a pro-slavery grand jury. This same grand jury had recommended the abatement of two Free-State newspapers published in Lawrence and of the Free State Hotel in the same city. As a result, several citizens of the city were arrested on charges of treason; the two newspaper offices destroyed; their presses, books and papers thrown into the river; the Free State Hotel bombarded by cannon and set afire; and the home of Charles Robinson razed.

John Brown and his sons, with others from their area, were on their way to the relief of Lawrence when they were met by a messenger on May 22, who informed them of the attack. Outraged by the news, as well as by previous depredations and killings—two young anti-slavery men named John Jones and John Stewart had been killed just prior to the attack on Lawrence—and disgusted by the timid refusal of Free-State leaders to defend themselves from the repeated outrages, Brown decided upon a reprisal which has come to be known as the Pottawatomie killings. On May 23, the day after receiving the news about Lawrence, he led a group of seven men,

10 James Ford Rhodes, *History of the United States*, (New York, 1904), II, 158. Quoted in Villard, *John Brown*, p. 145.

including his sons Owen, Frederick, Salmon, and Oliver, his son-in-law, Henry Thompson, and two others, Theodore Wiener and James Townsley, to the Pottawatomie settlement. On the night of May 24, at midnight, Brown and his men took from their cabins five pro-slavery men who had actively aided the invaders, defended the pro-slavery cause and threatened Free-State settlers in their area, and killed them with broadswords. Although Brown himself did not do any of the killing, he was the leader of the group and was undoubtedly responsible for the conception and execution of the deed.

Contemporary historians have tended to condemn Brown for the killing. At the time it occurred, the Free-State settlers of Kansas took a more sympathetic view of the matter. Judge James Hanway, a leading settler, had this to say in 1878 concerning the attitudes of the settlers in 1856 and later:

". . . So far as public opinion in the neighborhood, where the affair took place, is concerned, I believe I may state that the *first* news of the event produced such a shock that public opinion was considerably divided; but after the whole circumstances became known, there was a reaction in public opinion and the Free State settlers who had claims on the creek considered that Capt. Brown and his party of eight had performed a justifiable act, which saved their homes and dwellings from threatened raids of the pro-slavery party."[11] There is no doubt that if one judges the killings in isolation from other events of the day, the resulting judgment will be one of condemnation. However, if they are placed within their historical context, a different view will tend to emerge. What must have been Brown's state of mind on the night of the killings was expressed in a dispatch from Leavenworth, Kansas, on May 20, which appeared in the New York *Daily Tribune* on May 30, 1856: "No man's life is safe; no kind of property secure. A Guerrilla war exists in Kansas, and unless the people in the States come to our rescue and relief speedily, we shall all likewise perish." Brown, instead of supinely waiting for help from outside the Territory, took matters into his own hands.

Further insight into the situation is given by two hitherto unpublished letters. One is by Rev. Samuel Lyle Adair, John Brown's brother-in-law, as mild and decent a person as one could find in the Territory; the other, by his wife Florilla. Writing on May 16, 1856, Florilla Adair tells of the fear of death with which the Free-State settlers in and near Osawatomie lived. "It is believed that Osawa-

[11] Ms. by James Hanway in Kansas Historical Society. Quoted in Villard, *op. cit.*, p. 170.

31

tomie is in danger any day or night. You ask in one of your letters if we have any fear of our lives. I think now we are constantly exposed and we have almost no protection. . . . A few have their guns and revolvers, but as a people and place we are without even these and the place is known and called an *abolition nest.* . . ."[12]

The letter by Rev. Samuel Adair was written several days after the Pottawatomie killings.[13] It expresses what must also have been the reaction of many of Adair's neighbors: that the killings, as reprisals, were a hopeful sign of resistance to the pro-slavery terror. The letter first refers to a previous one in which the attack on Lawrence had been described. It then continues:

> I now add that the houses of citizens were entered, money, arms, & goods at the peril of life were demanded. And in this way the citizens were robbed of about Fifty Thousand Dollars in money, arms, & goods. Horses & cattle, etc., etc., were taken; & not only was this done in Lawrence, but also by guerilla parties that went in different directions among the people of the country.
>
> But, it has been found that gun which they have been firing is beginning to kick, & it is not certain whether it will not produce greater terror, & do more execution at the brick [breech] than it has yet done at the mussle [muzzle].
>
> The assassination of Jones a few weeks ago was a mere flash in a pan, or the bursting of a cap, as an experiment to see what the effect would be. You will recollect the murder of Dow last November—of Barber in Dec. of Brown in Jan. of Jones & Steward, last week; or a thousand other outrages. Five Free State men shot or butchered: not only did not [sic] did bogus authority refuse to lift a finger to bring to justice these murderers, but has shielded them. The U.S. territorial officers have done the same. Now what is the result? Guerilla parties are now forming & organizing through all the territory. A decent was made by one party on Saturday night last & five pro-slavery men were shot or butchered in one night. Some of them had made threats, had threatened the lives of Free State men—had acted most outrageously for some time past—they probably were dreaming of no danger to themselves. Some of them were taken from their beds and almost literally hewed to peices [sic] with broad swords. The scene of these desperate deeds, is only about eight miles from us. The excitement

12 Copy in the Villard Collection, Columbia University Library. The letter is addressed to " Dear Sister Martha."
13 Copy in the Villard Collection, Columbia University Library. It is addressed to " Dear Bro. & Sis. Hand & Other Friends."

produced has been most tremendous. Money, arms, horses, etc. were taken. Some pro-slavery men took the alarm & fled—many free state also left their houses for a few nights. Runners were sent to Missourie, for help.—And pro-slavery men in different localities gathered together or stood in fear of their lives. Missourie troops have not come and it is thought they will not come in large numbers and it is well for them not to. But if they do, they may expect to find one of their party dead when they return, a house burnt, a horse stolen, as the case may be when they return. As many pro-slavery men must die as free state men are killed by them, and they will not be particular who he is, so he is one who has made himself officious in Kansas matters. "Eye for eye, tooth for tooth" —dollar for dollar & compound interest in some cases may be demanded.

There is much reason to believe that John B. Sen. & sons—J-jun, & Jason excepted, who were with the company encamped near the Santa Fe road at the time of the transaction—were with the company that did the deed. John & Jason have been taken & are now before court at Batteeses—8 miles from here—. An effort was made to take Owen, but did not succeed. John & Jason can be proved clear of any participation in the act by more than one hundred men. Yet we know not what will be done with them. Their wives and children are with us. The rest of the men, are armed to the teeth & out some where, we know not where. Pro-slavery men are in terror, for if this is the beginning of the discharges of a gun they have been shooting when turned the other way they know not what the end will be.

During the ensuing months, Brown and his men went into hiding, but Jason and John, Jr., who had not participated in the killings, were captured by pro-slavery forces and Federal troops and imprisoned They were later released, Jason in June and John in September. In the meantime, John Brown's reputation as a guerrilla leader grew. On June 2, he defeated and captured a force of twenty-three pro-slavery men headed by Henry Clay Pate, a captain in the Missouri militia, deputy United States Marshal and newspaper correspondent. At the end of August, he fought a skirmish at Osawatomie in which he led a band of thirty or forty men against two hundred and fifty commanded by a Mexican War veteran, John W. Reid. Though badly outnumbered, Brown fought back hard and succeeded in escaping with the bulk of his force. Prior to the engagement, his son,

33

Frederick, had been killed by the vanguard of Reid's force, and afterward, Osawatomie itself was burned. Brown participated in other guerrilla engagements, but by the fall of 1856, under the vigorous administration of a new Governor, John W. Geary, much of the warfare had ceased and conditions in Kansas grew relatively quiet. Feeling that he was no longer needed, Brown decided to return East. Henry Thompson, Oliver and Salmon, fed up with the fighting and killing, had left in August and at the beginning of October, Brown, with John, Jr., Jason and Owen crossed over from Kansas to Iowa.

As he left Kansas, Brown was carrying a letter from Charles Robinson, a Free-State leader and first Governor of Kansas. About two decades after Brown's death, Robinson turned into a mortal enemy of Brown's memory, but in 1856, he wrote the following:[14]

Lawrence, Sept 15, 1856.

Capt. John Brown: My Dear Sir:—I take this opportunity to express to you my sincere gratification that the late report that you were among the killed at the battle of Osawatomie is incorrect.

Your course, so far as I have been informed, has been such as to merit the highest praise from every patriot, and I cheerfully accord to you my heartfelt thanks for your prompt, efficient and timely action against the invaders of our rights and the murderers of our citizens. History will give your name a proud place on her pages, and posterity will pay homage to your heroism in the cause of God and Humanity.

Trusting that you will conclude to remain in Kansas and serve during the war the cause you have done so much to sustain, and with earnest prayers for your health and protection from the shafts of Death that so thickly beset your path, I subscribe myself,

Very respectfully

Your Ob't Servant

C. Robinson

It was at the beginning of 1857 that Brown reached Boston. He met the city's outstanding philanthropists, scholars and anti-slavery leaders, and impressed them with his abilities as a leader of men and with his sincerity and devotion to the anti-slavery cause. During his stay in Boston and other Eastern cities he succeeded in enlisting the moral and financial support of a secret committee of men who served as his devoted backers during the ensuing years. These were

[14] Printed in Villard, op. cit., pp. 262-3.

Gerrit Smith, Dr. Samuel G. Howe, Thomas Wentworth Higginson, George L. Stearns, Theodore Parker and Franklin B. Sanborn. However, in 1857, their knowledge of his plans included only future forays in Kansas. It was not until the following year that they learned of the projected attack in Virginia.

In March, 1857, in New York, Brown met Hugh Forbes, a British soldier-of-fortune, who had fought under Garibaldi in Italy. Impressed by his knowledge and ability, Brown hired Forbes to train recruits for service in Kansas and Virginia. Ultimately, Forbes proved a greater hindrance than help. He broke with Brown in 1858, when the plan for the attack on Virginia had already matured, and then threatened to publicize the entire scheme. As a result, Brown was forced to postpone his plans for an entire year.

Brown spent a good part of the spring and summer of 1857 in raising funds for future campaigns in Kansas, and at the beginning of November he was back in the Territory. But he found little to do there. Conditions had quieted considerably, the Free-State settlers had scored significant successes at the polls, and Governor Robert J. Walker of Mississippi, who had succeeded Governor Geary, seemed sincerely interested in preventing fraudulent voting. Brown left Kansas before the end of November, but not before he had made another important decision: to launch the attack on Harpers Ferry as soon as possible. By the time he left Kansas, he had already enlisted ten recruits, including his son Owen.

He brought his men to Springdale, Iowa, found quarters for them and then headed East to meet with his supporters and to secure their financial help. He spent three weeks with Frederick Douglass in Rochester, visited with Gerrit Smith, Sanborn and others in Peterboro, New York, saw Higginson, Parker, Howe, Sanborn and Stearns in Boston, and spent some time in Canada, where he visited St. Catherine's, Ingersoll, Chatham and Toronto, and met many leaders of the Negro communities. He decided to hold a convention of his followers at Chatham, returned to Springdale where he gathered his men and brought them back to Chatham.

The convention opened on May 8, 1858. Present were Brown's party of twelve, including himself, and thirty-five Negroes. To allay suspicion, it was announced that the purpose of the convention was to organize a Masonic lodge among Negroes. The presiding officer was Rev. William Charles Munroe, pastor of a Detroit Negro church; the secretary, John H. Kagi, was later killed at Harpers Ferry. The proceedings included an address by Brown, in which he pre-

35

sented his plans, the adoption of a "Provisional Constitution and Ordinances for the People of the United States," and the election of officers.

Brown's plan, apparently, was to move from the convention to the point of attack in Virginia. But he had not reckoned on the intervention of Forbes. While the convention was yet in session it was learned that Forbes had revealed the substance of the plans to certain political leaders. Brown's backers, with the exception of Higginson, were terrified and demanded that the entire project be abandoned for the time being. Brown acceded to their demands and directed his steps toward Kansas, re-entering the territory at the end of June, where he lived under the name of Shubel Morgan. He spent most of his time in southeastern Kansas, where James Montgomery, a Free-State guerrilla leader, had been operating. Brown's most famous exploit while there was a foray into Missouri, on December 20, where he and his men forcefully liberated eleven Negro slaves, brought them safely to Canada—a distance of eleven hundred miles —in eighty-two days, with the authorities constantly on their heels and a price of $250.00 on Brown's head.

As the spring of 1859 approached, the fears occasioned by Forbes's revelations subsided, and Brown felt ready for the move which had been his ultimate goal for twenty years. He rented the Kennedy Farm in Maryland, at the beginning of July, used it as a base for preparations, and on the night of October 16 set out with eighteen of his men—leaving three behind at the farm—to capture Harpers Ferry. Harpers Ferry was chosen because within it were located a United States Armory and Arsenal, which could provide arms for the numerous slaves who were expected to flock to Brown's standard. The town was taken without difficulty, but Brown delayed unnecessarily. By Monday afternoon he was surrounded by the Virginia militia and escape became impossible. On Tuesday morning, the doors of the engine house in which Brown and his surviving men had taken refuge were battered down by U.S. Marines under the command of Colonel Robert E. Lee, and the battle was over.

The raid had proven a failure. The slaves had not been liberated nor did they rise to assist those who sought to free them. Of the twenty-two men comprising the "Army of Liberation," five escaped, ten were killed and seven, including Brown, captured and hanged later. Other casualties included seven dead—a free Negro, two slaves, a Marine and three white citizens—and ten wounded.

Brown was brought to trial on October 25, a week after capture, and was found guilty six days later of three crimes: conspiring with slaves to rebel, murder and treason. Though his lawyers sought to enter a plea of insanity on the basis of affidavits received from residents of Ohio, he rejected the attempts and refused to permit any such plea. Concerning the trial itself, Richard B. Morris, the well-known historian, notes that it was "flagrantly unfair."

The right of the accused to a reasonable time to prepare for trial was shockingly violated. Brown was forced to stand trial the very same day he was indicted. Scrupulous though the court was to provide the accused with competent trial counsel, it erroneously denied him the right to engage lawyers of his own choice. When, finally, his own counsel took over, they were given no time to familiarize themselves with the case against their client.

To this catalogue of judicial errors must be added a last one: John Brown was tried and sentenced for a crime of which he could not conceivably have been guilty. How the accused could have committed treason against Virginia when he was neither a citizen nor a resident of that state and owed it no allegiance was never clarified by the law-enforcement authorities. Objectivity and reason gave way to hysteria and vigilantism. This was no time for technicalities. It was enough that John Brown be convicted of a crime carrying the capital penalty and that the sentence of the court be carried out with expedition.[15]

Morris also suggests that Brown should have been examined by an alienist or psychiatrist, and implies that if he had been, he might never have been brought to trial. As has just been indicated, efforts were made during the trial to have him adjudged insane. On the second day of the trial, Brown's lawyer received a telegram from A. H. Lewis of Akron, Ohio, editor of the *Summit Beacon*, emphasizing that insanity was hereditary in Brown's family on his mother's side. After the trial, in a further attempt to secure clemency, nineteen affidavits, gathered by one of Brown's lawyers from relatives and friends in Ohio, repeated the same information and added that Brown was insane on the subject of slavery. At one point, Governor Wise issued an order to have Brown examined by an alienist, but then countermanded the order.

As to whether Brown was or was not insane, the best answer lies in an examination of his behavior at the trial and afterward. Cer-

15 Richard B. Morris, *Fair Trial*. (New York: Alfred A. Knopf, 1953), pp. 259-260.

tainly, his remarks and actions at the trial show no indication of insanity, nor has it ever been alleged that they do. His speech to the court before sentence was pronounced is regarded by many as one of the finest utterances in American literature; Emerson, indeed, compared it in later years to Lincoln's Gettysburg address. His letters from prison are models of lucidity and breathe a rare nobility of thought and character. " No lunatic," writes Villard, " ever penned such elevated and high-minded, and such consistent epistles."[16] Brown's concentration upon slavery and its evils throughout the latter part of his life, which is the usual reason given for alleging his insanity, was indeed intense and unusual for his day. But it was not unusual when compared to that of such men and women as William Lloyd Garrison, Wendell Phillips, Lydia Maria Child, Theodore Parker, Charles Sumner, Maria Weston Chapman and Parker Pillsbury, to name but a few, who devoted their lives to the anti-slavery cause, suffered hardships and privations for its sake, and at various occasions were also accused of being fanatics and insane on the subject of slavery. The lesson to be learned from their example is simply that to be deeply sensitive to injustice, to be willing to devote one's life to an unpopular cause, to give up the pursuit of one's own gain to alleviate the suffering of others, involves running the risk of being called fanatic and even insane by the smug, the callous and the well-placed members of society. " The prophet is a fool, the man of the spirit is mad! " has echoed through the ages, from the days of Hosea to our own.

Finally, perhaps the most important evidence as to the nature of John Brown's mind and character is to be found in the devotion to him of the twenty-one young men—intelligent, able and high-minded—who lived with him and knew him as a leader and a friend, and who followed him even unto death.[17]

[16] *Op. cit.*, p. 509.

[17] Among recent historians, Professors C. Vann Woodward and Allan Nevins have emphasized the case for Brown's insanity. Prof. Vann Woodward has made much of the nineteen affidavits testifying to insanity in Brown's family, especially on his mother's side, and to Brown's own insanity or " monomania " on the question of slavery. Putting aside the basic question of whether one's insanity may be established by the presence or absence of insanity in one's family, it may be noted that the affidavits are highly suspect as valid evidence. Their primary purpose was to save Brown from execution by showing him to be insane. They must, therefore, be regarded not as objective reports but as partisan statements made to achieve a certain purpose, with every possibility that the material they present may be biased in the direction of proving insanity. Moreover, their reliability as evidence is weakened still further by the fact that they include significant sections which are based, quite explicitly, not on direct knowledge but on hearsay and secondhand information.

By accepting the affidavits at their face value, Prof. Vann Woodward, though a very careful historian, is led into committing several errors. He states, for instance, that one of Brown's brothers was insane. This assertion is made in only one of the affidavits and is not substantiated by any evidence. The brother referred to was the editor of the New Orleans *Bee* and a prominent figure in New Orleans public affairs. All that we know of him indicates that he was quite sane. Prof. Vann Woodward also asserts that Brown's mother, grandmother, sister and sister's daughter were insane. Family letters and other records cast doubt upon that part of the assertion which refers to the grandmother and sister's daughter, while a careful reading of the affidavits them-

John Brown's end came on December 2, on a scaffold in Charlestown. His execution served as a visible demonstration by the state of Virginia of the condign punishment ultimately in store for those who sought to tamper with the institution of slavery; for the slave seeking to escape from bondage and for the free man, white or colored, who dared to aid him.

To the North, however, Brown's execution brought a far different lesson. For in John Brown, whose venture at Harpers Ferry it first saw as the desperate act of a demented old man oblivious to the realities of the world, the North came to see the embodiment of all that was noble, courageous, and self-sacrificing in man's love for his fellow man. It saw beyond the bloodshed and death into the heart of a man who had identified himself with the poorest, the lowliest, the most forsaken people of the land, had thrown in his lot with theirs, had given up his home, his possessions, his ambitions, his wife and children whom he loved, even life itself, to bring freedom and dignity to men, women and children who had known only the bitterness and hopelessness of slavery. As they saw the state of Virginia, in all of its majesty, proceed in indecent haste to exact the life of the man who had threatened its power, the people of the North learned, as little else could have taught them, that the structure of slavery remained intact primarily through the power of the whip, the gun and the gallows and that when these were gone there was little else left. They learned, too, that wealth and happiness derived from the sweat of slaves was not less easily relinquished than that gotten through more honorable means, and that the slaveholder would fight desperately, with all the means at his disposal, to maintain the foundation of his wealth and power. It was then that many in the North realized that the issue of slavery and freedom would be decided by the weapons that the South had chosen. The battle at Harpers Ferry demonstrated what those weapons were.

selves fails to reveal any reference to the insanity of Brown's mother. All available evidence affirms her sanity.

One may also question Prof. Nevins' evidence, which he has assiduously gathered, in seeking to prove Brown's insanity. Since limitations of space prevent an extended analysis, the following will have to suffice. Prof. Nevins writes that Brown " was subject to extravagant religious fixations. In 1852, worried because his son John did not exhibit piety, he spent an entire month writing a letter of pamphlet length to him, composed largely of scriptural quotations. We might question the sanity of a nearly penniless man with a large family who devotes a month to such an exhortation —which proved futile." A close reading of the letter in question, which is printed in full in F. B. Sanborn's *John Brown*, pp. 45-51, reveals the very opposite of what Prof. Nevins believes it to prove. In the letter Brown writes as follows: " It is now nearly a month since I began on another page. . . . I did mean that my letter should go off at once, but I have not become very stout, and have a great deal to look after, and have had many interruptions. We have done part of our sowing, and expect to get all our corn (of which we have a good crop) secure from frost this day." Prof. Vann Woodward's discussion of Brown is in " John Brown's Private War," *America in Crisis*, ed. by Daniel Aaron (New York: Alfred A. Knopf, 1952), pp. 109-130. Prof. Nevins evaluates Brown in *The Emergence of Lincoln* (New York and London: Charles Scribner's Sons, 1950), II, 5 ff.

When the war came, almost two years later, the man who had been hanged rose, as it were, from his grave to march again with those who had finally taken up the cause for which he had fought, and, by proffering the example of his life and work, helped to achieve the victory which he had lost in life but gained in death.

PART ONE

IN HIS OWN WORDS

THE STORY
OF JOHN BROWN
THROUGH HIS
LETTERS AND OTHER
WRITINGS

PRELUDE TO HARPERS FERRY

I T is fortunate for our knowledge of John Brown's early life that on his first
visit to the home of George Luther Stearns, the wealthy Boston businessman who became one of his dearest friends and benefactors, little Henry
Stearns was present when Brown told the story of his experiences in Kansas.
It was Henry who prevailed upon Brown to write of his childhood in the
remarkable letter which we reprint here. Many years later, on October 26,
1902, Henry wrote the following account of how the letter came to be
written:[1] "On Sunday, January 4th, 1857, John Brown came to our house
to consult with my father and mother about the troubles in Kansas. I was at
that time about twelve years old, and I listened attentively to the conversation, and to all he said about them, and young as I was I had some idea of
the meaning of it. Especially was I touched by what he said about the sufferings of the little children there. When he was about to take his leave, I went
to my father, and in a whisper asked him if I could give what pocket-money
I had, to Captain Brown. I received permission to do so, and running to the
place where I kept it, I took it to John Brown and said, ' Will you please buy
something with this for some poor little boy in Kansas? ' He patted me on the
head, and replied : ' I will, my son, and God bless you for your kind heart.'
Then I said : ' Captain Brown, will you sometime write me a letter, and tell
me what sort of a little boy you were? ' He smiled and said that he would
when he could spare the time. This letter, which is the only record of John
Brown's early life, was the result."

Although the letter to Henry Stearns is a late one chronologically, we
present it here because of the light it throws upon John Brown's earliest
years. The letters that follow it are in chronological order.

Red Rock, Iowa, 15th, July, 1857.
Mr Henry L Stearns   My Dear Young Friend
                                      I have not forgotten my
promise to write you; but my constant care, & anxiety : have obliged
me [to] put it off a long time. I do not flatter myself that I *can* write
anything that will very much interest you : but have concluded to
send you a short story of a certain boy of my acquaintance : & for
convenience & shortness of name, I will call him John. This story
will be mainly a naration of follies & errors; which it is to be hoped
you may avoid; but there is one thing connected with it, which will

[1] This account is in the Oswald Garrison Villard Collection, George L. Stearns folder, Columbia
University Library, New York City.

43

be calculated to encourage any young person to persevereing effort : & that is the degree of success *in accomplishing his objects* which to a great extent marked the course of this boy throughout my entire acquaintance with him; notwithstanding his moderate capacity; & still more moderate acquirements.

John was born May 9th 1800, at Torrington, Litchfield Co. Connecticut; of poor but respectable parents : a decendant on the side of his Father of one of the company of the Mayflower who landed at Plymouth 1620. His Mother was decended from a man who came at an early period to New England from Amsterdam, in Holland. Both his Fathers and his Mothers Fathers served in the war of the revolution : His Fathers Father; died in a barn at New York while in the service, in 1776.

I cannot tell you of anything in the first Four years of Johns life worth mentioning save that at that *early age* he was tempted by Three Large Brass Pins belonging to a girl who lived in the family & *stole them*. In this he was detected by his Mother; & after having a full day to think of the wrong : received from her a thorough whipping. When he was Five years old his Father moved to Ohio; then a wilderness filled with wild beasts, & Indians. During the long journey which was performed in part or mostly with an *Ox team*; he was called on by turns to assist a boy Five years older (who had been adopted by his Father & Mother) & learned to think he could accomplish *smart things* in driving the Cows; & riding the horses. Sometimes he met with Rattle Snakes which were very large; & which some of the company generally managed to kill. After getting to Ohio in 1805 he was for some time rather afraid of the Indians, & of their Rifles; but this soon wore off : & he used to hang about them quite as much as was consistent with good manners; & learned a trifle of their talk. His Father learned to dress Deer Skins & at 6 years old John was installed a young Buck Skin. He was perhaps rather observing as he ever after remembered the entire process of Deer Skin *dressing*; so that he could at any time dress his own leather such as Squirel, Raccoon, Cat, Wolf, or Dog Skins : & also learned to make Whip Lashes : which brought him some change at times; & was of considerable service in many ways. At Six years old John began to be quite a rambler in the wild new country finding birds and Squirels, & sometimes a wild Turkeys nest. But about this period he was placed in the School of *adversity* : which my young friend was a most necessary part of his early training. You may *laugh* when you come to read about it; but these were *sore trials* to John : whose earthly

44

treasures were very *few*, & *small*. These were the beginning of a severe but *much needed course* of dicipline which he afterward was to pass through; & which it is to be hoped has learned him before this time that the Heavenly Father sees it best to take all the little things out of his hands which he has ever placed in them. When John was in his Sixth year a poor *Indian boy* gave him a Yellow Marble the first he had ever seen. This he thought a great deal of; & kept it a good while; but at last *he lost it* beyound recovery. *It took years to heal the wound*; & I *think* he cried at times about it. About Five months after this he caught a young Squirel tearing off his tail in doing it and getting severely bitten at the same time himself. He however held on *to the little bob tail Squirrel*; & finally got him perfectly tamed, so that he almost idolized his pet. *This too he lost*; by its wandering away; or by getting killed: & for a year or Two John was *in mourning*; & looking at all Squirrels he could see to try & discover Bob tail, *if possible*. I must not neglect to tell you of a verry *bad* & *foolish* habbit to which John was somewhat addicted. I mean *telling lies*: generally to screen himself from blame; or from punishment. He could not well endure to be reproached; & I now think had he been oftener encouraged to be entirely frank; by making *frankness a kind of atonement* for some of his faults; he would not have been so often guilty of this fault; nor have been obliged to struggle *so long* in after life with *so mean* a habit.

John was *never quarrelsome*; but was *excessively* fond of the *hardest* & *roughest* kind of plays; & could *never get enough* [of] them. Indeed when for a short time he was sometimes sent to School the opportunity it afforded to wrestle, & Snow ball, & run, & jump, & knock off old seedy Wool hats; offered to him almost the only compensation for the confinement, & restraints of school. I need not tell you that with such feeling & but little chance of going to school *at all*: he did not become much of a schollar. He would always choose to stay at home & work hard rather than be sent to school; & during the warm season might generally be seen *barefooted*, & *bareheaded*: with Buckskin Breeches suspended often with one leather strap over his shoulder but sometimes with Two. To be sent off through the wilderness alone to very considerable distances was particularly his delight; & in this he was often indulged so that by the time he was Twelve years old he was sent off more than a Hundred Miles with companies of cattle; & he would have thought his character much injured had he been obliged to be helped in any such job. This was a boyish kind of feeling but characteristic however.

At Eight years old John was left a Motherless boy which loss was complete & permanent for not withstanding his Father again married to a sensible, inteligent, & on many accounts a very estimable woman: *yet he never addopted her in feeling*: but continued to pine after his own Mother for years. This opperated very unfavourably uppon him; as he was both naturally fond of females; & withall extremely diffident; & deprived him of a suitable conne[c]ting link between the different sexes; the want of which might under some circumstances have proved his ruin.

When the war broke out *with England*; his Father soon commenced furnishing the troops with beef cattle, the collecting & driving of which afforded him some opportunity for the chase (on foot) of wild steers, & other cattle through the woods. During this war he had some chance to form his own boyish judgment of *men* & *measures*: & to become somewhat familiarly acquainted with some who have figured before the country since that time. The effect of what he saw during the war was to so far disgust him with Military affairs that he would neither train, *or drill*; but paid fines; & got along like a Quaker untill his age finally has cleared him of Military duty.

During the war with England a circumstance occurred that in the end made him a most *determined Abolitionist*: & led him to declare, or *Swear*: *Eternal war* with slavery. He was staying for short time with a very gentlemanly landlord since a United States Marshall who held a slave boy near his own age very active, inteligent, & good feeling; & to whom John was under considerable obligation for numerous little acts of kindness. *The Master* made a great pet of John: brought him to table with his first company; & friends; called their attention to every little smart thing he *said or did*: & to the fact of his being more than a hundred miles from home with a company of cattle alone; while the *negro boy* (who was fully if not more than his equal) was badly clothed, poorly fed; & *lodged in cold weather*: & beaten before his eyes with Iron Shovels or any other thing that came first to hand. This brought John to reflect on the wretched, hopeless condition, of *Fatherless* & *Motherless* slave *children*: for such children have neither Fathers or Mothers to protect, & provide for them. He sometimes would raise the question: *is God their Father?*

At the age of Ten years, an old friend induced him to read a little history; & offered him the free use of a good library by; which he acquired some taste for reading: which formed the principle part of his early education: & diverted him in a great measure from bad company. He by this means grew to be very fond of the company, & conversation of old & inteligent persons. He never attempted to dance in his life; nor did he ever learn to know *one* of a pack of *Cards*, from *another*. He learned nothing of Grammer; nor did he get at school so much knowledge of comm[on] Arithmetic as the Four ground rules. This will give you some general idea of the first Fifteen years of his life: during which time he became very strong & large of his age & ambitious to perform the full labour of a man; at almost any kind of hard work. By reading the lives of great, wise, & good men their sayings, & writings; he grew to a dislike of vain & frivolous *conversation*, & *persons*; & was often greatly obliged by the kind manner in which older, & more inteligent persons treated him at their houses; & in conversation; which was a great relief on account of his extreme bashfulness.

He very early in life became ambitious to excel in doing anything he undertook to perform. This kind of feeling I would reccommend to all young persons both *male* & *female*: as it will certainly tend to secure admission to the company of the more inteligent; & better portion of every community. By all means endeavour to excel in some laudable pursuit.

I had like to have forgotten to tell you of one of Johns misfortunes which set rather hard on him while a young boy. He had by some means *perhaps* by gift of his Father become the owner of a little Ewe Lamb which did finely till it was about Two Thirds grown; & then sickened & died. This brought another protracted *mourning season*: not that he felt the pecuniary loss so heavily: for that was never his disposition: but so strong & earnest were his atachments.

John had been taught from earliest childhood to " fear God & keep his commandments;" & though quite skeptical he had always by turns felt much serious doubt as to his future well being; & about this time became to some extent a convert to Christianity & ever after a firm believer in the divine authenticity of the Bible. With this book he became very familiar: & possessed a most unusual memory of it[s] entire contents.

Now some of the things I have been *telling of*; were just such as I would reccommend to you: & I would like to know that you had selected those out; & adopted them as part of your own plan of life; & I wish you to have some *deffinite plan*. Many seem to have none: & others never stick to any that do they form. This was not the case with John. He followed up with *tenacity* whatever he set about so

47

long as it answered his general purpose : & hence he rarely failed in some good degree to effect the things he undertook. This was so much the case that he *habitually expected to succeed* in his undertakings. With this feeling *should be coupled*; the consciousness that our plans are right in themselves.

During the period I have named John had acquired a kind of ownership to certain animals of some little value but as he had come to understand that the *title of minors* might be a little imperfect; he had recourse to various means in order to secure a more *independant*; & *perfect* right of property. One of those means was to exchange with his Father for something of far less value. Another was by trading with other persons for something his Father had never owned. Older persons have sometimes found difficulty with *titles* :

From Fifteen to Twenty years old, he spent most of his time working at the Tanner & Curriers trade keeping Bachelors hall; & he officiateing as Cook; & for most of the time as foreman of the establishment under his Father. During this period he found much trouble with some of the bad habits I have mentioned & with some that I have not told you of : His con[s]cience urging him forward with great power in this matter : but his close attention to *business*; & success in its management : together with the way he got along with a company of men, & boys; made him quite a favorite with the serious & more inteligent portion of older persons. This was so much the case; & secured for him so many little notices from those he esteemed; that his vanity was very much fed by it; & he came forward to manhood quite full of self conceit; & self confident : notwithstanding his *extreme* bashfulness. A younger brother used sometimes to remind him of this : & to repeat to him *this expression* which you may somewhere find; " A King against whom there is no rising up." The habit so early formed of being obeyed rendered him in after life too much disposed to speak in an imperious or dictating way. From Fifteen years & upward he felt a good deal of anxiety to learn; but could only read, & studdy a little; both for want of time; & on account of inflamation of the eyes. He however managed by the help of books to make himse[lf] tolerably well acquainted with common Arithmetic; & Surveying; which he practiced more or less after he was Twenty years old.

At a little past Twenty years led by his own inclination & *prompted also* by his Father he married a *remarkably plain*; but neat industrious & economical girl; of excellent character; earnest piety; & good practical common sence; about one year younger than him-

48

self. This woman by her mild, frank, & *more than all else*: by her very consistent conduct; acquired; & ever while she lived maintained a most powerful; and good influence over him. Her plain but kind admonitions generally had the right effect; without arousing his haughty obstinate temper. John began early in life to discover a great liking to fine Cattle, Horses, Sheep; & Swine; & as soon as circumstances would enable him he began to be a practical *Shepherd*: *it being* a calling for which *in early life* he had a kind of *enthusiastic longing*: together with the idea that as a business it bid fair to afford him the means of carrying out his greatest or principle object. I have now given you a kind of general idea of the early life of this boy; & if I believed it would be worth the trouble; or afford much interest to any good feeling person; I might be tempted to tell you something of his course in after life; or manhood. I do not say that I *will do it.*

You will discover that in using up my *half* sheets to *save paper*; I have written Two pages, so that one does not follow the other as it should. I have no time to write it over; & but for unavoidable hindrances in travelling I can hardly say when I should have written what I have. With an honest desire for your best good I subscribe myself   Your Friend

J Brown

P S I had like to have forgotten to acknowledge your contribution in aid of the cause in which I serve. God Allmighty *bless you*; my Son :

J B

The letters that follow reveal John Brown in his relationship to members of his family, to friends, and to the anti-slavery enterprise. In the first, he writes to his father of the death of his first wife, Dianthe, in childbirth on August 10, 1832. Her death was preceded by that of the unnamed infant son to whom she had given birth.

Randolph, Pa., August 11, 1832

Dear Father :

We are again smarting under the rod of our Heavenly Father. Last night about eleven o'clock my affectionate, dutiful and faithful Dianthe (to use her own words) bade ' farewell to Earth.' My own health is so poor that I have barely strength to give you a short history of what passed since I wrote you last. Her health, I think mentioned in my last letter, was very poor, partly owing to her pregnancy but more perhaps to a difficulty about her heart. She however kept about a little. . . [The doctor] advised her situation was critical, but this information did not depress her spirits. She made answer ' I thought I might go to rest on God's Sabbath.' At her request the children were brought to her and she with heavenly composure gave faithful advice to each.

Our hopes were quite revived for the first twenty-four hours for her recovery. About that time her difficulty of the heart palpitation became so great that we thought her dying for some hours. She however revived but not to gain much strength after. Her reason was unimpaired and her mind composed with the Peace of God. Tomorrow she is to lay beside our little son.

From your sorrowing son
John Brown

To his brother, Frederick, of Hudson, Ohio. John Brown was then a successful businessman as well as the postmaster in Randolph (now New Richmond), Pennsylvania. This is the first written reference by Brown to any plan to assist Negroes.

Randolph, Nov. 21, 1834.

Dear Brother,—As I have had only one letter from Hudson since you left here, and that some weeks since, I begin to get uneasy and apprehensive that all is not well. I had satisfied my mind about it for some time, in expectation of seeing father here, but I begin to give that up for the present. Since you left me I have been trying to devise some means whereby I might do something in a practical way for my poor fellow-men who are in bondage, and having fully consulted the feelings of my wife and my three boys, we have agreed to get at least one negro boy or youth, and bring him up as we do our own,—viz., give him a good English education, learn him what we can about the history of the world, about business, about general subjects, and, above all, try to teach him the fear of God. We think of three ways to obtain one: First, to try to get some Christian slaveholder to release one to us. Second, to get a free one if no one will let us have one that is a slave. Third, if that does not succeed, we have all agreed to submit to considerable privation in order to buy one. This we are now using means in order to effect, in the confident expectation that God is about to bring them all out of the house of bondage.

I will just mention that when this subject was first introduced, Jason had gone to bed; but no sooner did he hear the thing hinted, than his warm heart kindled, and he turned out to have a part in the discussion of a subject of such exceeding interest. I have for years been trying to devise some way to get a school a-going here for blacks, and I think that on many accounts it would be a most favorable location. Children here would have no intercourse with vicious people of their own kind, nor with openly vicious persons of any kind. There would be no powerful opposition influence against such a thing; and should there be any, I believe the settlement might be so effected in future as to have almost the whole influence of the place in favor of such a school. Write me how you would like to join me, and try to get on from Hudson and thereabouts some first-rate abolitionist families with you. I do honestly believe that our united exertions alone might soon, with the good hand of our God upon us, effect it all.

This has been with me a favorite theme of reflection for years. I think that a place which might be in some measure settled with a view to such an object would be much more favorable to such an undertaking than would any such place as Hudson, with all its conflicting interests and feelings; and I do think such advantages ought to be afforded the young blacks, whether they are all to be immediately set free or not. Perhaps we might, under God, in that way do more towards breaking their yoke effectually than in any other. If the young blacks of our country could once become enlightened, it would most assuredly operate on slavery like firing powder confined in rock, and all slaveholders know it well. Witness their heaven-daring laws against teaching blacks. If once the Christians in the free States would set to work in earnest in teaching the blacks, the people of the slaveholding States would find themselves constitutionally driven to set about the work of emancipation immediately. The laws of this State are now such that the inhabitants of any township may raise by a tax in aid of the State school-fund any amount of money they may choose by a vote, for the purpose of common schools, which any child may have access to by application. If you will join me in this undertaking, I will make with you any arrangement of our temporal concerns that shall be fair. Our health is good, and our prospects about business rather brightening.

Affectionately yours,

John Brown

John Brown removed to Franklin Mills (now Kent), Ohio, in 1835, with his family. Although he had been successful in business, his financial position deteriorated seriously as a result of his speculations in land and the depression of 1837. Subjected to numerous lawsuits, he was declared bankrupt in 1842, and emerged stripped of all his property. During these years he turned to cattle-trading and sheep-raising for a livelihood. He made two trips to New England with herds of cattle—the first at the end of 1838, returning in February 1839, the second in March 1839, returning in July—in the course of which the following letters were written.

New York 5th Decem 1838

Dear Wife and Children

A kind & merciful God has kept me hitherto. I arrived here four days ago, but shall probably leave soon. I have not had the pleasure of hearing from you since I left or yet, hope I may before I leave. I have not yet succeeded in my business, but think the prospect such that I do not by any means despair of final success. As to that, may Gods holy will be done. My unceasing and anxious care for the present and everlasting welfare of evry [member] of my family seems to be threefold as I get seperated farther and farther from them. Forgive the many faults & foibles you have seen in me, and try to proffit by anything good in either my example, or my council; Try and not any of you get weary of well doing. Should the older boys read and coppy my old letters as I proposed to them, I want to have them all preserved with care. The time of my return is verry uncertain, but will be soon as is in any way consistent I will write you again, when I have opportunity. I know of no place where I shall be so likely to hear from you as at this place at present and God Allmighty bless and keep you all

your affectionate Husband and Father
JOHN BROWN

New Hartford, 12th June 1839

My dear wife and children;

I write to let you know that I am in comfortable health, and that I expect to be on my way home in the course of a week, should nothing befal me. If I am longer detained, I will write you again. The cattle business has succeeded about as I expected, but I am now somewhat in fear that I shall fail of getting the money I expected on the loan. Should that be the will of Providence, I know of no other

52

way but we must consider ourselves very poor; for our debts must be paid, if paid at a sacrifice. Should that happen (though it may not) I hope God, who is rich in mercy, will grant us grace to conform to our circumstances with cheerfulness and true resignation. I want to see each of my dear family very much, but must wait God's time. Try all of you to do the best you can, and do not one of you be discouraged; tomorrow may be a much brighter day. Cease not to ask God's blessing on yourselves and me. Keep this letter wholly to yourselves, excepting that I expect to start for home soon, and that I did not write confidently about my success, should any one inquire. Edward is well, and Oliver Mills. You may show this to my father, but to no one else. I am not without great hopes of getting relief, I would not [now] have you understand, but things have looked more unfavorable for a few days. I think I shall write again before I start. Earnestly commending you every one to God and to his mercy, which endureth forever, I remain

Your affectionate husband and father
John Brown

The friends here I believe are all well

J. B.

Winchester, Ct. 19th June 1839.

My Dear Wife and Children;

Through the great goodness of God, I am once more on my way home, and should nothing befall me, I hope to see you all by about the 1st of July. I expect to return by way of our place in Pa.

I have left no stone unturned to place my affairs in a more settled and comfortable shape, and now should I, after all my sacrifice of body and mind be compelled to return, a very poor man, how would my family receive me? I do not say that such will be the fact, but such may be the fact. I expect at any rate to bring all of you that can read, a book that has afforded me great support and comfort during my long absence.

I have got the book for John that he wanted me to get for him and mean to get the truss at Albany for Jason.

Should nothing hinder me on the road, perhaps you may not hear from me till I return.

Your affectionate husband and father,
John Brown

53

In June 1839, John Brown received $2800.00 from the New England Woolen Company at Rockville, Connecticut, through their agent George Kellogg. He used the sum for his personal needs and was then unable to repay it. The following letters reveal the desperate circumstances underlying that action and the subsequent poverty to which he and his family were reduced.

Franklin Mills, 27th Aug 1839

George Kellogg, Esqr
    Dear Sir :

        Yours of the 2nd was received in season, & I have no excuse for not answering it promptly, except that I have found it hard to take up my pen to record, & to publish, my own shame, & abuse of the confidence of those whom I esteem, & who have treated me as a friend, & as a brother. I flattered myself till now, with the hope that I might be able to render a more favorable account of myself, but the truth, & the whole truth, shall be told. When I saw you at Vernon, I was in dayly expectation of receiving a number of thousands of dollars from Boston, something over five of which I owed for money I had used belonging to our cattle company, (viz Wadsworth, Wells & myself). On the day I was to set out for home, as I was disappointed of the money I expected, I found no alternative but to go to jail, or to pledge the money the money [sic] you had confided to my trust, & in my extremity I did so with the most of it, pledging it for thirty days, believing that in less than that time I could certainly redeem it, as I expected a large amount from a source I did believe I could depend uppon. Though I have been waiting in painful anxiety I have been disappointed still, & as the best course I could take, I have made an assignment of all my real & personal property for the benefit of my creditors generally, as our laws forbid any preference. I think my property much more than sufficient to satisfy all demands, & that I shall not have to subject you to anything worse in the end than disappointment & delay. I am determined that shall be all, if I & my family work out by the month, & by the day, to make up a full return. I have yet hopes of relief from Boston, & should that be, it will set matters in measure to right again. I have disposed of about 40 yards of your cloth, & find it would go well if my affairs had stood as I expected. Wool has sold at much higher prices here than was expected, & higher than I should have dared to pay had your money been in my possession when I got home.

        Unworthily yours
        JOHN BROWN

Seeking a way out of his financial difficulties, Brown endeavoured to negotiate the purchase of one thousand acres of Virginia land from Oberlin College. On April 3, 1840, the trustees of the college accepted his offer to survey the land "for one dollar per day, and a modest allowance for necessary expenses."[2] The next few months found him engaged in making his surveys, which were received by the trustees on July 14. It was in the course of a survey that he wrote to his family from Ripley (now Alma), Tyler County, Virginia.

Because of Brown's hesitancy in accepting the land when the trustees of the college offered it to him, and a subsequent change of heart by the trustees, the transaction fell through.

Tyler Co Va 27th April 1840

My Dear Wife & Children

I arived on the 17th at this place. Have been well ever since I lef[t] you & every where kindly used. Have made some progress in my business; but do not now expect to get through before the 8 or 9 of May. I like the country as well as I expected, & its inhabitants rather better I think we can find a place in it that will answer all the purposes for which we kneed this world, & have seen the spot where if it be the will of Providence, I hope one day to live with my family. I do not find the season so forward as I expected compared with our Ohio country but to enable you to compare a little I would say that some have planted their Corn more than a week since. Onion tops are pretty well grown, & I saw Potatoes out of the ground more than a week ago on the river. Apples are about the size of large Peas & other things about in the same proportion Were the inhabitants as resolute and industrious, as the northern people, & did they understand how to manage as well, they would become rich, but they are not generally so. They seem to have no Idea of improvement in their Cattle Sheep, or Hogs nor to know the use of enclosed pasture fields for their stock, but spend a large portion of their time in hunting for their Cattle, Sheep & Horses, & the same habit continues from Father to Son. They have so little idea of moveing off any thing they have to sell, or of going away for any thing they kneed to buy, that their Merchants extort uppon them prodigiously. By compareing them with the people of other parts of the Country, & world, I can see new and abundant proof that knowledge is power. I think we might be verry useful to them on many accounts, were we so disposed. May God in mercy keep us all, & enable us to get wisdom, and with all our getting or looseing to get understanding

Affectionately yours

John Brown

2 Oswald Garrison Villard, *op. cit.*, p. 31.

I intended to have left word to have some one go to Dazlys for Upper leather so that Jason might have a pair of boots made, but forgot it

Yours J B

Advice to his eldest son, John, Jr.

Hudson 18th Jany 1841

Dear Son John

Since I parted with you at Hudson some thoughts have passed through my mind which my intence anxiety for your welfare prom[p]ts me to communicate by writing. I think the situation in which you have been placed by Providence at this early period of your life will afford to yourself and others some little test of the sway you may be expected to exert over mind in after life, & I am glad on the whole to have you brought in some measure to the test in your youth. If you cannot now go into a disordered country school and gain its confidence, & esteem, & reduce it to good order, & waken up the energies & the verry soul of every rational being in it yes of every mean ill behaved, ill governed, snotty, boy & girl that compose it; & secure the good will of the parents, then how how how are you to stimulate Asses to attempt a passage of the Alps. If you run with footmen & they should we[a]ry you how should you contend with horses. If in the land of peace they have wearied you, then how how how will you do in the swelling of Jordan. Shall I answer the question myself. If any man lack wisdom let him ask of God who giveth liberally unto all and upbraideth not. Let me say to you again love them all & commend them, & yourself to the God to whom Solomon sought in his youth & he shall bring it to pass. You have heard me tell of dividing a school into two great spelling classes & of its effects if you should think best & can remember the process you can try it. Let the grand reason that one course is right, & another wrong be kept continueally before your own mind & before your school

From your affectionate father
John Brown

Brown was declared bankrupt on Sept. 28, 1842. He nevertheless felt morally obligated (as the following documents indicate) to pay his debts to the New England Woolen Company and to a business partner, Heman Oviatt.

Richfield, Oct. 17, 1842

Whereas I, John Brown, on or about the 15th day of June, A.D. 1839, received of the New England Company (through their agent, George Kellogg, Esq.), the sum of twenty-eight hundred dollars for the purchase of wool for said company, and imprudently pledged the same for my own benefit, and could not redeem it; and whereas I have been legally discharged from my obligations by the laws of the United States,—I hereby agree (in consideration of the great kindness and tenderness of said Company toward me in my calamity, and more particularly of the moral obligation I am under to render to all their due), to pay the same and the interest thereon, from time to time, as Divine Providence shall enable me to do. Witness my hand and seal

John Brown

Annexed to this agreement was the following letter:

Richfield, Summit County, Ohio, Oct. 17, 1842

George Kellogg, Esq.

Dear Sir,—I have just received information of my final discharge as a bankrupt in the District Court, and I ought to be grateful that no one of my creditors has made any opposition to such discharge being given. I shall now, if my life is continued, have an opportunity of proving the sincerity of my past professions, when legally free to act as I choose. I am sorry to say that in consequence of the unforeseen expense of getting the discharge, the loss of an ox, and the destitute condition in which a new surrender of my effects has placed me, with my numerous family, I fear this year must pass without my effecting in the way of payment what I have encouraged you to expect (notwithstanding I have been generally prosperous in my business for the season).

Respectfully your unworthy friend,

John Brown

Richfield 29th Oct 1842

Whereas Heman Oviatt of this place on or about 17th September A D 1839 paid on my account the sum of $5667.96 and costs of Court, and whereas I have since been discharged from all legal obligations by a decree of the United States Court I hereby (in consideration of numerous favors received of said Oviatt, but more particularly on account of the ever binding moral obligation I am under to render to all their due) agree to pay the same and the interest thereon from time to time (together with all other equitable claims of said Oviatt against me) as Divine Providence shall hereafter enable me to do.

*   Witness my hand and Seal

John Brown   Seal

A poignant letter from John Brown to John, Jr., telling of the deaths of four of his children, three of whom were buried at one time. They were nine, six, three and one year old respectively.

Richfield 25th Sept 1843

Dear Son

God has seen fit to visit us with the pestilence since you left us, and Four of our number sleep in the dust, and Four of us that are still living have been more or less unwell but appear to be nearly recovered. On the 4th Sept Charles was taken with the Dysentery and died on the 11th, about the time that Charles died Sarah, Peter, & Austin were taken with the same complaint. Austin died on the 21st, Peter on the 22d & Sarah on the 23d and were all buried together in one grave. This has been to us all a bitter cup indeed, and we have drunk deeply, but still the Lord reigneth and blessed be his great and holy name forever. In our sore affliction there is still some comfort. Sarah (like your own Mother) during her sickness discovered great composure of mind, and patience, together with strong assureance at times of meeting God in Paradise. She seemed to have no idea of recovering from the first, nor did she ever express the least desire that she might, but rather the reverse. We fondly hope that she is not disappointed. They were all children towards whom perhaps we might have felt a little partial but they all now lie in a little row together. Jason wants to add a few lines & I shall be short. I am yet feeble from the same disorder which may account for some of my blunders. We hope to see you when your term is out, it perhaps will not be best before. May you be enabled to cleanse your way

[signature cut out]

Dear Brother

These days are days of rebuke and severe trial with us. A few days ago you parted with us all in good health and cheerfulness, but now how different. Little did any of us think that that parting would be final with four of our number) I will not be lengthy, let us not murmur, The Judge of all the Earth, has done, and will do right. But let us give glory and honor and power and thanks unto him that sitteth on the throne forever and ever.

Your Brother
Jason Brown

On January 9, 1844, John Brown entered into a business partnership with Simon Perkins. It lasted ten years and proved to be Brown's longest and last business venture. Soon after it ended he went to Kansas. On April 10, 1844, the Brown family moved into a house owned by Perkins not far from the Perkins' house, in Akron, Ohio.

AGREEMENT—JOHN BROWN & SIMON PERKINS

The undersigned, Simon Perkins, Jr. and John Brown have this day agreed as follows viz. They agree to place the flocks of sheep which they each now have in a joint concern at their value, and to share equally the gain or loss yearly, commencing on the 15th day of April of each year.

Said Perkins agrees to furnish all the food and shelter that shall be necessary for the good of the flock from the 1st of December of each year to the 15th of April of each year.

Said Brown agrees on his part to furnish throughout the year all the care and attention of every description which the good of the flock may require, wash the sheep, shear the wool, sack and ship the same for market in the neatest and best manner, an equal set-off against the food &c. necessary for the wintering of the flock.

The said parties agree to share equally the pasturing, and all other expenses of said flock yearly, and to improve and increase the same from time to time as the business will justify, and they may agree.

Said Perkins agrees to let said Brown the frame dwelling-house on his farm (south of the house in which he now lives) door-yards, garden grounds, and the privilege of getting wood for fuel, for the rent of thirty-dollars a year commencing on the First of April next.

Said Brown agrees to pay that amount yearly, so long as he may continue to occupy said house, from his share of the proceeds of said flock.

Said Brown agrees to harvest the turnips and potatoes which said Perkins may raise yearly for the use of said flock.

This agreement to remain in force for full years until the parties shall think proper to alter or dissolve it.

Witness our names this ninth day of January 1844

[Signed] Simon Perkins, Junior
John Brown

Richfield 11th Jany. 1844

Dear Son

Your Letter dated 21st Dec was received some days ago but I have purposely delayed till now in order to comply the better with your request that I should write you about every thing. We are all in health; amongst the number is a new sister[3] about three weeks old. I know of no one of our friends that is not comfortably well. I have just met with Father he was with us a few days since & all were then well in that quarter. Our flock is well and we seem to be overtakeing our business in the tanery. Divine Providence seems to smile on our works at this time, I hope we shall not prove unthankful for any favour, nor forget the giver. I have gone to sleep a great many times while writing the above. The boys and Ruth are trying to improve some this winter & are effecting a little I think I have lately entered into a copartnership with Simon Perkins Jr of Akron with a view to carry on the Sheep business extensively He is to furnish all the feed, & shelters for wintering as a set off against our taking all the care of the flock. All other expences we are to share equally, & to divide the proffits equally This arangement will reduce our cash rents at least $250, yearly & save our hireing help in Haying. We expect to keep the Capt Oviatt farm for pasturing, but my family will go into a verry good House belonging to Mr Perkins say from half a mile, to a mile, out of Akron. I think this is the most comfortable and the most favourable arangement of my worldly concerns that I ever had, and calculated to afford us more leisure for improvement, by day, & by Night, than any other I do hope that God has enabled us to make it in mercy to us, & not that he should send leanness into our

3 Anne Brown, housekeeper at the Kennedy Farm; married Samuel Adams; died at Shively, California, October 5, 1926.

soul. Our time will all be at our own command except the care of the flock. We have nothing to do with providing for them in the winter excepting harvesting Rootabaga and Potatoes. This I think will be considered no mean alliance for our family & I most earnestly hope they they [sic] will have wisdom given to make the most of it. It is certainly endorseing the poor Bankrupt & his family three of whom were but recently in Akron jail[4] in a manner quite unexpected, & proves that notwithstanding we have been a company of Belted Knights, our industrious & steady endeavours to maintain our integrity & our character have not been wholly overlooked. Mr P[erkins] is perfectly advised of our poverty, & the times that have passed over us. Perhaps you may think best to have some connection with this business : I do not know of ANY person in (Richfield) that you would be likely to be fond of hearing from in particular excepting one at (Cleaveland) and if hearing from ANY person prove to be (a verry up stream) business I would advise not to worry at present. Will you let me know how it stands between you & all parties concerned.[5]

Your Father John Brown

I will try to send at least $1, the next time I write you. Do not pay the Postage on what you write me

J B

Akron 23d May 1845

Dear Son John

Yours of the 28th April we did not get verry seasonably as we have been verry busy, & not at the P office often. We are all obliged for your letter & I hope thankful for any comforts or success that may attend you. If the days of mourning have in deed & in truth *ceased*; then I trust all is well. all is well, as it should be, & I have known fair days to follow after verry foul wether. The great trouble is we are apt to get too damp in a wet foggy spell. We are all well but little Anne who is afflicted with a singular eruption of the skin : & is withall quite unwell. We get along in our business as well as we ever have done I think. We loose some sheep but not as many as for two seasons past. Matters seem to go well betwixt us, & our friend Perkins, & for any thing that I know our worldly prospects are as good as we can bear. I hope that entire leanness of soul may

<hr>

4 For an interesting account of this event, see Oswald Garrison Villard, *John Brown*, New York, 1943, pp. 37-41.
5 Refers to a love affair in which John, Jr., was then involved.

not attend any little success in business. I do not know as we have yet any new plans. When we have we will let you hear. We are nearly through another yeaning time, & have lost but verry few. Have not yet counted Tails: Think there may be about Four Hundred. Never had a finer, or more thrifty lot. Expect to begin washing next week. Have received our medals, & Diploma. They are splendid toys, & appear to be knock down arguments among the sheep folk who have seen them. All were well at Hudson a few days since. Father was here, & had just moved into the Humiston house out west. You did not say in your letter whether you ever conversed with him in regard to his plans for his old age, as was talked of when you were here, & was helping pick sheep. Should like to know if you did, &c. Cannot tell you much more now, except it be that we all appear to think a great deal more about this world than about the next which proves that we are still verry foolish. I leave room for some others of the family to write if they will. Affectionately Yours

John Brown

In June 1846, the firm of Perkins and Brown opened an office in Springfield, Mass., with Brown in charge. Brown's function was to receive wool from growers, sort it and sell it according to grade. The wool was sold at a commission of two cents a pound. It was the hope of the wool growers of Pennsylvania, New York and Virginia who participated, that by selling graded wools to the manufacturers they would receive much higher prices for their wools than had previously been the case. At first only Jason and John, Jr. accompanied their father to Springfield. In July 1847 the rest of the family moved there.

Springfield Mass 23d July 1846

Friend Perkins

Dear Sir

Yours of the 10th is received for which we are much obliged & we now are anxiously looking for another. I did not write you last week as I intended in consequence of the extreme press of business. Your kind hint about coppying the letters we write on business is exactly right and will be accepted, & I hope you will continue to give any hints you may think of. We had however commenced doing so on the first day after our arrival here, & I have never found our coppies worth more even now than they have cost. We have received so much wool that our freight bills have given us a good deal of anxiety, & trouble, but have got over that for the present by the sale of our wool yesterday (I mean) our own clip. We sold for 69 cents all round, & are to get 70 cents if the new Tarriff bill does not pass. This is as well as we could do while the bill is pending, & makes the whole business *drag*, & we were badly cramped. We have bargained off some 20 odd thousand lbs to be taken as fast as we can class it. Our experiment will work finely, but we have been a little lame for want of the whole building we occupy only in part, & for want of some 10 to 20 thousand Dollars to deal out in safe advances on wool as received here. Had we been fixed right in these two things our most sanguine expectations would have been exceeded. Our business would yet be vastly increased could we make advances. Please say whether you would think it worth while to undertake it, or whether you would advise to have me affect some arrangement of that kind here. I have no doubt I could find abundance of partners here that would find the means if that were *best*, but I have never named the thing to any one, & do not intend to till you may advise to such steps. I might perhaps arrange with one of the banks here, *if that were best*. However would it suit one of your brothers to come on here, & take hold with us in such an operation. There is no mistake about doing a vast business, & perfectly safe. I have got a standing insurance on $15,000 worth of wool for three months. Cost $23. I intended most of what I have said above for your own ear *exclusively*. The immediate want of some money, & the fear of delay is what will take away perhaps 3/4 of the customers we should otherwise get this year. Persons being so much in a hurry is the principal objection any one raises to the measure. As it now is, it is not bad. It might not do any harm to let it be publicly known what our wool has sold at, with all the panic that now exists in the wool market on account of the Tarriff. The prospects of good & brisk sales is very different from what it was before the Dough faces passed the bill through the house. If you are not more pressed for time than we are, please let me hear all about matters at home &c &c on receipt of this. We shall neglect to coppy this into our book. If wool sells low we shall feel it more in our own clip than in business here.

Respectfully Yours
JOHN BROWN

P S We shall find no difficulty in selling the inferior grades of wool here at some price, & we get the same for it as for selling fine. Can not yet say what Col Dodger wool is worth. Will write again soon.

Yours

J B

Sabbath evening

MY DEAR AFFLICTED WIFE & CHILDREN

I yesterday at night returned after an absence of several days from this place & am uterly unable to give any expression of my feelings on hearing of the dreadful news contained in Owens letter of the 30th & Mr. Perkins of the 31st Oct. I seem to be struck almost dumb.

One more dear little feeble child I am to meet no more till the dead small & great shall stand before God.[6] This is a bitter cup indeed, but blessed be God : a brighter day shall dawn; & let us not sorrow as those that have no hope. Oh that we that remain, had wisdom wisely to consider; & to keep in view our latter end. Divine Providence seems to lay a heavy burden; & responsibility on you *my dear Mary*; but I trust you will be enabled to bear it in some measure as you ought. I exceedingly regret that I am unable to return, & be *present* to share your trials with you : but anxious as I am to be once more at home I do not feel at liberty to return yet. I hope to be able to get away before verry long; but cannot say when. I trust that none of you will feel disposed to cast an unreasonable blame on my dear Ruth on account of the dreadful trial we are called [to] suffer; for if the want of proper care in each, & all of us has not been attended with fatal consequenses it is no thanks to us. If I had a right sence of my habitual neglect of my familys Eternal interests; I should probably go crazy. I humbly hope this dreadful afflictive Providence will lead us all more properly to appreciate the amazeing, unforseen, untold, consequences; that hang upon the right or wrong doing of things seemingly of trifling account. Who can tell or comprehend the vast results for good, or for evil; that are to follow the saying of one little word. Evrything worthy of being done *at all*; is worthy of being done in *good earnest*, & in the best possible manner. We are in midling health & expect to write some of you again soon. Our warmest thanks to our kind friends Mr. & Mrs. Perkins & family. From your affectionate husband, & father

JOHN BROWN

[6] The child who died was Amelia Brown, born June 22, 1845, at Akron, Ohio. Her death was due to accidental scalding by her sister, Ruth.

Dear Mary

It is once more Sabbath evening, & kneed I say that with its return my mind is more than ever filled with the thoughts of home, of my wife, & my children. In immagination I seem to be present with you; to share with you the sorrows, or joys you experience. Your letter dated the 20th was received last night, & afforded one *a real* though a mournful satisfaction. That you had received; or were to receive a letter from either John, or Jason, I was in perfect ignorance of; till you informed me; & I am glad to learn that wholly uninfluencd by me; they have shown a disposition to afford you all the comfort in your *deep affliction* which the nature of the case would admit of. Nothing is scarsely equ[a]l with *me*; to the satisfaction of seeing that one portion of my *remaining* family are not disposed to exclude from their sympathies, & their warm affections, another portion. I accept it as one of the most grateful returns that can be made to me; for any care or exertions on my part to promote either their present or their future well being; & while I am able to discover such a feeling, I feel assured that notwithstanding God has chastised us *often*, & *sore*; yet he has not *himself* entirely withdrawn from us, nor forsaken us *utterly*. The sudden, & dreadful manner in which he has seen fit to call *our dear little Kitty* to take her leave of us, is I kneed not tell you how much on mind; but before *Him*; *I* will bow my head in submission, & hold my peace. I suppose Jason is with you before this can reach you, & I trust that nothing on his part, or on the part of *any one* of my older children will be wanting to render your situation as comfortable as may be. Of the motives that lead one into such business as will, or does deprive me of the society of my family I will say nothing, but any ideas that *to me* the separation is not a painful one are wholly mistaken ones. I have sailed over a somewhat stormy sea for nearly half a century, & have experienced enough to teach me thoroughly that I may most reasonabl[y] buckle up & be prepared for the tempest. Mary let us try to maintain a cheerful self command while we are tossing up & down, & let our motto still be Action, Action; as we have but one life to live. How long I shall yet feel constrained to stay *here*, I am not yet able to foresee, sometimes the prospect seems quite disheartening, & at other times it brightens. Since Jason left things look a little more encourageing than at that time. When the day *comes* that will afford me an opportunity to return I shall be awake to greet the earliest dawn; if not its *midnight birth*. I want to have you write me oftener; & as there is another man belonging in Springfield of the same name as myself, & son, who sometimes opens my letters; you might direct to care of Perkins & Brown. I want to hear how Jason got home, (as he appeared lately to be in rather a poor state of health) & whether you have received the cloth, fish & Tea I had tried to send you or not. Mr. Perkins has done us a great kindness in writing us so often; & has manifested the kindest feeling in all that he has written, & in being midling particular about things at home. I hope he will not get tired of it. I mean to write him again shortly. I neither forget him, nor Mrs. P, or any of their family.

Affectionately Yours
JOHN BROWN

I think Ruth promised to write me again

Springfield Mass 5th Jany 1847

Dear Daughter Ruth

Your dated 20th & Jasons dated 16th Decem were both received in season, & were verry grateful to our feelings; as we are anxious to hear from home often; & had become verry uneasy before we got word from Jason. We are midling well & verry much pressed with our work, accounts, & correspondence. We expect now to go home if our lives, & health are spared next month, & we feel rejoiced that the time is so near when we hope to meet you all once more. Sometimes my immagination follows those of my family who have passed behind the scenes, & I would almost rejoice to receive permision to make them a personal visit. I have outlived nearly half of all my numerous family, & I ought to realize that in any event a large proportion of my journey is traveled over. You say you would like verry much to have a letter from me; with as much good advice as I will give.

Well what do you suppose I feel most anxious *for*; in regard to yourself, & all at home? Would you believe that I ever had any such care on my mind about them, as we read that Job had about his family? (Not that I would ever think to compare myself with Job.) Would you believe that the long story would be that ye *sin* not; that you form no foolish atachment; & that you be not a companion of Fools

Your Affectionate Father
John Brown

Springfield, Mass 7th March 1844 [1847][7]

My Dear Mary

It is once more Sabbath evening & nothing so much accords with my feelings as to spend a portion of it converseing with the partner of my own choice, & the sharer of my poverty, trials, discredit, & sore afflictions; as well as what of comfort, & seeming prosperity has fallen to my lot; for quite a number of years. I would you should realise that notwithstanding I am absent in boddy I am verry much of the time present in spirit. I do not forget the firm attachment of her who has remained my fast, & faithful affectionate friend, when others said of me (now that he lieth he shall rise up no more.) When I reflect on these things together with the verry considerable difference in our age, as well as all the follies, & faults with which I am justly chargeable, I really admire at your constancy; & I really feel notwithstanding I sometimes chide you severely that you ar[e] *really* my better half. I now feel encouraged to believe that my absence will not be verry long. After being so much away, it seems as if I knew pretty well how to appreciate the quiet of home. There is a peculiar music in the world which a half years absence in a distant country would enable you to understand. Millions there are who have no such thing to lay claim to. I feel considerable regret by turns that I have lived so many years, & have in reality done so verry little to increase the amount of human happiness. I often regret that my manner is no more kind & affectionate to those I really love, & esteem; but I trust my friends will overlook my harsh rough ways when I cease to be in their way; as an occasion of pain, & unhappiness. In immagination I often see you in your room with Little Chick; & that strange Anna. You must say to her that Father means to come home before long, & kiss someboddy. I will close for this time by saying what is my growing resolution to endeavour to promote my *own* happiness by doing what I can to render those around me more so. If the large boys do wrong call them alone into your room, & expostulate with them kindly, & see if you cannot reach them by a kind but powerful appeal to their honor. I do not claim that such a theory accords verry much with *my practice. I frankly confess it does not*; but I want *your face* to shine even if my own should be dark, & cloudy. You can let the family read this letter, & perhaps you may not feel it

[7] This letter was probably written after Brown was established in the wool business in Springfield and should therefore be dated 1847.

a great burden to answer it & let hear me [sic] all about how you get along.

Affectionately Yours
JOHN BROWN

Springfield Mass 2d April 1847

Dear Father

Your verry kind as well as rational letter I received last evening. I trust I do in some small measure realize that only a few, *verry few* years will of necessity bring to me a literal accomplishment of the sayings of the Preacher. I am quite sensible of the truth of your remark that my family are quite as well off as though we possessed millions. I hope we may not be left to a feeling of ingratitude or greediness of gain, & I feel unconcious of a desire to become rich. I hope my motive for exerting myself is higher. I feel no inclination to move my family to Springfield on account of any change that I am itching for; & think it verry doubtful whether I ever conclude on it as the last course. My only motive would be to have them with me, if I continue in my present business; *which I am by no means atached too*. I seem to get along midling well, & hope to return in short time. Wrote Jeremiah some days since. I shall pay ten cents[8] verry cheerfully to hear that you are alive, & well at any time; & should not grudge to pay more for such kind & ever seasonable pointing me to the absolùte vanity of this worlds treasures; as well as the sollemn picture, which is before me. It affords me great satisfaction to get a letter from you at this period of your life, so handsomely written, so well worded, & so exactly in point both as to manner, & (what is much more) and matter. I intend to preserve it carefully

Your Affectionate Son
John Brown

[8] Postage.

While living in Springfield, John Brown contributed an essay entitled "Sambo's Mistakes" to *The Ram's Horn*, a New York anti-slavery newspaper edited by Negroes which appeared from January 1847 to June 1848. In this essay, by posing as a Negro who is offering the benefit of his experience in life to his fellow Negroes, he points out what he regards as mistaken attitudes and practices prevalent among Negroes. A copy of the essay in Brown's handwriting was found in a search of the Kennedy farm, whence Brown set out for his attack on Harpers Ferry. The original copy, from a photostat of which the following has been taken, is in the possession of the Maryland Historical Society in Baltimore.

Chapter 1st.

Sambos Mistakes   For the Rams Horn

Mess Editors Notwithstanding I may have committed a few mistakes in the course of a long life like others of my colored brethren yet you will perceive at a glance that I have always been remarkable for a seasonable discovery of my errors & quick perception of the true course. I propose to give you a few illustrations in this & the following chapters. For instance when I was a boy I learned to read but instead of giving my attention to sacred & profane history by which I might have become acquainted with the true character of God & of man learned the true course for individuals, societies, & nations to pursue stored my mind with an endless variety of rational and practical ideas, profited by the experience of millions of others of all ages, fitted myself for the most important stations in life & fortified my mind with the best & wisest resolutions, & noblest sentiments, & motives, I have spent my whole life devouring silly novels & other miserable trash such as most of newspapers of the day & other popular writings are filled with, thereby unfitting myself for the realities of life & acquiring a taste for nonsense & low wit, so that I have no rellish for sober truth, useful knowledge or practical wisdom. By this means I have passed through life without proffit to myself or others, a mere blank on which nothing worth peruseing is written. But I can see in a twink where I missed it. Another error into [which] I fell in early life was the notion that chewing & smoking tobacco would make a man of me but little inferior to some of the whites. The money I spent in this way would with the interest of it have enabled me to have relieved a great many sufferers supplied me with a well selected interesting library, & pa[i]d for a good farm for the support & comfort of my old age; whereas I have now neith[er] books, clothing, the satisfaction of having benefited others, nor where to lay my hoary head. But I can see in a moment where I missed it. Another of the few errors of my life is that I have joined the Free Masons Odd Fellows Sons of Temperance, & a score of other secret societies instead of seeking the company of inteligent wise & good men from whom I might have learned much that would be interesting, instructive, & useful & have in that way squandered a great amount of most precious time; & money enough sometime in [a] single year which if I had then put the same out on interest & kept it so would have kept me always above board given me character, & influence amongst men or have enabled me to pursue some respectable calling so that I might employ others to their benefit & improvement, but as it is I have always been poor, in debt, & now obliged to travel about in search of employment as a hostler shoe black & fidler. But I retain all my quickness of perception I can see readily where I missed it.

Chapter 2d

Sambos Mistakes

Another error of my riper years has been that when any meeting of colored people has been called in order to consider of any important matter of general interest I have been so eager to display my spouting talents & so tenacious of some trifling theory or other that I have adopted that I have generally lost all sight of the business in hand consumed the time disputing about things of no moment & thereby defeated entirely many important measures calculated to promote the general welfare; but I am happy to say I can see in a minute where I missed it. Another small error of my life (for I never committed great blunders) has been that I never would (for the sake of union in the furtherance of the most vital interests of our race) yield any minor point of difference. In this way I have always had to act with but a few, or more frequently alone & could accomplish nothing worth living for, but I have one comfort, I can see in a minute where I missed it. Another little fault which I have committed is that if in anything another man has failed of coming up to my standard that notwithstanding he might possess many of the most valuable traits & be most admirably adapted to fill some one important post, I would reject him entirely, injure his influence, oppose his measures, & even glory in his defeats while his intentions were good, & his plans well laid. But I have the great satisfaction of being able to say without fear of contradiction that I can see *verry quick* where I missed it.

Chapter 3d

Sambos Mistakes

Another small mistake which I have made is that I could never bring myself to practice any present self denial although my theories have been excellent. For instance I have bought expensive gay clothing nice Canes, Watches, Safety Chains, Finger rings, Breast Pins, & many other things of a like nature, thinking I might by that means distinguish myself from the vulgar as some of the better class of whites do. I have always been of the foremost in getting up expensive parties, & running after fashionable amusements, have indulged my appetite freely whenever I had the means (& even with borro[w]ed means) have patronized the dealers in Nuts, Candy, &c freely & have sometimes bought good suppers & was always a regular customer at Livery stables. By these & many other means I have been unable to benefit my suffering Brethren, & am now but poorly able to keep my own Soul & boddy together; but do not think me thoughtless or dull of appre[he]ntion for I can see at once where I missed it.

Another trifling error of my life has been that I have always expected to secure the favour of the whites by tamely submitting to every species of indignity contempt & wrong instead of nobly resisting their brutal aggressions from principle & taking my place as a man & assuming the responsibilities of a man a citizen, a husband, a father, a brother, a neighbour, a friend as God requires of every one (if his neighbour will allow him to do it:) but I find that I get for all my submission about the same reward that the Southern Slaveocrats render to the Dough faced Statesmen of the North for being bribed & browbeat, & fooled & cheated, as the Whigs & Democrats love to be. & think themselves highly honored if they may be allowed to lick up the spittle of a Southerner. I say I get the same reward. But I am uncomm[only] quick sighted I can see in a minute where I missed it. Another little blunder which I made *is*, that while I have always been a most zealous Abolitionist I have been constantly at war with my friends about certain religious tenets. I was first a Presbyterian but I could never think of acting with my Quaker friends for they were the rankest heretiks & the Baptists would be in the water, & the Methodists denied the doctrine of Election. & of later years since becoming enlightened by Garrison Abby Kelley & other really benevolent persons I have been spending all my force on my friends who love the Sabbath & have felt that all was at stake on that point just as it has proved to be of late in France in the abolition of Slavery in their colonies. Now I cannot doubt Mess Editors notwithstanding I have been unsuccessful that you will allow me full credit for my *peculiar* quick sightedness. I can see in one second where I missed it.

Letters from Brown to his father and to Joshua Giddings, an anti-slavery Congressman from the Western Reserve of Ohio. In March, 1859, just a few months prior to the attack on Harpers Ferry, Brown accepted an invitation from Rep. Giddings to speak at a meeting in Jefferson, Ohio. After the talk, which dealt with his experiences in Kansas, Brown visited with the Congressman and his wife at their home, and received a contribution of three dollars to further his work.

Springfield, Mass., 16th Jan., 1848.

Dear Father,—It is Sabbath evening; and as I have waited now a long time expecting a letter from you, I have concluded to wait no longer for you to write to me. I received the Hudson paper giving an account of the death of *another* of our family.[9] I expected to get a letter from you, and so have been waiting ever since getting the paper. I never seemed to possess a faculty to console and comfort my friends in their grief; I am inclined, like the poor comforters of Job, to sit down in silence, lest in my miserable way I should only add to their grief. Another feeling that I have in your case, is an entire consciousness that I can bring before your mind no new source of consolation, nor mention any which, I trust, you have not long since made full proof of. I need not say that I know how to sympathize with you; for that you equally well understand. I will

[9] Refers to death in December, 1847, of Lucian Brown, John Brown's half-brother.

only utter one word of humble confidence,—"Though He slay me, yet will I trust in Him, and bless His name forever." We are all in health here, but have just been taking another lesson on the uncertainty of all we hold here. One week ago yesterday, Oliver found some root of the plant called hemlock, that he supposed was carrot, and eat some of it. In a few minutes he was taken with vomiting and dreadful convulsions, and soon became senseless. However, by resorting to the most powerful emetics he was recovered from it, like one raised from the dead, almost.

The country in this direction has been suffering one of the severest money pressures known for many years. The consequence to us has been, that some of those who have contracted for wool of us are as yet unable to pay for and take the wool as they agreed, and we are on that account unable to close our business. This, with some trouble and perplexity, is the greatest injury we have suffered by it. We have had no winter as yet scarcely, the weather to-day being almost as warm as summer. We want to hear how you all are very much, and all about how you get along. I hope to visit you in the spring. Farewell.

Your affectionate, unworthy son,
John Brown

Springfield, Mass 22d June 1848.

Hon. J. R. Giddings.

Dear Sir

I have at my command a fund of One Thousand Dollars & some thing over to be expended in premiums of from Three to Ten Eagles each on the best cases of American Woolen goods manufactured from American grown wools *exclusively*. I wish to manage the business in such a way as to benefit the abolition cause to which I am most thoroughly devoted; whilst at the same time I wish to encourage American tallent, & industry. I have thought that were this fund or these premiums to be offered by you in some way as an encouragement to American Tallent, & industry, it might do a two fold good by showing that you are an *American* to the *core*; as well as an abolitionist. It seems to me that it might be so used at this time as to secure favour to the cause of humanity which you have *nobly* defended often. I know perfectly well that I am not the man to offer them but I feel so deeply interested in having the thing done *right* that I will go to Washington if need be to consult about it. Now sir you will see at once that some of the strong interests of the country are to be both *flattered*, & *benefited*, by the encouragement these premiums offer. All the controll I wish over the matter is to advise as to the kinds of goods that may compete, & who are to be the Judges to award the premiums; & at what time the exhibition shall come off.

Now Dear Sir will you think this matter over & write *me* on the subject directing your letter to care of Perkins & Brown, Springfield Mass *without* putting on your *Frank* as I wish the whole matter to be kept a most *profound secret.*————The premiums will be of a much more liberal character than any heretofore offered in the United States. Perhaps you may think of something that will be of service in carrying out my plan. I do not wish to impose any burden on you that you would not cheerfully bear, & will at any time you *wish* explain to you my reasons for wishing myself to be kept *wholly & absolutely out of sight*. The fund may be increased if best

Verry Respectfully Yours
John Brown of the
Firm of Perkins & Brown

Mr. H. Clay has been called an *American. Why* may not Abolitionists?

Springfield Mass 7th Sept 1848

Hon. Joshua R. Giddings
Dear Sir

I have by no means given up the measure I proposed to you at Springfield,[10] but ill health prevented my going to Washington to see you as I intended. Please say to me at what time or times I may find you at home, or at any other points nearer to this place. I wrote you by Telegraph at Washington after I recovered, but it seems that you had then left.

Verry Respectfully Yours
John Brown

Please direct to care of Perkins & Brown as before

Yours in truth
J B

10 There is no evidence that anything further was done regarding this proposal or that Brown went to Washington to see Giddings about it.

Dear Father

Your verry kind & excellent letter of the 1st inst is received & as you say you never loved letters so well as you do now, I will send you one, even though it be a verry poor one. We have had considerable poor health this winter, arising from hard colds mostly. Our youngest child is verry much out of order in the lungs so that we have a good deal of fear that she will not be able to hold out till warm weather. Owens arm is (we think a little) better. We feel a good deal of spirit about the oppressions, & cruelties that are done in the land, but in regard to other verry important interests we are quite too indifferent. I suppose it may well be questioned whether any one duty can be *acceptably* performed; while most others are, neglected. I was on some of the Gerrit Smith lands[11] lying opposite Burlington Vt last fall that he has given away to the blacks & found no objection to them but the high Northern Lattitude in which they lie. They are indeed rather inviting on many accounts. There are a number of good colored families on the ground; most of whom I visited. I can think of no place where I think I would sooner go; *all things considered* than to live with those poor despised Africans to try, & encourage them; & show them a little so far as I am capable how to manage. You kneed not be surprised if at some future day I should do so. Our business is prosperous; to all appearance. Money is becoming more easy. Write us often; the oftener the better. Dr. Humphrey has called twise.

From your Affectionate but unworthy Son   John Brown

The following letters refer to Brown's plans for a trip to Europe, undertaken in the attempt to sell American wool there, to outwit American cloth manufacturers who had sought to force down the prices of American-grown wool.

Springfield, Mass. 24th May 1849

Friend Perkins

Dear Sir

Your favour of the 12th inst received, & will now proceed to answer your questions (without repeating) them, in the order in which they come. Those who send wool pay all expenses. The

[11] At North Elba, Essex County, N.Y. Brown moved his family there in the spring of 1849.

Exchange will cover all expenses of Insurance, Freight, Commission &c &c less by about 2 per cent as near as we can get at it, from Proforma Bills of Sale sent us by two first rate English Houses recommended to us by the Banks in New York. The prospect now is that wool will nett in England full our 1847 prices. Prices have been there about those rates within the last three months. I do not think the present moment as favourable as though they were in a more settled state. Still I think a good sale may be effected, & valuable acquaintances formed even under present circumstances. At any rate we *must do so*, or put the wool under the hammer, the very thing the manufacturers have boasted they would drive us to. All business at Springfield will be closed except the selling of some graded wool for a few who decline sending it to Europe. I do not think of starting until after I see you, which will be (I think) in about three weeks or thereabouts. I should expect to be gone Eight or Nine weeks, & to close up the sales there before returning. Have corresponded with the greater part of those who have sent us fine wool, & as a general thing they say " send off the fine wool & get what you can for it." *I shall pay off all our indebtedness* before leaving by advances of about 50 per cent on the value of the wool here; made by the English Houses to whom we ship. Have begun to ship already. Have hired a farm in Essex Co N. Y. at $50 a year, bought me some cows & an ox team, & started my family on to it for a home until I can close up the wool business here. The small Pox is raging in Springfield. We mean to embrace every opportunity of selling out here & to send for none to Europe who do not fully approve of the measure. I believe however that nineteen out of twenty will choose to have their wool go out of the country under all the circumstances.

Yours Truly
JOHN BROWN

Boston 15th Aug 1849

Simon Perkins Esqr

Dear Sir

I write you as follows viz Sail today by Steamer Cambria for Liverpool. Have settled up wool business so far as it could be done at present. Have left matters so at Springfield that I think you will have no trouble with them except it be with Fowler of Westfield. He has been calculating to get a lawyers job out of the business for a good while; & I know of no way to prevent him as we have offered to pay those men either here or in Ohio, unless by your making to them at Medina a specie tendery of the nett proceeds of their wool. John will write you whether they will accept payment here or not; & the amount due each. We have given Fowler from the first candid, & true statements, & such as would satisfy any body *but a little trifling Pettifogger* but he represents things so to those men at Medina that that [sic] they accuse us of fraud. Explanation with them is to no purpose while he contradicts what we say, & they are determined to give him a job. Perhaps were you to see them, & show them my letters to you it might have some good effect. Have reduced our indebtedness at this time to about $13000, all told. Due in Sept with opportunity to renew for 60 days in order to close up some more accounts this indebtedness may have for a time to be some increased. This is provided for should it be needed. Most persons do not expect their accounts closed till we get returns from England. . . .

Your Friend

John Brown

Letters written while Brown was in Europe.

London, Aug. 29, 1849.

Dear Son John,—I reached Liverpool on Sabbath day, the 26th inst., and this place the 27th at evening,—a debtor to Grace for health and for a very pleasant and quick passage. Have called on the Messrs. Pickersgill, and find they have neither sold any wool nor offered any. They think that no time has been lost, and that a good sale can yet be expected. It is now the calculation to offer some of it at the monthly sale, September next, commencing a little before the middle of the month. I have had no time to examine any wools as yet, and can therefore express no opinion of my own in the matter. England is a fine country, so far as I have seen; but nothing so very wonderful has yet appeared to me. Their farming and stone-masonry are very good; cattle, generally more than middling good. Horses, as seen at Liverpool and London, and through the fine country betwixt these places, will bear no comparison with those of our Northern States, as they average. I am here told that I must go to the Park to see the fine horses of England, and I suppose I must; for the streets of London and Liverpool do not exhibit half the display of fine horses as do those of our cities. But what I judge from more than anything is the numerous breeding mares and colts among the growers. Their hogs are generally good, and mutton-sheep are almost everywhere as fat as pork. Tell my friend Middleton and wife that England affords me plenty of roast beef and mutton of the first water, and done up in a style not to be exceeded. As I intend to write you very often I shall not be lengthy; shall probably add more to this sheet before I seal it. Since writing the above, I find that it will be my best way to set out at once for the Continent, and I expect to leave for Paris this evening. So farewell for this time,—now about four o'clock P.M.

Your affectionate father,
John Brown.

London Oct 1849

Simon Perkins Esqr
    Dear Sir

        I expect to get through with the sale of wool today, & was in hopes of doing it so as to get on my way homeward by steamer tomorrow, but find it cannot be brought about. I find that with all the prejudices that exist against American wools that have come to this country for the most part, that a good sale is out of the question. Many manufacturers that have lately paid from $.74 to more than One Dollar per lb I cannot persuade even to take a single bag to try at $.50. Some are less fearful, & particularly the French & belgians who I expect will probably take it all. I know they want to get it, but they want it as they get the Colonial wools here. I expect to get from about $.30 to a little over $.50 & to let it slide. However much I may be blamed for doing poorly with the wool, I believe the wool business in the country (U S) will be permanently helped by the means; & at any rate I have done every thing in my power. I do not expect to write again before I leave for home. Am in good health.

Respectfully Yours
JOHN BROWN

Forced to sell his wool at a disastrously low price, Brown's trip to Europe proved a fiasco. The firm of Perkins & Brown, according to Oswald Garrison Villard's estimate, lost about $40,000.00 in the venture. Brown returned to the United States at the end of October, landing in Boston "shortly after midnight on the 26th." His wife and children, having moved from Springfield to North Elba in the spring of 1849. remained there until March 1851. However, before the end of 1850, as is shown in his letter of November 28, 1850, Brown's business difficulties were already forcing him to consider moving his family back to Akron, Ohio. The move was made in March 1851.

Burgettstown, Penn., April 12, 1850.

Dear son John and Wife,—When at New York, on my way here, I called at Messrs. Fowler & Wells's office, but you were absent. Mr. Perkins has made me a visit here, and left for home yesterday. All well at Essex when I left; all well at Akron when he left, one week since. Our meeting together was one of the most cordial and pleasant I ever experienced. He met a full history of our difficulties and probable losses without a frown on his countenance, or one syllable of reflection; but, on the contrary, with words of comfort and encouragement. He is wholly averse to any separation of our business or interest, and gave me the fullest assurance of his undiminished confidence and personal regard. He expresses strong desire to have our flock of sheep remain undivided, to become the joint possession of our families when we have gone off the stage. Such a meeting I had not dared to expect, and I most heartily wish each of my family could have shared in the comfort of it. Mr. Perkins has in the whole business, from first to last, set an example worthy of a philosopher, or of a Christian. I am meeting with a good deal of trouble from those to whom we have over-advanced, but feel nerved to face any difficulty while God continues me such a partner. Expect to be in New York within three or four weeks.

Your affectionate father,
John Brown

Springfield, Mass. 28th Nov. 1850

Dear Wife;

As I cannot yet say how soon I can return, or what the prospect is of our moving at all this winter, I write to let you hear from me, as you said. I have been well, and have effected a sale of our wool at about 60¢ per lb. Since leaving home I have thought that under all the circumstances of doubt attending the time of our removal; and the possibility that we may not remove at all that I had perhaps encouraged the boys to feed out the potatoes too freely. I now wish them to stop when they have fed out the small ones, as, should anything prevent our moving longer than we have expected, or prevent it entirely I do not wish to be obliged to buy. When the small potatoes are fed out, the boys can mess the cows that give milk with cleaned vats. I want to have them very careful to have no hay or straw wasted, but I would have them use enough straw for bedding the cattle to keep them from lying in the mire. I heard from Ohio a few days since; all were then well. It now seems that the fugitive slave law was to be the means of making more abolitionists than all the lectures we have had for years. It really looks as if God had his hand in this wickedness also. I of course keep encouraging my friends to " trust in God and keep their powder dry " I did so today at thanksgiving meeting.publicly. I may get ready to go home the middle of next month, but am wholly in the dark about it yet: do not mean that idleness shall prevent me. While here, and at almost all places where I stop, I am treated with all kindness and attention, but it all does not make home. I feel lonely and restless, no matter how neat and comfortable my room and bed, nor how richly loaded may be the table; they have very few charms for me. Away from home, I can look back to our log cabin at the centre of Richfield with a supper of Porridge and Johnny-cake as to a place of far more interest to me than the Massasoit[12] of Springfield. But, " there's mercy in every place, and mercy, encouraging thought." I shall endeavor when I come home to bring the things that Owen and others of the family stood in need of. I told Mr. Cutting of Westport he might have either of the yearling heifers for thirty dollars. I want Owen to get the largest bull in order, if he can do it by any means. May God in very deed bless and keep all my family is the continued prayer of

Your affectionate husband
John Brown

Will any of them write me here? I should think they might afford to, some one of them.

12 A well-known inn.

Dear Sons John, Jason, & Frederick, & daughters

I this moment received the Letter of John, & Jason, of the 29th Nov, & feel grateful not only to learn that you are all alive, & well, but also for almost every thing your letters communicate. *I am much pleased* with the reflection that you are all three once more together, & all engaged in the same calling that the old Patriarchs followed, & will say but one word more on that score, & that is taken from their history. "See that ye fall not out by the way" & all will be exactly right in the end. I should think matters were brightening a little in this direction in regard to our claims but I have not yet been able to get any of them to a final isue. I think too that the prospect for the fine wool business rather improves. What burdens me *most of all is*; the apprehension that Mr Perkins expects of me in the way of bringing matters to a close what no living man can possibly bring *about*; in a short time, & that he is getting out of patience, & becoming distrustfull. If I could be with him in all I do, or could possibly attend to all my cares, & give him full explanations by letter of all my movements I should be greatly relieved. He is a most noble spirited man, to whom I feel most deeply indebted, & no amount of money would attone to my feelings for the loss, of a feeling of confidence, & cordiality on his part. If my sons who are so near him conduct wisely, & faithfully, & kindly, in what they have undertaken, they will beyond the possibility of a doubt secure to themselves a full reward if they should not be the means of entirely relieveing a Father of his burdens. I will once more repeat an idea I have often mentioned in regard to business of life in general. A world of pleasure, & of success is the sure, & constant attendant upon *early rising*. It makes all the business of the day go off with a peculiar cheerfulness, while the effects of the contrary course are a great, & constant draught upon ones "vitality" & good temper. When last at home in Essex I spent every day but the first afternoon Surveying, or in tracing out old lost boundaries about which I was very successful; working early, & late at $2,00 per day. This was of the utmost service to both boddy and mind; It exercised me to the full extent, & for the time being almost entirely diverted my mind from its burdens so that I returned to my task verry greatly refreshed, & invigorated. John asks me about Essex. I will say that the family there were living upon the Bread, Milk, Butter, Pork, Chickens, Potatoes, Turnips, Carrots &c of their own raising; & *the most of them* abundant in quantity, & of superior quality. I have no where seen such Potatoes. Essex Co so abounds in Hay, Grain, Potatoes, Rutabaga, &c that I find unexpected difficulty in selling for cash Oats, & some other things we have to spare. Last year it was exactly the reverse. The weather was charming up to the 15th Nov when I left, & never before did the country seem to hold out so many things to entice me to stay on its soil. *Nothing* but the strong sence of duty, obligation, & propriety, would keep me from laying my bones to rest there; but I shall cheerfully endeavour to make that sense my guide; God always helping. It is a source of the utmost comfort to feel that I retain a warm place in the sympathies, affections, & confidence of my own most familiar acquaintance, *my family*; & allow me to say that a man can hardly get into difficulties too big to be surmounted if he has a firm foothold at home. *Remember that*. . . . I am sorry for Johns trouble in his throat, & hope he will get relieved of that. I have some doubt about the Cold Water practice in cases of that kind, but do not suppose a resort to medicines of much account. Regular out of Door labour I believe to be one of the best medicines of all that God has as yet provided. As to Essex I have no question at all. For stock growing, & dairy business considering its healthiness, cheapness of price, & nearness to the two best markets in the Union (New York, & Boston,) I do not know where one could go to do better. I am much refreshed by your letters, & untill you hear from me to the contrary, shall be glad to have you write me here often. Last night I was up till after midnight writing to Mr Perkins, & perhaps used some expressions in my rather *cloudy* state of feeling, that I had better not have used. I mentioned to him that Jason understood he disliked his management of the flock somewhat, & was worried about that, & about the poor Hay he would have to feed out during the Winter. I did not mean to write him any thing offensive, & hope he will so understand me. There is now a fine Plank Road completed from Westport to Elisabethtown. We have no hired person about the family in Essex. Henry Thompson is clearing up a piece of ground that the "colored Brethren" choped for me. he boards with the family, & by the way he gets Ruth out of bed so as [to] have Breakfast before light mornings. It is again getting late at night, & I close by wishing every present as well as future good.

[Signature cut out]

PS I want to have you *save or secure* the first real prompt, fine looking, Black, Shepherd Puppy whose Ears stand erect that you can get. I do not care about his training at all further than to have him learned to come to you when bid, to set down & lie down, when told; or something in the way of play. Mess Cleaveland, & Titus our Lawyers in New York are verry anxious to get one for a play thing & I am well satisfied that should I give them one as a matter of friendship it would be more appreciated by them, & do more to secure their best services in our suit with Pickersgill than would a hundred Dollars paid them in the way of fees. I want to have Jason obtain from Mr Perkinses or any where he can get them Two good Junk Bottles have them thoroughly cleaned & filled with the Cherry Wine being verry careful not to rile it up before filling the Bottles providing good Corks & filling them perfectly full. These I want him to pack safely in a verry small strong Box he can make: direct them to Perkins & Brown Springfield Mass & send them by Express. We can effect something to purpose by producing unadulterated Domestic Wines. They will command great prices.

JB

The following letter, from John Brown to his wife, undoubtedly refers to the formation by Brown on January 15, 1851, of the League of Gileadites, an organization for the protection of Negro fugitive slaves in Springfield. The nature of the organization is described in the succeeding statement.

Springfield, Mass., Jan. 17, 1851.

Dear Wife,— . . . Since the sending off to slavery of Long from New York, I have improved my leisure hours quite busily with colored people here, in advising them how to act, and in giving them all the encouragement in my power. They very much need encouragement and advice; and some of them are so alarmed that they tell me they cannot sleep on account of either themselves or their wives and children. I can only say I think I have been enabled to do something to revive their broken spirits. I want all my family to imagine themselves in the same dreadful condition. My only spare time being taken up (often till late hours at night) in the way I speak of, has prevented me from the gloomy homesick feelings which had before so much oppressed me: not that I forget my family at all.

WORDS OF ADVICE

Branch of the United States League of Gileadites.
Adopted Jan. 15, 1851, as written and
recommended by John Brown.

"Union is Strength"

Nothing so charms the American people as personal bravery. Witness the case of Cinques, of everlasting memory, on board the "Amistad." The trial for life of one bold and to some extent successful man, for defending his rights in good earnest, would arouse more sympathy throughout the nation than the accumulated wrongs and sufferings of more than three millions of our submissive colored population. We need not mention the Greeks struggling against the oppressive Turks, the Poles against Russia, nor the Hungarians against Austria and Russia combined, to prove this. *No jury can be found in the Northern States that would convict a man for defending his rights to the last extremity. This is well understood by Southern Congressmen, who insisted that the right of trial by jury should not be granted to the fugitive.* Colored people have ten times the number of fast friends among the whites than they suppose, and would have ten times the number they now have were they but half as much in earnest to secure their dearest rights as they are to ape the follies and extravagances of their white neighbors, and to indulge in idle show, in ease, and in luxury. Just think of the money expended by individuals in your behalf in the past twenty years! Think of the number who have been mobbed and imprisoned on your account! Have any of you seen the Branded Hand? Do you remember the names of Lovejoy and Torrey?

Should one of your number be arrested, you must collect together as quickly as possible, so as to outnumber your adversaries who are taking an active part against you. Let no able-bodied man appear on the ground unequipped, or with his weapons exposed to view: let that be understood beforehand. Your plans must be known only to yourself, and with the understanding that all traitors must die, wherever caught and proven to be guilty. "Whosoever is fearful or afraid, let him return and part early from Mount Gilead" (Judges, vii. 3; Deut. xx. 8). Give all cowards an opportunity to show it on condition of holding their peace. *Do not delay one moment after you are ready; you will lose all your resolution if you do. Let the first blow be the signal for all to engage; and when engaged do not do your work by halves, but make clean work with your enemies,— and be sure you meddle not with any others.* By going about your business quietly, you will get the job disposed of before the number that an uproar would bring together can collect; and you will have the advantage of those who come out against you, for they will be wholly unprepared with either equipments or matured plans; all with them will be confusion and terror. Your enemies will be slow to attack you after you have done up the work nicely; and if they should, they will have to encounter your white friends as well as you; for you may safely calculate on a division of the whites, and may by that means get to an honorable parley.

Be firm, determined, and cool; but let it be understood that you are not to be driven to desperation without making it an awful dear job to others as well as to you. Give them to know distinctly that those who live in wooden houses should not throw fire, and that you are just as able to suffer as your white neighbors. *After effecting a rescue, if you are assailed, go into the houses of your most prominent and influential white friends with your wives; and that will effectually fasten upon them the suspicion of being connected with you, and will compel them to make a common cause with you, whether they would otherwise live up to their profession or not. This would leave them no choice in the matter.* Some would doubtless prove themselves true of their own choice; others would flinch. That would be taking them at their own words. You may make a tumult in the court-room where a trial is going on, by burning gunpowder freely in paper packages, if you cannot think of any better way to create a momentary alarm, and might possibly give one or more of your enemies a hoist. But in such case the prisoner will need to take the hint at once, and bestir himself; and so should his friends improve the opportunity for a general rush.

A lasso might possibly be applied to a slave-catcher for once with good effect. Hold on to your weapons, and never be persuaded to leave them, part with them, or have them far away from you. *Stand by one another and by your friends, while a drop of blood remains; and be hanged, if you must, but tell no tales out of school. Make no confession.*

Union is strength. Without some well-digested arrangements nothing to any good purpose is likely to be done, let the demand be never so great. Witness the case of Hamlet and Long in New

York, when there was no well-defined plan of operations or suitable preparation beforehand.

The desired end may be effectually secured by the means proposed; namely, the enjoyment of our inalienable rights.

AGREEMENT

As citizens of the United States of America, trusting in a just and merciful God, whose spirit and all-powerful aid we humbly implore, *we will ever be true to the flag of our beloved country, always acting under it.* We, whose names are hereunto affixed, do constitute ourselves a branch of the United States League of Gileadites. That we will provide ourselves at once with suitable implements, and will aid those who do not possess the means, if any such are disposed to join us. We invite every colored person whose heart is engaged in the performance of our business, whether male or female, old or young. The duty of the aged, infirm, and young members of the League shall be to give instant notice to all members in case of an attack upon any of our people. We agree to have no officers except a treasurer and secretary *pro tem.*, until after some trial of courage and talent of able-bodied members shall enable us to elect officers from those who shall have rendered the most important services. Nothing but wisdom and undaunted courage, efficiency, and general good conduct shall in any way influence us in electing our officers.

Boston, Mass. 22d Dec. 1851

Dear Mary;

I shall take a few moments to write as prompted by my inclination rather than from feeling that I have any other sufficient reason. My prospects about getting back soon are rather poor at this moment, but still it may be I shall be on my way within a day or two. . . . I wrote to Fred'k Douglas a few days since to send on his paper, which I suppose he has done before this, as he very promptly acknowledged the receipt of my letter. There is an unusual amount of very interesting things happening in this and other countries at present, and no one can foresee what is yet to follow. The great excitement produced by the coming of Kossuth, and the last news of a new revolution in France, with the prospect that all Europe will soon again be in blaze seem to have taken all by surprise. I have only to say in regard to these things that I rejoice in them from the full belief that God is carrying out his eternal purpose in them all. . . . I know of nothing unfavorable in our prospects except the slow progress we make and the great expense attending it.

Your affectionate husband
John Brown

Letters to Ruth and Henry Thompson.

Troy N Y 23 Jany 1852

Dear Children

I returned here on the evening of the 19th inst & left Akron on the 14th the date of your letters to John. I was very glad to hear from you again in that way, not having received any thing from you while at home. I left all in usual health & as comfortable as could be expected; but am afflicted *with you* on account of your little Boy. Hope to hear by return mail that you are all well. As in this trouble you are only tasteing of a Cup I have had to drink of deeply, & very often; I need not tell how fully I can sympathize with you in your anxiety. My atachments to this world have been very strong, & Divine Providence has been cutting me loose one Cord after another, up to the present time, but notwithstanding I have so much to remind me that all ties must *soon* be severed; I am still clinging like those who have hardly taken a single lesson. I really hope some of my family may understand that this world is not the *Home* of man; & act in accordance. *Why* may I not hope this of you? When I look forward as regards the religious prospects of my numerous family (the most of them) I am forced to say, & to feel too; that I have *little, very little* to cheer. That this should be so, is I perfectly well understand the legitimate fruit of my own planting; and that only increases my punishment. Some Ten or Twelve years *ago*, I was cheered with the belief that my elder children had chosen the *Lord*, to be their *God*; & I valued much on their influence & example in attoning for my deficiency, & bad example with the younger children. But; *where are we now?* Several have gone to where neither a good or bad example from me will better their condition or prospects or make them the worse. The younger part of my children seem to be far less thoughtful, & disposed to reflection than were my older children at their age. I will not dwell longer on this distressing subject but only say that so far as I *have* gone; it is from no disposition to reflect on any one but myself. I think I can clearly discover where I wandered from the Road. How to now get on it with my family is beyond my ability to *see*; or my courage to *hope*. God grant you *thorough* conversion from sin, & full purpose of heart to continue steadfast in his ways through the *very short* season of trial you will have to pass.

How long we shall continue here is beyound our ability to foresee, but think it very probable that if you write us by return mail we shall get your letter. Something may *possibly* happen that may enable us, (or one of us) to go & see you but do not look for us. I should feel it a great privilege if I could. We seem to be getting along well with our business *so far*; but progress miserably slow. My journeys back & forth this Winter have been very tedious. If you find it difficult for you to pay for Douglas paper, I wish you would let me know *as I know I took* some *liberty* in ordering it continued. You have been very Kind in helping me, & I do not mean to make myself a burden

Your Affectionate Father
John Brown

Brown's move to Akron seems to have been intended as a temporary measure, to permit him to wind up his business with Mr. Perkins, and attend to various lawsuits which had been brought against the firm.

In 1853, he was making arrangements to have his daughter and her husband, Ruth and Henry Thompson, who had been living in North Elba, secure a home there for him and his family. It was not until June 1855, however, that he was able to move the family back to North Elba.

To Ruth and Henry Thompson.
———

Akron, Ohio, June 30, 1853.

Dear Children,—Your very welcome letters were received last night. In regard to a house, I did not prefer a log one, only in view of the expense; and I would wish Henry to act according to his own best judgment in regard to it. If he builds a better house than I can pay for, we must so divide the land as to have him keep it. I would like to have a house to go into next spring, if it can be brought about comfortably. I ought to have expressed it more distinctly in better season, but forgot to do so. We are in comfortable health, so far as I know, except father, Jason, and Ellen, all of whom have had a run of ague. Father, when I saw him last, was very feeble; and I fear that in consequence of his great age he will never get strong again. It is some days since I went to see him. We are not through sheep-shearing or hoeing, and our grass is needing to be cut now. We have lately had very dry weather. . . . I am much rejoiced at the news of a religious kind in Ruth's letter; and would be still more rejoiced to learn that all the sects who bear the Christian name would have no more to do with that mother of all abominations—man-stealing. I hope, unfit and unworthy as I am, to be allowed a membership in your little church before long; and I pray God to claim it as his own, and that he will most abundantly bless all in your place who love him in truth. " If any man love not his brother whom he *hath* seen, *how* can he love God whom he *hath not* seen? " I feel but little force about me for writing or any kind of business, but will try to write you more before long. Our State fair commences at Dayton the 20th of September, and will be held open four days.

Your affectionate father,
John Brown

Akron, Ohio, Aug. 26, 1853.
Dear Son John,—Your letter of the 21st instant was received yesterday, and as I may be somewhat more lengthy than usual I begin my answer at once. The family have enjoyed as good health as usual since I wrote before, but my own health has been poor since in May. Father has had a short turn of fever and ague; Jason and Ellen have had a good deal of it, and were not very stout on Sunday last. The wheat crop has been rather light in this quarter; first crop of grass light; oats very poor; corn and potatoes promise well, and frequent rains have given the late grass a fine start. There has been some very fatal sickness about, but the season so far has been middling healthy. Our sheep and cattle have done well; have raised five hundred and fifty lambs, and expect about eighty cents per pound for our wool. We shall be glad to have a visit from you about the time of our county fair, but I do not yet know at what time it comes. Got a letter from Henry dated the 16th of August; all there well. Grain crops there very good. We are preparing (in our minds, at least) to

go back next spring. Mrs. Perkins was confined yesterday with another boy, it being her eleventh child. The understanding between the two families continues much as formerly, so far as I know.

In Talmadge there has been for some time an unusual seriousness and attention to future interests. In your letter you appear rather disposed to sermonize; and how will it operate on you and Wealthy if I should pattern after you a little, and also quote some from the Bible? In choosing my texts, and in quoting from the Bible, I perhaps select the very portions which " another portion " of my family hold are not to be wholly received as *true*. I forgot to say that my younger sons (as is common in this " progressive age ") appear to be a *little in advance* of my older, and have thrown off the *old shackles* entirely; after THOROUGH AND CANDID investigation they have discovered the Bible to be ALL a fiction! Shall I add, that a letter received from *you* some time since gave me little else than pain and sorrow? " The righteous shall hold on his way;" " By and by he is offended."

My object at this time is to recall your particular attention to the fact that the earliest, as well as all other, writers of the Bible seem to have been impressed with such ideas of the character of the religion they taught, as led them to apprehend a want of steadfastness among those who might profess to adhere to it (no matter what may have been the motives of the different writers). Accordingly we find the writer of the first five books putting into the mouth of his Moses expressions like the following,—and they all appear to dwell much on the idea of two distinct classes among their reputed disciples; namely, a genuine and a spurious class:—

" Lest there should be among you man, or woman, or family, or tribe, whose heart turneth away this day from the Lord our God, to serve the gods of these nations; lest there should be among you a root that beareth gall and wormwood." " Then men shall say, because they have forsaken the covenant of the Lord God of their fathers." " But if thine heart turn away so that thou wilt not hear, but shalt be *drawn away*, and worship other gods, and serve them." . . . .

The writer here makes his *Moses* to dwell on this point with a most remarkable solicitude, a most heart-moving earnestness. The writer of the next book makes his *Joshua* to plead with Israel with the same earnestness. " Choose you this day whom you will serve." " Ye are witnesses against yourselves that ye have chosen you the Lord, to serve him." The writer of the book called Judges uses strong language in regard to the same disposition in Israel to backslide: "And it came to pass when the judge was dead, that they returned and corrupted themselves more than their fathers; they ceased not from their own doings, nor from their stubborn way." The writer of the book Ruth makes Naomi say to Orpah, "Thy sister-in-law is gone back unto her people and unto her gods." The writer of the books called Samuel represents Saul as one of the same spurious class. Samuel is made to say to him, "Behold, to obey is better than sacrifice; and to hearken, than the fat of rams,"—clearly intimating that all service that did not flow from an obedient spirit and an honest heart would be of no avail. He makes his Saul turn out faithless and treacherous in the end, and finally consult a woman "having a familiar spirit," near the close of his sad career. The same writer introduces Ahitophel as one whose counsel "was as if a man had inquired at the oracle of God;" a writer of the Psalms makes David say of him, "We took sweet counsel together, and walked to the house of God in company;" but he is left advising the son of David to incest publicly, and soon after hangs himself. The spot of those men seems not to be genuine.

. . . .

Akron, Ohio, Sept. 13, 1853.

Dear Children,—It is now nearly a month since I began on another page. Since writing before, father has seemed quite well, but Jason, Ellen, Owen, and Frederick have all had more or less of the ague. They were as well as usual, for them, yesterday. Others of the family are in usual health. . . .

I hope that through the infinite grace and mercy of God you may be brought to see the error of your ways, and be in earnest to turn many to righteousness, instead of leading astray; and then you might prove a great blessing to Essex County, or to any place where your lot may fall. I do not feel "estranged from my children," but I cannot flatter them, nor "cry peace when there is no peace." My wife and Oliver expect to set out for Pennsylvania before long, and will probably call on you; but probably not until after the fair. We have a nice lot of chickens fattening for you, when you come.

Your affectionate father,

John Brown

To Frederick Douglass, the Negro leader.

Akron, O., Jan. 9, 1854.

F. Douglass, Esqr., Dear Sir:-I have thought much of late of the extreme wickedness of persons who use their influence to bring law and order and good government, and courts of justice into disrespect and contempt of mankind, and to do what in their power lies to destroy confidence in legislative bodies, and to bring magistrates, justices, and other officers of the law into disrespect amongst men. Such persons, whoever they may be, would break down all that opposes the passions of fallen men; and could they fully carry out their measures, would give to the world a constant succession of murder, revenge, robbery, fire and famine; or, first, of anarchy in all its horrid forms; and then of the most bloody despotisms, to be again succeeded by anarchy, and that again to terminate in a despotism. What punishment ever inflicted by man or even threatened of God, can be too severe for those whose influence is a thousand times more malignant than the atmosphere of the deadly Upas-for those who hate the right and the Most High.

I will now enquire who are such malignant spirits-such fiends clothed in human form? Among the first are men who, neglecting honorable and useful labor to seek office and electioneer, have come to be a majority in our national Legislature, and in most of our State Legislatures, and who there pass unjust and wicked enactments, and call them laws. Another set are from the same description of men, and who fill the offices of Chief Magistrate of the United States, and of different States, and affix the official signature to such enactments. Next comes another set from the same horde, who fill the offices of judge, justices, commissioners, &c., who follow that which is altogether unjust. Next comes a set of Capt. Rynders men—marshals, sheriffs, constables and policemen—brave cat paws of the last named, ever prompt to execute their decisions. Another set are such as sometimes succeed in getting *nominated* for some office, and are very loud at hotels, in cars, on steam-boats, and in stages, urging upon others the duty of fulfilling all our solemn engagements, and "last but not least" comes the devil's drummers and fifers—such fellows as in *black cloth* get in the "sacred desk" there to publish the Gospel, (no doubt): for numbers of them are Doctors of Divinity. But what Gospel do they preach? Is it the Gospel of God, or the Son of God? God commands "That which is altogether just shall thou follow," and every man's conscience says Amen! God commanded "That thou shalt not deliver unto his master the servant which is escaped from his master unto thee. He shall dwell with thee, even among you in that place which he shall choose, in one of thy gates where it liketh him best. *Thou shalt not oppress him.*" Every man's conscience says Amen to that command. The Son of God said - "Therefore all things whatsoever ye would that men should do to you, do ye even so to them; for this is the law and the Prophets." The conscience of every man that ever heard or read that command says Amen! But what say these so-called Divines? You must obey the enactments of the United States Congress, even to the violation of conscience, and the trampling under foot of the laws of our final Judge. "Remember them, O my God, because they have defiled the priesthood."

There is one other set of the same throngers of the "broad way" which I have not mentioned. (Would to God I had already done!) I mean Editors of, and writers in the pro - slavery newspapers and periodicals. These seem to vie with each other in urging men on to greater and still greater lengths in stifling conscience, and insulting God. What, I ask, could possibly tend so to destroy all possible respect for legislators, presidents, judges, or other magistrates or officers - or to root out all confidence in the integrity of civil rulers and courts, as well as legislative bodies, as the passing of enactments which it is self - evident are most abominably wicked and unjust, dignifying them with the name of laws, and then employing the public purse and sword to execute them? But I have done. I am too destitute of words to express the tithe of what I feel, and utterly incapable of doing the subject any possible degree of justice, in my own estimation. My only encouragement to begin, was the earnest wish that if I might express, so that it may be understood to all, an important fact, that you or some friend of God and the right, will take it up and clothe it in the suitable language to be noticed and felt. I want to have the enquiry everywhere raised - Who are the men that are undermining our truly republican and democratic institutions at their very foundations? I forgot to head my remarks "Law and Order."

Yours in Truth
JOHN BROWN

It was in August 1854 that John Brown, Jr. first mentioned to his father his plan to move to Kansas. Because of the latter's feeling that he had a prior commitment to North Elba, he refused, although with reluctance, to join his son.

To John Brown, Jr.

Akron, August 21,1854

If you or any of my family are disposed to go to Kansas or Nebraska, with a view to help defeat *Satan* and his legions in that direction, I have not a word to say; *but I feel committed to operate in another part of the field.* If I were not so committed, I would be on my way this fall. Mr. Adair [who married Brown's half sister Florilla] is fixing to go, and wants to find "good men and true" to go along. I would be glad If Jason would give away his Rock and go. Owen is fixing for some move; I can hardly say what.

To Ruth and Henry Thompson at North Elba.

Akron, Ohio, 30th Sept 1854

Dear Children

After being hard pressed to go with my family to Kansas as more likely to benefit the colored people *on the whole* than to return with them to North Elba; I have consented to ask for your *advice & feeling* in the matter; & also to ask you to learn from Mr. Epps & all the colored people (so far as you can) how they would wish, & advise me to act in the case, all things considered. As I volunteered in their service; (or the service of the colored people); they have a right to vote, as to course I take. I have just written Gerrit Smith, Fredk Douglas, & Dr McCune Smith, for their advice. We have a new daughter now Five days old.[13] Mother & child, are both doing well to appearance. Other friends well so far as I know. John & Wealthy are still with us. Will you write as soon as you can? Have not received your reply to my other questions.

Your Affectionate Father

John Brown

[13] The daughter was Ellen, twentieth and last child of John Brown, and the second of his children to bear that name; born at Akron, Ohio, September 25, 1854. She removed to California with her mother in 1864; married James Fablinger at Rohnersville, Cal., in 1876; died at Saratoga, Cal., July 15, 1916.

Dear Children,—I feel still pretty much determined to go back to North Elba; but expect Owen and Frederick will set out for Kansas on Monday next, with cattle belonging to John, Jason, and themselves, intending to winter somewhere in Illinois. . . . Gerrit Smith wishes me to go back to North Elba; from Douglass and Dr. McCune Smith I have not yet heard. . . .

Your affectionate father,

John Brown

Motivated by a desire to aid the anti-slavery cause in Kansas, to which may be added the desire to share in the unexploited wealth of that newly-opened territory, John Brown's sons, Owen, Frederick, and Salmon, left Ohio for Kansas in October, 1854, wintered in Illinois, and entered Kansas on April 20, 1855. On May 7, Jason and John, Jr. joined them at Osawatomie. Early in 1855, touched by the contagion that had already seized his sons, John Brown changed his mind about staying in North Elba and decided to join his sons in Kansas. He raised money for arms at an anti-slavery convention in Syracuse at the end of June, and by the middle of August he was in Cleveland on the way to Kansas with his son-in-law, Henry Thompson. They were later joined by Oliver Brown, and all three arrived in Kansas on October 6.

Brownsville Kansas Territory 19th Oct 1855

Dear Father

We arrived here Two Weeks ago Tomorrow Evening; & finding but Two well persons in all the number, with no Houses to shelter them; nor any crop of Hay, Corn, Beans, or Potatoes, secured for Winter; I have felt driven to neglect writing almost entirely; & have only written One Letter before this (this one to my Wife) since I got on. I might have written before day Mornings but had no place with the cold chilling Winds shut out where I could improve such Hours. I felt very much disappointed at finding all my children here in such very uncomfortable circumstances. We are doing all we can to help them; & that is not much as Henry Thompson, & Oliver have both had something of the Ague since we got on. I was at Mr. Adairs over Sunday last; & found them all more or less sick; but all able to be up, & about a little. I think all here are on the gain slowly; Frederick however has it on him now while I am writing. Mr. Adairs family are much more comfortable situated. I think much of the sickness in my family out here is from most unreasonable exposure; but from what we learn the sickness has been quite general over the more Eastern country. We hear that you have been sick and not expected to live but that you had got about a little. We shall be looking anxiously to hear from you again. We had a slow tedious journey out on account of our heavy load and our Horse having the distemper. He has got well. We used all the money we had, & all you sent in getting on but Sixty cents. Think I can soon sell something Horse, or Waggon, so as to replace what we used. We came by the place where Austin[14] was buried, & took him up; & brought him on with us; which seems to have had a good effect on Jason, & Ellen. We reached in time to be at the *Free State* election & hearing that trouble was expected we turned out powerfully armed; but no enemy appeared. From what we can learn not only Missouri but other Slave States are getting quite discouraged about Kansas; & I think there is no doubt of a favourable result, if Free State folks will hold on patiently. The country is much like the upland portion of Illinois where you have been; but I have seen no wet or Marchy lands as yet, & I may say on the whole is just about as good as I expected, & better timbered. I do not think this is the only desirable spot on Earth I have seen but believe that in the end it will be a good country; & generally healthy. I should think a majority of the settlers were of the poorer class, & will have to submit to some privations for some little time. Jason thinks the prospect for a sale of fruit Trees will not be very good for some time yet. I think there is no doubt that stock growing & dairy business will do well here for those who take hold of them right in connection with corn growing. We are all anxious to hear from you; & we know that you will write if you are able. My advantages for writing at present are so very poor that I hope this letter will answer for as many of the friends as is consistent; & that you will accept it as in some measure from all here. I hope the afflictions of Jason & Wife will not be wholly lost on them. Wishing you & all our Ohio friends the full blessing; & the peace of God; I remain

Your Affectionate but unworthy Son
JOHN BROWN

In the following letter, which appeared originally in the *Summit Beacon*, Akron, Ohio (now *Akron Beacon-Journal*), in early 1856, John Brown tells of his early experiences in Kansas.

[14] Jason's son, four years old, who died of the cholera on the way to Kansas.

Editor of Summit *Beacon*:

My Dear Sir:—You will greatly oblige me by allowing me the use
of your columns in order to give a little account of my movements
to my numerous friends in Akron and vicinity, who, as well as yourself, contributed towards supplying arms and ammunition to the
Free State men of Kansas. It would afford me the utmost pleasure
were it in my power to write each a letter individually, to show my
strong regard for all those numerous friends; but I *must beg* them
to accept this as a substitute.

Soon after leaving Chicago with the arms and ammunition, in
company with a son-in-law and son, one of our company was taken
sick. This rendered our journey through Illinois, Iowa and Missouri
so slow, that, when we finally reached their neighborhood, October
5th, we had between us all but sixty cents. We got the most valuable
part of the arms and ammunition through safe, and just in time to
have them on hand at the Free State Election, at Pottawatomie,
October 8th, where difficulty was expected; but no disturbance
occurred.

When we reached the territory there was not, among the five sons
I had already there, one well person; and they had not been able to
provide themselves comfortable houses, or to secure their crops.
Since then, for much of the time, I have been the only well man out
of eight. Since the cold weather commenced four of the young men
have become middling strong, and the other three have improved.
The care of my friends has prevented my being as active among the
emigrants generally as I intended.

You have doubtless learned of the late invasion of Kansas, and
something of its results; but I will give you a little of my version of
the affair. Free State men here, as all well know, had openly avowed
their determination to disregard the enactments of the Bogus Legislature, and to resist their enforcement; and, as *reports say*, it was
contrived in what they call the Blue *Lodge* in Missouri (in the White
House it is likely), to have some three or four Free State men killed
in Kansas, in order to have an opportunity of showing before the
country and the world that those enactments *could and would be
enforced*—just before the sitting of Congress. Be that as it may,
about four weeks since, news came around that a Free State man
named Dow, had been deliberately murdered by a Missourian, who

had given himself up to Governor Shannon; that the only Free State witness of the murder had been arrested, under a warrant issued by a justice of bogus origin, on complaint of pro-slavery men swearing that they were afraid he would take their lives, etc.; that such excessive bail had been required as he could not give; that he had been started for jail by a bogus sheriff named Jones, with a party of fifteen armed men, taking a circuitous route through Lawrence, on purpose to let the people of that place see that the bogus laws would be enforced; that some eight men with Sharp's rifles, had met their company and rescued the man; that Governor Shannon had ordered out the pro-slavery men of Kansas; called on the Government for troops, and on Missouri to help him : that a force of about two thousand had collected under Governor Shannon, near Lawrence; that the Free State men had collected in nearly equal numbers; that it was supposed a battle had been or would be fought immediately. This news proved in the main to be correct. The numbers were overstated; but Coleman, the murderer, was made a leader in the Governor's camp. When this news came I was here, a distance of ten miles from where my boys are located. I left immediately, intending to set out next morning for Lawrence to learn the facts; but as J. Brown, jun. was acquainted with the road and the people of Lawrence he was started on horseback : but before going many rods he was met with news by a runner, asking for help immediately. We at once set about preparing bread, meat, blankets and horsefeed, running bullets, loading all the guns and pistols and packing them in a one-horse wagon. All of us who were able to walk, five in all, set off on foot the same afternoon. Our guns, ammunition, baggage, &c., made a fair load for our horse. We walked that afternoon and all the following night, except for a short time spent in cooking our supper and resting our horse. We reached Lawrence the next forenoon, having traveled in a dark night (for the most part) a distance of from 35 to 40 miles.

On our way an accident occurred at a bridge about three miles from Lawrence, which will serve a little, in connection with other circumstances, to show the real character of those *dreadful Missourians*, who have invaded Kansas in time past. We had to pass the bridge (so far as we had information of the road) and it was guarded, as differently reported, by from 15 to 25 of the enemy, armed, and in a log house at the end of the bridge next to us. We had no means of counting them, part being in the log house and part at the door. On our approach a small boy ran ahead, and gave the men notice.

We each carried a good gun, two large revolvers in a belt, and one small revolver in our pockets, all loaded. We were prepared to give from 95 to 100 shots without reloading, and were certainly well equipped. As we moved directly on the bridge without making any halt, they silently suffered us to pass *with the free will offerings* of our dear friends at Akron and elsewhere, without any interruption save that of looking very earnestly at us. In a few hours after, five more of a volunteer company to which we belonged passed the same bridge and received similar respectful treatment. They, however, stopped a boy of 15 or 16 years, and carefully examined him the same day; but the evening before some 15 or 20 of them, armed, attacked three or four men (mostly without arms) and killed a Mr. Barber from Ohio, who had no arms. From these and numerous other circumstances, I am led to conclude that *even Missourians* are amused with trinkets, or with those who wear them.

We learned on our arrival in Lawrence that numerous demands had been sent in from the Governor's camp, viz: that the rescued man, and those who rescued him, should be given up: that the people should allow some forty or fifty warrants to be served; that the Sharp's rifles should be surrendered; that certain buildings and fortifications should be destroyed by the inhabitants; the printing presses should be demolished and thrown into the river, and that the inhabitants generally should swear to support the enactments of the so-called Kansas Legislature. Some of these demands were officially made, the others, however, emanating from his camp. We were told that Governor Shannon had signified to the inhabitants repeatedly that if they had any business to transact with him, to come to his camp and attend to it; and that word had so often been returned, that if he had business with any person in Lawrence, to come in and see to it.

After thus parleying for some days, Governor Shannon sent word that he wished to visit town, and an escort was sent from Lawrence, which conducted him in. During this time eleven companies of Free State Volunteers had collected in Lawrence, who were employed, (with the inhabitants) night and day, under the direction of Colonel Lane, in the construction of embankments and earthworks, and which they had in a good degree completed. After Governor Shannon had met some of the principal inhabitants, they very soon 'found him out'; and taking advantage of his weakness, frailties and fear of the result of an engagement, together with some resort on their part to Yankee ingenuity, and his own consciousness of the awkward fix he had got himself into, and a most *horrible* supply of *Brandy*, they got him quite elated, and succeeded in making just about such a treaty with him as they desired. Among the conditions agreed to on his part, was the ordering home of the pro-slavery force he had called out; the issuing of a proclamation, requiring the foreign invaders to quit the Territory immediately, with a promise from him no more to call for such aid. In short, he abandoned his entire ground; recognized the volunteers, as the militia of Kansas, and empowered the officers in command to call them out at their discretion, for the protection of Lawrence and the Territory. Governor Shannon in return, got a promise from two individuals, for the people of Lawrence and the Territory, that they would assist him in the execution of the laws of the Territory.

How much of truthfulness or sincerity characterized these negotiations, I will not say. The invaders soon left, covered over with glory, after suffering great expenses, hardships and privations; not having fulfilled any of their threatenings, or fought any battles, or accomplished anything for which they set out, save the commission of certain robberies, and a few acts of violence on the defenceless inhabitants in the neighborhood of their camps, and the killing of one unarmed man, leaving the Territory entirely in the power of the Free State men, with an organized militia, armed, equipped, and in full force for its protection; but the result is not yet fully known. What now remains for the Free State men of Kansas, and their friends in the State, and the world to do, is to *hold* the ground they now possess, *and Kansas is free.*

A great part of the volunteers were strong, hardy farmers and mechanics, who had left their work and their homes (on hearing of the invasion) without even waiting to change their clothes; and were, as a whole, the most intelligent, sober and orderly set of men I have ever seen collected, in equal number, except at religious worship. They were sober, earnest thinking men, betraying no anxiety as to the result of what they had undertaken, as composed and quiet as though they had been collected from some first rate country neighborhood, to raise a house or barn. Here were developed such a set of determined men as I had no idea this Territory could boast of, in any such numbers. They now know their own members, and their condition for self-government and self-defence. They have now become acquainted, and in their feelings, strongly knit together, the result of having shared together some of the conditions of war in actual service. Many of those volunteers were sterling Free State men from several of the Slave States. They have my warmest blessing. *35271*

We are exceedingly anxious to learn how matters go off in the States and in Congress this winter. We are very much shut away from news. Please acknowledge this by sending one number of the *Beacon*, for which I would subscribe had I the means.

Yours truly,   JOHN BROWN

Osawatomie Kansas Territory 1st Feby 1856

Dear Wife & Children every One

Your & Watsons Letter to the Boys, & Myself of Decem 30th & Jany 1st were received by last Mail. We are all very glad to hear again of your welfare; & I am particularly grateful when I am noticed by a Letter from *you*. I have just taken out Two Letters for Henry One of which I suppose is from Ruth. Salmon & myself are so far on our way home from Missouri; & only reached Mr Adairs last night. They are all well & we know of nothing but all are well at the Boys Shantees. The weather continues very severe : & it is now nearly Six Weeks that the Snow has been almost constantly driven (like dry Sand) by the fierce Winds of Kansas. Mr. Adair has been collecting Ice of late from the Osage River; which is 9½ Inches thick, of perfect clean sollid Ice, formed under the Snow. By means of the sale of our Horse & Waggon : our present wants are tolerably well met; so that if health is continued to us we shall not probably suffer much. The idea of again visiting those of my dear family at North Elba; is so calculated to unMan me that I seldom allow my thoughts to dwell uppon it : & I do not think best to write much about it. "Suffise it to Say"; that God is *abundantly* able to keep both us, & you : & *in him let us all trust*. We have just learned of some *new*; & shocking outrages at Leavenworth : & that the Free State people there have fled to Lawrence : which place is again threatened with an attack. *Should* that take place we may soon again be called uppon to "buckle on our Armor"; which by the help of God we will do : when I suppose Henry, & Oliver will have a chance. *My judgement is*; that we shall have no more general disturbance until warmer weather. I have more to say; but not time now to say it. So farewell for this time. *Write*

Your Affectionate Husband & Father
John Brown

101

The following letter was written after the Pottawatomie killings, in which five pro-slavery men on Pottawatomie Creek were killed by a party of eight under John Brown's leadership.

Near Brown's Station, K. T., June, 1856.

DEAR WIFE AND CHILDREN, EVERY ONE,—It is now about five weeks since I have seen a line from North Elba, or had any chance of writing you. During that period we here have passed through an almost constant series of very trying events. We were called to the relief of Lawrence, May 22, and every man (eight in all), except Orson[15] turned out; he staying with the women and children, and to take care of the cattle. John was captain of a company to which Jason belonged; the other six were a little company by ourselves. On our way to Lawrence we learned that it had been already destroyed, and we encamped with John's company overnight. Next day our little company left, and during the day we stopped and searched three men.

Lawrence was destroyed in this way: Their leading men had (as I think) decided, in a very *cowardly* manner, not to resist any process having any Government official to serve it, notwithstanding the process might be wholly a bogus affair. The consequence was that a man called a United States marshal came on with a horde of ruffians which he called his posse, and after arresting a few persons turned the ruffians loose on the defenceless people. They robbed the inhabitants of their money and other property, and even women of their ornaments, and burned considerable of the town.

On the second day and evening after we left John's men we encountered quite a number of proslavery men, and took quite a number prisoners. Our prisoners we let go; but we kept some four or five horses. We were immediately after this accused of murdering five men at Pottawatomie, and great efforts have since been made by the Missourians and their ruffian allies to capture us. John's company soon afterwards disbanded, and also the Osawatomie men.[16]

Jason started to go and place himself under the protection of the Government troops; but on his way he was taken prisoner by the Bogus men, and is yet a prisoner, I suppose. John tried to hide for several days; but from feelings of the ungrateful conduct of those

---

[15] Mr. Orson Day, a brother of Mrs. John Brown.

[16] F. B. Sanborn makes the following comment in a note at this point: " In the original something has been erased after this, to which this note seems to have been appended: ' There are but very few who wish real facts about these matters to go out.' Then is inserted the date ' June 26,' as below." (*John Brown*, p. 237.)

who ought to have stood by him, excessive fatigue, anxiety, and constant loss of sleep, he became quite insane, and in that situation gave up, or as we are told, was betrayed at Osawatomie into the hands of the Bogus men. We do not know all the truth about this affair. He has since, we are told, been kept in irons, and brought to a trial before a bogus court, the result of which we have not yet learned. We have great anxiety both for him and Jason, and numerous other prisoners with the enemy (who have all the while had the Government troops to sustain them). We can only commend them to God.

The cowardly mean conduct of Osawatomie and vicinity did not save them; for the ruffians came on them, made numerous prisoners, fired their buildings, and robbed them. After this a picked party of the Bogus men went to Brown's Station,[17] burned John's and Jason's houses, and their contents to ashes; in which burning we have all suffered more or less. Orson and boy have been prisoners, but were soon set at liberty. They are well, and have not been seriously injured. Owen and I have just come here for the first time to look at the ruins. All looks desolate and forsaken,—the grass and weeds fast covering up the signs that these places were lately the abodes of quiet families. After burning the houses, this self-same party of picked men, some forty in number, set out as they supposed, and as was the fact, on the track of my little company, boasting, with awful profanity, that they would have our scalps. They however passed the place where we were hid, and robbed a little town some four or five miles beyond our camp in the timber.[18] I had omitted to say that some murders had been committed at the time Lawrence was sacked.

On learning that this party were in pursuit of us, my little company, now increased to ten in all, started after them in company of a Captain Shore, with eighteen men, he included (June 1). We were all mounted as we travelled. We did not meet them on that day, but took five prisoners, four of whom were of their scouts, and well armed. We were out all night, but could find nothing of them until about six o'clock next morning, when we prepared to attack them at once, on foot, leaving Frederick and one of Captain Shore's men to guard the horses. As I was much older than Captain Shore, the principal direction of the fight devolved on me. We got to within about a mile of their camp before being discovered by their scouts, and then moved at a brisk pace, Captain Shore and men forming our

17 Ten miles west of Osawatomie. 18 Palmyra.

left, and my company the right. When within about sixty rods of the enemy, Captain Shore's men halted by mistake in a very exposed situation, and continued the fire, both his men and the enemy being armed with Sharpe's rifles. My company had no long-shooters. We (my company) did not fire a gun until we gained the rear of a bank, about fifteen or twenty rods to the right of the enemy, where we commenced, and soon compelled them to hide in a ravine. Captain Shore, after getting one man wounded, and exhausting his ammunition, came with part of his men to the right of my position, much discouraged. The balance of his men, including the one wounded, had left the ground. Five of Captain Shore's men came boldly down and joined my company, and all but one man, wounded, helped to maintain the fight until it was over. I was obliged to give my consent that he[19] should go after more help, when all his men left but eight, four of whom I persuaded to remain in a secure position, and there busied one of them in shooting the horses and mules of the enemy, which served for a show of fight. After the firing had continued for some two to three hours, Captain Pate with twenty-three men, two badly wounded, laid down their arms to nine men, myself included,—four of Captain Shore's men and four of my own. One of my men (Henry Thompson) was badly wounded, and after continuing his fire for an hour longer was obliged to quit the ground. Three others of my company (but not of my family) had gone off. Salmon was dreadfully wounded by accident, soon after the fight; but both he and Henry are fast recovering.

A day or two after the fight, Colonel Sumner of the United States army came suddenly upon us, while fortifying our camp and guarding our prisoners (which, by the way, it had been agreed mutually should be exchanged for as many Free-State men, John and Jason included), and compelled us to let go our prisoners without being exchanged, and to give up their horses and arms. They did not go more than two or three miles before they began to rob and injure Free-State people. We consider this as in good keeping with the cruel and unjust course of the Administration and its tools throughout this whole Kansas difficulty. Colonel Sumner also compelled us to disband; and we, being only a handful, were obliged to submit.

Since then we have, like David of old, had our dwelling with the serpents of the rocks and wild beasts of the wilderness; being obliged to hide away from our enemies. We are not disheartened, though

[19] Captain Shore.

nearly destitute of food, clothing, and money. God, who has not given us over to the will of our enemies, but has moreover delivered them into our hand, will, we humbly trust, still keep and deliver us. We feel assured that He who sees not as men see, does not lay the guilt of innocent blood to our charge.

I ought to have said that Captain Shore and his men stood their ground nobly in their unfortunate but mistaken position during the early part of the fight. I ought to say further that a Captain Abbott, being some miles distant with a company, came onward promptly to sustain us, but could not reach us till the fight was over. After the fight, numerous Free-State men who could not be got out before were on hand; and some of them, I am ashamed to add, were very busy not only with the plunder of our enemies, but with our private effects, leaving us, while guarding our prisoners and providing in regard to them, much poorer than before the battle.

If, under God, this letter reaches you so that it can be read, I wish it at once carefully copied, and a copy of it sent to Gerrit Smith. I know of no other way to get these facts and our situation before the world, nor when I can write again.

Owen has the ague to-day. Our camp is some miles off. Have heard that letters are in for some of us, but have not seen them. Do continue writing. We heard last mail brought only three letters, and all these for proslavery men. It is said that both the Lawrence and Osawatomie men, when the ruffians came on them, either hid or gave up their arms, and that their leading men counselled them to take such a course.

May God bless and keep you all!

Your affectionate husband and father,
John Brown

P. S. Ellen and Wealthy are staying at Osawatomie.

The above is a true account of the first regular battle fought between Free-State and proslavery men in Kansas. May God still gird our loins and hold our right hands, and to him may we give the glory! I ought in justice to say, that, after the sacking and burning of several towns, the Government troops appeared for their protection and drove off some of the enemy.

J. B.

June 26. Jason is set at liberty, and we have hopes for John. Owen, Salmon, and Oliver are down with fever (since inserted); Henry doing well.

Topeka, Kansas Ter, 4th July, 1856

Dear Wife & Children every one

I have again through the mercy of God opportunity to write you a few words. Wrote you in pencil somewhat at length a few days ago : but have no assurance that anything I send will ever meet your eyes. Have seen nothing that came from you since some time in May last. Since I wrote you last we have had more of quiet; but in the mean time Salmon, Owen, Fred^k & Oliver have all been sick; Owen *very* sick & was still so, when Oliver & I left our camp about four or Five days since. We are very anxious about him, Henry & Salmon are both much better of their wounds. We came here with Free State men collected to attend the convening of the Free State Legislature who were threatened with general arrest if they met again. A large number of U S troops are on the ground to enforce Bogus Legislation; & to scatter the Free State men, who are also on the ground in considerable force. Today will probably decide whether the Free State Legislature is to be broken up or not. *If they are* : It will be done by the *government troops;* as I have no idea of the Bogus men fighting us at all without them. A dreadful state of things exists here but I have no doubt but that in the end *Right* will triumph. We are near where John is held prisner by U S troops, but no Free State friends are allowed to visit him for some days past. None of us have seen him since he was taken. Jason has been set at liberty I here stop hoping to report further before I close.

July 5th 1856

Yesterday Col Sumner of the US army with his men took possession of the Hall or rooms to be occupied by the Free State Legislature; then called in the members, & in the name of Franklin Pierce, & as he said by his direction commanded the Legislature to disperse to which they submitted. There was no fighting. We leave today for our camp. Are in hopes John will soon now be liberated. May God Keep & bless You all

Your Affectionate Husband & Father   John Brown

John Brown writes of the death of his son, Frederick, and tells the story of his battle at Osawatomie with the border ruffians.

Lawrence K T 7th Sept 1856

Dear Wife & Children every one

I have one moment to write you to say that I am yet alive that Jason & family were well yesterday John; & family I hear are well; (he being yet a prisoner.[20] On the morning of the 30th Aug an attack was made by the ruffians on Osawatomie numbering some 400 by whose scouts our dear Fred[k] was shot dead without warning he supposing them to be Free State men as near as we can learn. One other man a Cousin of Mr Adair was murdered by them about the same time that Fred[k] was killed & one badly wounded at the same time. At this time I was about 3 miles off where I had some 14 or 15 men over night that I had just enlisted to serve under me as regulars. There I collected as well as I could with some 12 or 15 more & in about 3/4 of an Hour attacked them from a wood with thick undergroth., with this force we threw them into confusion for about 15 or 20 Minuets during which time we killed & wounded from 70 to 80 of the enemy *as they say* & then we escaped as well as we could with one killed while escaping; Two or Three wounded; & as many more missing. Four or Five Free State men were butchered during the day in all. Jason fought bravely by my side during the fight & escaped with me he being unhurt. I was struck by a partly spent, Grape, Canister, or Rifle shot which bruised me some but did not injure me seriously. "Hitherto the Lord hath helped me" notwithstanding my afflictions. Things now seem rather quiet just now; but what another Hour will bring I cannot say - I have seen Three or four letters from Ruth & One from Watson of July or Aug which are all I have seen since in June. I was very glad to hear once more from you & hope you will continue to write to some of the friends so that I may hear from you. I am utterly unable to write you for most of the time. May the God of of [sic] our Fathers bless & save you all

Your Affectionate Husband & Father

John Brown

Monday Morning 8th Sept/56

Jason has just come in. Left all well as usual Johns trial is to come off or commence today

Yours ever

John Brown

[20] Parenthesis omitted in original.

A speech reportedly delivered by John Brown in Lawrence, on Sunday afternoon, September 13, prior to an anticipated attack by 2,800 Missourians on the city.

"GENTLEMEN,—It is said there are twenty-five hundred Missourians down at Franklin, and that they will be here in two hours. You can see for yourselves the smoke they are making by setting fire to the houses in that town. Now is probably the last opportunity you will have of seeing a fight, so that you had better do your best. If they should come up and attack us, don't yell and make a great noise, but remain perfectly silent and still. Wait till they get within twenty-five yards of you; get a good object; be sure you see the hind sight of your gun,—then fire. A great deal of powder and lead and very precious time is wasted by shooting too high. You had better aim at their legs than at their heads. In either case, be sure of the hind sights of your guns. It is from the neglect of this that I myself have so many times escaped; for if all the bullets that have ever been aimed at me had hit, I should have been as full of holes as a riddle."

On leaving Kansas for the East.

Tabor, Iowa, 11th Oct 1856

Dear Wife & Children every one

I am *through Infinite grace*, once more in a Free State; & on my way to make you a visit. I left Kansas a day or Two since by a waggon in which I had a bed; as I was so unwell that I had to lie down. I first had the Dysentary, & then Chill Fever. Am now rapidly improveing. Wealthy & Ellen with their little boys started for home by way of the River about Ten day since. John, Jason, & Owen; all came out with me. John & Jason have gone on towards Chicago with a horse but *expects* to meet me next week on the Rail Road on the East line of the State. *I expect* to go by stage. *Owen* thinks of wintering here. *Mr Adair and family* were all midling well Two Weeks ago. Mr. Day and *Family have* been sick but were better. When we left there seemed to be a little calm *for the present* in Kansas; Cannot say how long it will last. You need not be anxious about me if I am some time on the road as I have to stop at several places; & go some out of my way; having left partly on business expecting to return if the troubles continue in Kansas; & my health will admit. Now that I am where I can write you, I may do it midling often. May God bless & Keep you all. Your Affectionate Husband & Father-

John Brown

P S Ruths letter to John of 16th Sept was received
Yours
J B

In 1857, after reaching the East, John Brown delivered speeches in Hartford, Boston, Concord and other cities, in which he described conditions in Kansas and sought to raise funds for his future efforts there. In Connecticut, where he felt more at home, he ended his talks with the following appeal for funds.

" I am trying to raise from twenty to twenty-five thousand dollars in the free States, to enable me to continue my efforts in the cause of freedom. Will the people of Connecticut, *my native State*, afford me some aid in this undertaking? Will the gentlemen and ladies of Hartford, where I make my first appeal in this State, set the example of an earnest effort? Will some gentleman or lady take hold and try what can be done by small contributions from counties, cities, towns, societies, or churches, or in some other way? I think the little beggar-children in the streets are sufficiently interested to warrant their contributing, if there was any need of it, to secure the object. I was told that the newspapers in a certain city were dressed in mourning on hearing that I was killed and scalped in Kansas, but I did not know of it until I reached the place. Much good it did me. In the same place I met a more cool reception than in any other place where I have stopped. If my friends will hold up my hands while I live, I will freely absolve them from any expense over me when I am dead. I do not ask for pay, but shall be most grateful for all the assistance I can get."

In seeking funds, he also published the following statement in the New York *Tribune* (March 4, 1857) and other newspapers.

TO THE FRIENDS OF FREEDOM

The undersigned, whose individual means were exceedingly limited when he first engaged in the struggle for Liberty in Kansas, being now still more destitute and no less anxious than in time past to continue his efforts to sustain that cause, is induced to make this earnest appeal to the friends of Freedom throughout the United States, in the firm belief that his call will not go unheeded. I ask all honest lovers of *Liberty and Human Rights, both male and female*, to hold up my hands by contributions of pecuniary aid, either as counties, cities, towns, villages, societies, churches or individuals.

I will endeavor to make a judicious and faithful application of all such means as I may be supplied with. Contributions may be sent in drafts to W. H. D. Callender, Cashier State Bank, Hartford, Ct. It is my intention to visit as many places *as I can* during my stay in the States, provided I am first informed of the disposition of the inhabitants to aid me *in my efforts*, as well as to receive my visit. Information may be communicated to me (care of Massasoit House) at Springfield, Mass. Will editors of newspapers friendly to the cause kindly second the measure, and also give this some half dozen insertions? Will either gentlemen or ladies, or both, who love the cause, volunteer to take up the business? It is with *no little sacrifice of personal feeling* that I appear in this manner before the public.

John Brown

New York, March, 1857.

To his wife, who had written him that his sons were unwilling to do any more fighting.

Springfield, Mass, 31st March, 1857.

Dear Wife

Your letter of the 21st inst is just received. I have only to say as regards the resolution of the boys to " learn, & practice war no more "; that it was not at my solicitation that they engaged in it at the first : & that while I may *perhaps* feel no more love of the business than they do; still I think there may be *possibly* in their day that which is more to be dreaded : if such things *do not now exist.* I have all along intended to make the best provision I may be capable of; for all my family. What I may hereafter be able *to effect*; I cannot now say. I now enclose a Draft on New York for $30, Thirty Dollars payable to the order of Watson. I have wholly forgotten how much I had of his sheep money; but I think I made an account of it in my book. If I do not send enough; perhaps Henry will spare him a little for a few days, until I get back again; if he has it on hand. I cannot well send any more just now; & get the articles that have been sent for since I left home. I expect more soon. I have just got a long letter from Mr. Adair. All midling well March 11th; but had fears of further trouble after a while. Your Affectionate Husband

John Brown

An inscription in a Bible which John Brown gave to his daughter, Ellen.

This Bible, presented to my dearly beloved daughter Ellen Brown, is not intended for common use, but to be carefully preserved *for her* and *by her*, in remembrance of her father (of whose care and attentions she was deprived in her infancy), he being absent in the territory of Kansas from the summer of 1855.

May the Holy Spirit of God incline your heart, *in earliest child-hood*, "to receive the truth in the love of it," and to form your thoughts, words, and actions by its wise and holy precepts, is *my best wish* and *most earnest* prayer to Him in whose care I leave you. Amen.

From your affectionate father,

John Brown

April 2, 1857

Boston, Mass. 3d April, 1857

Wm Barnes Esqr
  Albany, N. Y.

My Dear Sir

I expect soon to return West; & to [go] back without securing even an outfit. I go with a *sad heart* having failed to secure even the means of equiping; to say nothing of feeding men. I had when I returned no more that I could peril; & could make no further sacrifice, except to go about in the attitude of a beggar; & that I have done, humiliating as it is. You once in conversation mentioned the propriety of my taking a claim in Kansas, but I have no means of securing a claim; & shall be obliged to leave my Wife & Three little Girls dependent on the charities of friends to a great extent. If persons in your place are disposed to encourage me so far as to enable me to secure a claim in Kansas; it may enable me to avail myself of some State appropriations for actual Settlers. *I am prepared to expect nothing but bad faith* from the National Kansas Committee at Chicago, as I will show you hereafter. *This* is for the present *confidential.*

Very respectfully Yours
John Brown

P. S. Shall be glad to hear from you at Springfield, Mass., care of Massasoit House.

Yours   J B

West Newton, Mass, 15th April 1857

Dear Son John

I received your welcome letter of the 6th inst. last night, at Boston; & am very glad of all the information it gives. I have had no letters from home for several days; but when I last heard from N, E, all were well. I am much gratified to learn of Mr. Giddings full redemption from Slavery. I am also very glad at the kind feeling expressed by your "Bail" towards you; & have no doubt of the correctness of your ideas about *not going back* to stand trial. That would never do. If any of us are hereafter to be tried in Kansas;

I would much rather it should be with Irons *in* rather than *uppon* our hands. The old Monument (perhaps I forgot to say) is an old fashioned Granite, Grave Stone; with a short old style account of Capt John Brown who died at New York (*almost to a day*) Eighty years from the death of his *Great, Grand, Son, Fred^k Brown*; in Kansas. I value the old relic, much the more for its *age, & homeliness*; & it is of sufficient size to contain more *brief* inscriptions. One Hundred years from 1856 should it then be in the possession of the same posterity: it will be a great curiosity. Your remarks about the value & importance of dicipline, I fully appreciate; & I had been making arangements to secure the assistance, & instruction; of a distinguished Scotch officer;[21] & *author* quite popular *in this country*. I am quite sanguine of my success in the matter. My collections I may safely put down at $13000, & I think I have got matters in such a train that it will soon reach $30,000, I have had a good deal of discouragement; & *have often* felt quite depressed; *but " hither to God hath helped me."* About the *last* of last Week, I gave vent to those feelings in a short piece (which you may yet see in the prints,) headed Old Browns, Farewell: to the Plymouth Rocks; Bunker Hill, Monuments; Charter Oaks; & Uncle Toms Cabbins. The effect on a Boston Merchant who saw the manuscript was that he immediately sent me a letter authorizing me to draw on him at sight for $7000, & others were also moved to be in earnest: *Wendell Phillips*; & *Theodore Parker* (who though sick) said of the merchant (above named) that his *" name* had been written in the Lambs Book of life." A. A. Lawrence & Brother have started a Subscription to provide for my Wife, & little Girls in my *absence; & in case I never return to them*. About these things *I do not wish any remarks made*. Jason wrote me that Charly had been sick "unto death;" but appeared better & that one of "U.S. Hounds" had been at Cleveland going East *after me*. I have been hideing about a week for my track to get cold; & the papers gave it out last Week that I had left en Route for Kansas. I think I shall not "be delivered into the hands of the wicked"; & feel quite easy; but mean to make it very difficult to follow me. I mean if I can to call on you. Jeremiah wrote me that Abi was very sick. Hope to hear soon of her recovery. Write me through *Henry*. May God abundantly bless you all. Train up the Wolf hunter "in the way he *should go*.

Your Affectionate Father
John Brown

[21] Hugh Forbes, with whom he later quarreled.

This is the "short piece" referred to above. It was written by Brown in April while in hiding at the home of Judge and Mrs. Thomas Russell of Boston.

Old Browns Farewell
to
The Plymouth Rocks, Bunker Hill Monuments, Charter Oaks, and Uncle Thoms Cabbins.

He has left for Kansas. Has been trying since he came out of the territory to secure an outfit or in other words; the means of arming and thoroughly equipping his regular Minuet men, who are mixed up *with the people of Kansas*, and *he leaves* the States, *with a feeling of deepest sadness*; that after having exhausted *his own small means* and with his *family and his brave men*; suffered hunger, cold, naked-ness, *and some* of them sickness, wounds, imprisonment *in irons*; with extreme cruel treatment, *and others death* : that after lying on the ground for months in the most sickly, unwholesome, and un-comfortable places; *some of the time with sick and wounded* desti-tute of any shelter; and hunted like wolves; sustained in part by Indians : that after all this; in order to sustain a cause which every citizen of this " *glorious Republic*," is under equal moral obligation to do : *and for the neglect of which, he will be held accountable by God* : a cause in which every man, woman, and child; of the *entire human family* has a *deep* and *awful* interest; that when *no wages* are asked; or expected; he cannot secure, amidst all the wealth, luxury, and extravagance of this " Heaven exalted," people; even the necessary supplies of the common soldier. " How are the mighty fallen "?

Boston, April, A. D. 1857.

On the way to Kansas.

HUDSON, OHIO, May 27, 1857.

DEAR WIFE AND CHILDREN, EVERY ONE,—. . . I have got Salmon's letter of the 19th instant, and am much obliged for it. There is some prospect that Owen will go on with me. If I should never return, it is my particular request that no other monument be used to keep me in remembrance than the same plain one that

114

records the death of my grandfather and son; and that a short story, like those already on it, be told of John Brown the fifth, under that of grandfather. I think I have several good reasons for this. I would be glad that my posterity should not only remember their parentage, but also the cause they labored in. I do not expect to leave these parts under four or five days, and will try to write again before I go off. I am much confused in mind, and cannot remember what I wish to write. May God abundantly bless you all! . . .

Your affectionate husband and father,

JOHN BROWN.

On his way to Kansas, Brown wrote to Franklin B. Sanborn.

TABOR, FREMONT COUNTY, IOWA, Aug. 13, 1857.

Much as I love to communicate with you, it is still a great burden for me to write when I have nothing of interest to say, and when there is something to be active about. Since I left New England I have had a good deal of ill-health; and having in good measure exhausted my available means toward purchasing such supplies as I should certainly need if again called into active service, and without which I could accomplish next to nothing, I had to begin my journey back with not more than half money at any time to bear my expenses through and pay my freights. This being the case, I was obliged to stop at different points on the way, and to go to others off the route to solicit help. At most places I raised a little; but it consumed my time, and my unavoidable expenses so nearly kept pace with my incomes that I found it exceedingly discouraging. With the help of Gerrit Smith, who supplied me with sixty dollars at Peterboro', and two hundred and fifty dollars at Chicago, and other smaller amounts from others, I was able to pay freights and other expenses to this place; hiring a man to drive one team, and driving another myself; and had about twenty-five dollars on hand, with about one hundred dollars' worth of provisions, when I reached here. Among all the good friends who had promised to go with me, *not one* could I get to stick by me and assist me on my way through. I have picked up, at different times on the way, considerable value in articles (indispensable in active service) which were scattered on the way, and had been provided either by or for the National Committee. On reaching here I found one hundred and ten dollars, sent me by Mr. Whitman, from sale of articles in Kansas, sent there by the National Committee. This is all the money I have got from them on their appropriation at New York. On the road one of my horses hurt himself so badly that I lost about ten days in consequence, not being in condition to go on without him, or to buy or to hire another. I find the arms and ammunition voted me by the Massachusetts State Committee nearly all here, and in middling good order,—some a little rusted. Have overhauled and cleaned up the worst of them, and am now waiting to know what is best to do next, or for a little escort from Kansas, should I and the supplies be needed. I am now at last within a kind of hailing distance of our Free-State friends in Kansas.

On the way from Iowa City I and my third son (the hired man I mentioned), in order to make the little funds we had reach as far as possible, and to avoid notice, lived exclusively on herring, soda crackers, and sweetened water for more than three weeks (sleeping every night in our wagons), except that twice we got a little milk, and a few times some boiled eggs. Early in the season, in consequence of the poor encouragement I met with, and of their own losses and sufferings, my sons declined to return; and my wife wrote me as follows: "The boys have all determined both to practise and learn war no more." This I said nothing about, lest it should prevent my getting any further supplies. After leaving New England I could not get the scratch of a pen to tell whether anything had been deposited at Hartford, from New Haven and other places, for me or not; until, since I came here, a line comes from Mr. Callender, dated 24th July, saying nothing has been deposited, in answer to one I had written June 22, in which he further says he has answered all my letters. The parting with my wife and young uneducated children, without income, supplies of clothing, provisions, or even a comfortable house to live in, or money to provide such things, with at least a fair chance that it was to be a *last and final separation*, had lain heavily on me, and was about as much a matter of self-sacrifice and self-devotion on the part of my wife as on my own, and about as much her act as my own. When Mr. Lawrence, of his own accord, proposed relieving me on that score, it greatly eased a burdened spirit; but I did not rely upon it absolutely, nor make any certain bargain on the strength of it, until after being positively assured by Mr. Stearns, in writing, that it should, and by yourself that it would, certainly be done.

It was the poor condition of my noble-hearted wife and of her young children that made me follow up that encouragement with a tenacity that disgusted him and completely exhausted his patience. But after such repeated assurances from friends I so much respected that I could not suspect they would trifle with my feelings, I made a positive bargain for the farm; and when I found nothing for me at Peterboro', I borrowed one hundred and ten dollars of Mr. Smith for the men who occupied the farm, telling him it would certainly be refunded, and the others that they would get all their money very soon, and even before I left the country. This has brought me only extreme mortification and depression of feeling; for all my letters from home, up to the last, say not a dime has been paid in to Mr. Smith. Friends who never know the lack of a sumptuous dinner little comprehend the value of such trifling matters to persons circumstanced as I am. But, my noble-hearted friend, I am " though faint, yet pursuing." My health has been much better of late. I believe my anxiety and discouragements had something to do with repeated returns of fever and ague I have had, as it tended to deprive me of sleep and to debilitate me. I intend this letter as a kind of report of my progress and success, as much for your committee or my friend Stearns as yourself. I have been joined by a friend[22] since I got here, and get no discouraging news from Kansas.

Your friend,

J. BROWN.

John Brown arrived in Kansas about November 5. Because of the peaceful state of affairs in the Territory, there was little for him to do, and he left Kansas after about two weeks. Thereafter, all his efforts were concentrated upon plans for the attack upon slavery in Virginia.

ROCHESTER, N. Y., Jan. 30, 1858.

MY DEAR WIFE AND CHILDREN, EVERY ONE,—I am (praised be God!) once more in York State. Whether I shall be permitted to visit you or not this winter or spring, I cannot now say; but it is some relief of mind to feel that I am again so near you. Possibly, if I cannot go to see you, I may be able to devise some way for some one or more of you to meet me somewhere. The anxiety I feel to see my wife and children once more I am unable to describe. I want exceedingly to see my big baby and Ruth's baby, and to see how that little company of sheep look about this time. The cries of my

22 This friend was Col. Hugh Forbes, British soldier-of-fortune, whom Brown had employed to prepare a manual on guerrilla warfare and to train his men. Brown and Forbes soon parted, and Forbes, piqued, made disclosures which threatened to expose the whole plan, and did cause postponement of operations for more than a year.

poor sorrow-stricken despairing children, whose "tears on their cheeks" are ever in my eyes, and whose sighs are ever in my ears, may however prevent my enjoying the happiness I so much desire. But, courage, courage, courage!—the great work of my life (the unseen Hand that "guided me, and who has indeed holden my right hand, may hold it still," though I have not known him at all as I ought) I may yet see accomplished (God helping), and be permitted to return and "rest at evening."

O my daughter Ruth! could any plan be devised whereby you could let Henry go "to school" (as you expressed it in your letter to him while in Kansas), I would rather now have him "for another term" than to have a hundred average scholars. I have a particular and very important, but not dangerous, place for him to fill in the "school," and I know of no man living so well adapted to fill it. I am quite confident some way can be devised so that you and your children could be with him, and be quite happy even, and safe; but God forbid me to flatter you into trouble! I did not do it before. My dear child, could you face such music if, on a full explanation, Henry could be satisfied that his family might be safe? I would make a similar inquiry of my own dear wife; but I have kept her tumbling here and there over a stormy and tempestuous sea for so many years that I cannot ask her such a question. The natural ingenuity of Salmon in connection with some experience he and Oliver have both had, would point him out as the next best man I could now select; but I am dumb in his case, as also in the case of Watson and all my other sons. Jason's qualifications are, some of them, like Henry's also.

Do not noise it about that I am in these parts, and direct to N. Hawkins, care of Frederick Douglass, Rochester, N. Y. I want to hear how you are all supplied with winter clothing, boots, etc.

God bless you all!

Your affectionate husband and father,

JOHN BROWN.

To Thomas Wentworth Higginson, the anti-slavery Unitarian minister at Worcester, Mass.

Rochester, N. Y. 12th Feb'y, 1858.
MY DEAR SIR,—I have just read your kind letter of the 8th inst., and will now say that Rail Road business on a *somewhat extended*

scale is the *identical* object for which I am trying to get means. I have been connected with that business as *commonly conducted* from my boyhood and *never* let an opportunity slip. I have been opperating to some purpose *the past season*; but I now have a measure on *foot* that I feel *sure* would awaken in you something more than a *common interest* if you could understand it. I have just written my friends G. L. Stearns and F. B. Sanborn asking them to meet me for consultation at Gerrit Smith's, Peterboro' [N. Y.]. I am very anxious to have *you come along; certain as I feel*, that you will never regret having been one of the council. I would most gladly pay your expenses had I the means to spare. *Will you come on?* Please write as before.

Your Friend   John Brown.

This Constitution was adopted at a convention of John Brown's followers, consisting of forty-six Negro and white men, in Chatham, Canada West, held on May 8-10, 1858. It was intended to govern the areas which Brown hoped to liberate from Southern slavery. It consisted of forty-eight Articles, of which seven are reprinted here.

Provisional Constitution and Ordinances for the people of the United States

PREAMBLE

Whereas slavery, throughout its entire existence in the United States, is none other than a most barbarous, unprovoked, and unjustifiable war of one portion of its citizens upon another portion—the only conditions of which are perpetual imprisonment and hopeless servitude or absolute extermination—in utter disregard and violation of those eternal and self-evident truths set forth in our Declaration of Independence :

Therefore we, citizens of the United States, and the oppressed people who, by a recent decision of the Supreme Court, are declared to have no rights which the white man is bound to respect, together with all other people degraded by the laws thereof, do, for the time being, ordain and establish for ourselves the following Provisional Constitution and Ordinances, the better to protect our persons, property, lives, and liberties, and to govern our actions :

ARTICLE I

Qualifications for membership

All persons of mature age, whether proscribed, oppressed, and enslaved citizens, or of the proscribed and oppressed races of the United States, who shall agree to sustain and enforce the Provisional Constitution and Ordinances of this organization, together with all minor children of such persons, shall be held to be fully entitled to protection under the same.

ARTICLE II

Branches of government

The provisional government of this organization shall consist of three branches, viz.: legislative, executive, and judicial.

ARTICLE III

Legislative

The legislative branch shall be a Congress or House of Representatives, composed of not less than five nor more than ten members, who shall be elected by all citizens of mature age and of sound mind connected with this organization, and who shall remain in office for three years, unless sooner removed for misconduct, inability, or by death. A majority of such members shall constitute a quorum.

ARTICLE IV

Executive

The executive branch of this organization shall consist of a President and Vice-President, who shall be chosen by the citizens or members of this organization, and each of whom shall hold his office for three years, unless sooner removed by death or for inability or misconduct.

ARTICLE V

Judicial

The judicial branch of this organization shall consist of one Chief Justice of the Supreme Court and of four associate judges of said court, each constituting a circuit court. They shall each be chosen in the same manner as the President, and shall continue in office until their places have been filled in the same manner by election of the citizens. Said court shall have jurisdiction in all civil or criminal causes arising under this constitution, except breaches of the rules of war.

ARTICLE VI

Validity of enactments

All enactments of the legislative branch shall, to become valid during the first three years, have the approbation of the President and of the Commander-in-chief of the army.

ARTICLE VII

Commander-in-chief

A Commander-in-chief of the army shall be chosen by the President, Vice-President, a majority of the Provisional Congress, and of the Supreme Court, and he shall receive his commission from the President, signed by the Vice-President, the Chief Justice of the Supreme Court, and the Secretary of War, and he shall hold his office for three years, unless removed by death or on proof of incapacity or misbehavior. He shall, unless under arrest, (and until his place is actually filled as provided for by this constitution,) direct all movements of the army and advise with any allies. He shall, however, be tried, removed, or punished, on complaint of the President, by at least three general officers, or a majority of the House of Representatives, or of the Supreme Court; which House of Representatives, (the President presiding,) the Vice-President, and the members of the Supreme Court, shall constitute a court-martial for his trial; with power to remove or punish, as the case may require, and to fill his place, as above provided.

Because of a quarrel and open break with Hugh Forbes, and Forbes' threat to make public the entire plot, Brown and his backers decided to postpone the attack in Virginia. On June 25, 1858, Brown was again in Kansas, wearing a white beard, and using the name of Shubel Morgan. The following letter refers to one of his most spectacular exploits, in which he freed eleven slaves in Missouri and brought them, in the middle of March, after eighty-two days and eleven-hundred miles of wandering in the dead of winter, to safety in Canada. The letter appeared in the New York Daily *Tribune*, Saturday, January 22, 1859.

OLD BROWN'S PARALLELS

Correspondence of The N.Y. Tribune.

Trading Post, Kansas, Jan., 1859.

The editor of The N.Y. Tribune will greatly oblige a humble friend by allowing me the use of his columns while I briefly state two parallels, in my poor way.

Not one year ago, eleven quiet citizens of this neighborhood, viz: Wm. Calfsetzer [Colpetzer], Wm. Robertson, Amos Hall, Austin Hall, John Campbell, Asa Snyder, Thomas Stilwell, William Hairgrove, Asa Hairgrove, Patrick Ross and B. L. Reed were gathered up from their work and their homes, by an armed force under one Hamilton, and, without trial or opportunity to speak in their own defense, were formed into a line, and all but one shot—five killed and five wounded. One fell unharmed, pretending to be dead. All were *left for dead*. The only crime charged against them was that of being Free-State men. Now, I inquire, what action has ever, since the occurrence in May last, been taken by either the President of the United States, the Governor of Missouri, the Governor of Kansas, or any of their tools, or by any Pro-Slavery or Administration man, to ferret out and punish the perpetrators of this crime?

Now for the other parallel. On Sunday, the 19th of December, a negro man named Jim, came over to the Osage settlement, from Missouri, and stated that he, together with his wife, two children and one other negro man, were to be sold within a day or two, and begged for help to get away. On Monday, the following night, two small companies were made up to go to Missouri, and forcibly liberate the five slaves, *together with other slaves*. One of these companies I assumed to direct. We proceeded to the place, surrounded the buildings, liberated the slaves, and also took certain property supposed to belong to the estate. We, however, learned before leaving, that a portion of the articles we had taken belonged to a man living on the plantation as a tenant, and who was supposed to have no interest in the estate. We promptly returned to him *all we had taken*. We then went to another plantation, where we freed five more slaves, took some property, and two white men. We moved slowly away into the Territory, for some distance, and then sent the white men back, telling them to follow us as soon as they chose to do so. The other company freed one female slave, took some property, and, as I am informed, killed one white man (the master), who fought against the liberation.

Now for a comparison. Eleven persons are forcibly restored to their "natural and inalienable rights," with but one man killed, and all "Hell is stirred from beneath." It is currently reported that the Governor of Missouri has made a requisition upon the Governor of Kansas for the delivery of all such as were concerned in the last-named "dreadful outrage." The Marshal of Kansas is said to be collecting a posse of Missouri (not Kansas) men at West Point, in Missouri, a little town about ten miles distant, to "enforce the laws." All Pro-Slavery, conservative Free-State, and doughface men, and Administration tools, are filled with holy horror.

Consider the two cases, and the action of the Administration party.

Respectfully yours,   JOHN BROWN.

On April 19, about a month after the group of slaves had been safely seen into Canada, Brown reached his home at North Elba. Thereafter, he made plans for the foray into Virginia, spending much of his time travelling about, raising funds and securing arms. On one of his trips, he wrote to his daughter, Ellen, who was not quite five years old.

Boston, Mass, 13th May, 1859.

My Dear Daughter Ellen
> I will send you [a] short letter.

> I want very much to have you *grow* good every day : to have you learn to mind your mother very quick : & sit very still at the table; & to mind what all older persons say to you; that is right. I hope to see you soon again; & if I should bring some little thing that will please you; it would not be very strange. I want you to be uncommon *good natured. God* bless you my child.

Your Affectionate Father
John Brown

Brown's last parting with his family, at the beginning of his journey to Harpers Ferry, took place probably on June 16. Proceeding to Ohio, with his son, Oliver, he visited several of the state's towns and cities, and spent some time with his sons, Owen and John, Jr. He continued to Pennsylvania, and arrived at Harpers Ferry on July 3. A day or two later he rented the Kennedy Farm, in Maryland, which served as his rendezvous and point of departure for the attack on Harpers Ferry. The letters he wrote thereafter were datelined Chambersburg, Pa., and signed I.S., or Isaac Smith, the name he used at that time.

Chambersburg, Pa. 8th Sept. 1859

Dear Wife & Children All

I write to say that we are all well: & are getting along as well as we could reasonably expect. It now appears likely that Martha,[23] & Anne: will be on their way home in the course of this month: but they may be detained to a little later period. I do not know what to advise about fattening the old Spotted cow: as much will depend on what you have *to feed her with*; whether your heifers will come in or not; next Spring: also upon her present condition. You must exercise the best judgment you have in the matter: as I know but little about your crops. *I should like* to know more as soon as I can. I am now in hopes of being able to send you something in the way of help before long. May God abundantly bless you all. *Ellen I want you to be very good*. Your Affectionate husband & Father.

I S

Sept 9th Bells[24] letter of 30th Aug to Watson is received
Sept 20th 1859. All well. Girls will probably start for home soon.

I S

II

HARPERS FERRY, PRISON AND DEATH

I T was on Sunday night, October 16, 1859, that John Brown, at the head of a group of twenty-one men—three of whom were left, as a rear-guard, at the Kennedy Farm in charge of arms and supplies—made his attack on Harpers Ferry. Although meeting with initial success, Brown soon lost the

23 Martha, Oliver Brown's wife, and Anne, John Brown's daughter, seventeen and sixteen years old respectively, joined Brown about two weeks after he bought the Kennedy Farm. They did the cooking and housekeeping and served to avert suspicion while arms were being moved into the house.
24 Bell was the wife of Watson Brown.

initiative, and by noon the next day, he and his men were surrounded by the Virginia Militia. On Tuesday morning, the U.S. Marines, under the command of Col. Robert E. Lee, battered down the doors of the engine house in the Armory yard in which Brown and his surviving men had taken refuge, and the fight was over. Of the original army of twenty-two men (including Brown), ten were killed outright, seven, including Brown, were captured and later hanged, and five escaped.

Brown was interviewed by Southern leaders a day after his capture, as he lay in the office of the Armory. Present were Robert E. Lee, J. E. B. Stuart, Senator J. M. Mason, Governor Wise, Congressman C. L. Vallandigham, of Ohio, Colonel Lewis Washington, Andrew Hunter, and Congressman Charles James Faulkner, of Virginia.

Harper's Ferry, Oct. 19, 1859.

"Old Brown," or "Ossawattomie Brown," as he is often called, the hero of a dozen fights or so with the "border ruffians" of Missouri, in the days of "bleeding Kansas," is the head and front of this offending—the commander of the abolition filibuster army. His wounds, which at first were supposed to be mortal, turn out to be mere flesh wounds and scratches, not at all dangerous in their character. He has been removed, together with Stephens, the other wounded prisoner, from the engine room to the office of the armory, and they now lie on the floor, upon miserable shake-downs, covered with some old bedding.

Brown is fifty-five years of age, rather small sized, with keen and restless gray eyes, and a grizzly beard and hair. He is a wiry, active man, and should the slightest chance for an escape be afforded, there is no doubt that he will yet give his captors much trouble. His hair is matted and tangled, and his face, hands and clothes all smouched and smeared with blood. Colonel Lee stated that he would exclude all visiters from the room if the wounded men were annoyed or pained by them, but Brown said he was by no means annoyed; on the contrary he was glad to be able to make himself and his motives clearly understood. He converses freely, fluently and cheerfully, without the slightest manifestation of fear or uneasiness, evidently weighing well his words, and possessing a good command of language. His manner is courteous and affable, and he appears to make a favorable impression upon his auditory, which, during most of the day yesterday, averaged about ten or a dozen men.

When I arrived in the armory at Harper's Ferry, shortly after two o'clock in the afternoon of October 19, Brown was answering questions put to him by Senator Mason, who had just arrived from his residence at Winchester, thirty miles distant; Colonel Faulkner,

member of Congress, who lives but a few miles off; Mr. Vallandigham, member of Congress from Ohio; and several other distinguished
gentlemen. The following is a verbatim report of the conversation:—

BROWN'S INTERVIEW WITH MASON, VALLANDIGHAM, AND OTHERS

Senator Mason. Can you tell us who furnished money for your
expedition?

John Brown. I furnished most of it myself; I cannot implicate
others. It is by my own folly that I have been taken. I could easily
have saved myself from it, had I exercised my own better judgment
rather than yielded to my feelings.

Mason. You mean if you had escaped immediately?

Brown. No. I had the means to make myself secure without any
escape; but I allowed myself to be surrounded by a force by being
too tardy. I should have gone away; but I had thirty odd prisoners,
whose wives and daughters were in tears for their safety, and I felt
for them. Besides, I wanted to allay the fears of those who believed
we came here to burn and kill. For this reason I allowed the train
to cross the bridge, and gave them full liberty to pass on. I did it
only to spare the feelings of those passengers and their families, and
to allay the apprehensions that you had got here in your vicinity a
band of men who had no regard for life and property, nor any
feelings of humanity.

Mason. But you killed some people passing along the streets
quietly.

Brown. Well, sir, if there was anything of that kind done, it was
without my knowledge. Your own citizens who were my prisoners
will tell you that every possible means was taken to prevent it. I did
not allow my men to fire when there was danger of killing those we
regarded as innocent persons, if I could help it. They will tell you
that we allowed ourselves to be fired at repeatedly, and did not
return it.

A Bystander. That is not so. You killed an unarmed man at the
corner of the house over there at the water-tank, and another besides.

Brown. See here, my friend; it is useless to dispute or contradict
the report of your own neighbors who were my prisoners.

Mason. If you would tell us who sent you here,—who provided
the means,—that would be information of some value.

Brown. I will answer freely and faithfully about what concerns myself,—I will answer anything I can with honor,—but not about others.

Mr. Vallandigham (who had just entered). Mr. Brown, who sent you here?

Brown. No man sent me here; it was my own prompting and that of my Maker, or that of the Devil,—whichever you please to ascribe it to. I acknowledge no master in human form.

Vallandigham. Did you get up the expedition yourself?

Brown. I did.

Vallandigham. Did you get up this document that is called a Constitution?

Brown. I did. They are a constitution and ordinances of my own contriving and getting up.

Vallandigham. How long have you been engaged in this business?

Brown. From the breaking out of the difficulties in Kansas. Four of my sons had gone there to settle, and they induced me to go. I did not go there to settle, but because of the difficulties.

Mason. How many are there engaged with you in this movement?

Brown. Any questions that I can honorably answer I will,—not otherwise. So far as I am myself concerned, I have told everything truthfully. I value my word, sir.

Mason. What was your object in coming?

Brown. We came to free the slaves, and only that.

A Volunteer. How many men, in all, had you?

Brown. I came to Virginia with eighteen men only, besides myself.

Volunteer. What in the world did you suppose you could do here in Virginia with that amount of men?

Brown. Young man, I do not wish to discuss that question here.

Volunteer. You could not do anything.

Brown. Well, perhaps your ideas and mine on military subjects would differ materially.

Mason. How do you justify your acts?

Brown. I think, my friend, you are guilty of a great wrong against God and humanity,—I say it without wishing to be offensive,—and it would be perfectly right for any one to interfere with you so far as to free those you wilfully and wickedly hold in bondage. I do not say this insultingly.

Mason. I understand that.

Brown. I think I did right, and that others will do right who interfere with you at any time and at all times. I hold that the

Golden Rule, "Do unto others as ye would that others should do unto you," applies to all who would help others to gain their liberty.

Lieutenant Stuart. But don't you believe in the Bible?

Brown. Certainly I do.

.   .   .   .

Mason. Did you consider this a military organization in this Constitution? I have not yet read it.

Brown. I did, in some sense. I wish you would give that paper close attention.

Mason. You consider yourself the commander-in-chief of these "provisional" military forces?

Brown. I was chosen, agreeably to the ordinance of a certain document, commander-in-chief of that force.

Mason. What wages did you offer?

Brown. None.

Stuart. "The wages of sin is death."

Brown. I would not have made such a remark to you if you had been a prisoner, and wounded, in my hands.

A Bystander. Did you not promise a negro in Gettysburg twenty dollars a month?

Brown. I did not.

Mason. Does this talking annoy you?

Brown. Not in the least.

Vallandigham. Have you lived long in Ohio?

Brown. I went there in 1805. I lived in Summit County, which was then Portage County. My native place is Connecticut; my father lived there till 1805.

Vallandigham. Have you been in Portage County lately?

Brown. I was there in June last.

Vallandigham. When in Cleveland, did you attend the Fugitive Slave Law Convention there?

Brown. No. I was there about the time of the sitting of the court to try the Oberlin rescuers. I spoke there publicly on that subject; on the Fugitive Slave Law and my own rescue. Of course, so far as I had any influence at all, I was supposed to justify the Oberlin people for rescuing the slave, because I have myself forcibly taken slaves from bondage. I was concerned in taking eleven slaves from Missouri to Canada last winter. I think I spoke in Cleveland before the Convention. I do not know that I had conversation with any of

128

the Oberlin rescuers. I was sick part of the time I was in Ohio with the ague, in Ashtabula County.

Vallandigham. Did you see anything of Joshua R. Giddings there?

Brown. I did meet him.

Vallandigham. Did you converse with him?

Brown. I did. I would not tell you, of course, anything that would implicate Mr. Giddings; but I certainly met with him and had conversations with him.

Vallandigham. About that rescue case?

Brown. Yes; I heard him express his opinions upon it very freely and frankly.

Vallandigham. Justifying it?

Brown. Yes, sir; I do not compromise him, certainly, in saying that.

Vallandigham. Will you answer this: Did you talk with Giddings about your expedition here?

Brown. No, I won't answer that; because a denial of it I would not make, and to make any affirmation of it I should be a great dunce.

Vallandigham. Have you had correspondence with parties at the North on the subject of this movement?

Brown. I have had correspondence.

A Bystander. Do you consider this a religious movement?

Brown. It is, in my opinion, the greatest service man can render to God.

Bystander. Do you consider yourself an instrument in the hands of Providence?

Brown. I do.

Bystander. Upon what principle do you justify your acts?

Brown. Upon the Golden Rule. I pity the poor in bondage that have none to help them: that is why I am here; not to gratify any personal animosity, revenge, or vindictive spirit. It is my sympathy with the oppressed and the wronged, that are as good as you and as precious in the sight of God.

Bystander. Certainly. But why take the slaves against their will?

Brown. I never did.

Bystander. You did in one instance, at least.

(Stephens, the other wounded prisoner, here said, " You are right. In one case I know the negro wanted to go back.")

Bystander. Where did you come from?

Stephens. I lived in Ashtabula County, Ohio.

Vallandigham. How recently did you leave Ashtabula County?

Stephens. Some months ago. I never resided there any length of time; have been through there.

Vallandigham. How far did you live from Jefferson?

Brown. Be cautious, Stephens, about any answers that would commit any friend. I would not answer that.

(Stephens turned partially over with a groan of pain, and was silent.)

Vallandigham. Who are your advisers in this movement?

Brown. I cannot answer that. I have numerous sympathizers throughout the entire North.

Vallandigham. In northern Ohio?

Brown. No more there than anywhere else; in all the free States.

Vallandigham. But you are not personally acquainted in southern Ohio?

Brown. Not very much.

A Bystander. Did you ever live in Washington City?

Brown. I did not. I want you to understand, gentlemen, and (to the reporter of the " Herald ") you may report that,—I want you to understand that I respect the rights of the poorest and weakest of colored people, oppressed by the slave system, just as much as I do those of the most wealthy and powerful. This is the idea that has moved me, and that alone. We expected no reward except the satisfaction of endeavoring to do for those in distress and greatly oppressed as we would be done by. The cry of distress of the oppressed is my reason, and the only thing that prompted me to come here.

Bystander. Why did you do it secretly?

Brown. Because I thought that necessary to success; no other reason.

Bystander. Have you read Gerrit Smith's last letter?

Brown. What letter do you mean?

Bystander. The "New York Herald" of yesterday, in speaking of this affair, mentions a letter in this way :—

" Apropos of this exciting news, we recollect a very significant passage in one of Gerrit Smith's letters, published a month or two ago, in which he speaks of the folly of attempting to strike the shackles off the slaves by the force of moral suasion or legal agitation, and predicts that the next movement made in the direction of negro emancipation would be an insurrection in the South."

Brown. I have not seen the "New York Herald" for some days past; but I presume, from your remark about the gist of the letter, that I should concur with it. I agree with Mr. Smith that moral suasion is hopeless. I don't think the people of the slave States will ever consider the subject of slavery in its true light till some other argument is resorted to than moral suasion.

Vallandigham. Did you expect a general rising of the slaves in case of your success?

Brown. No, sir; nor did I wish it. I expected to gather them up from time to time. and set them free.

Vallandigham. Did you expect to hold possession here till then?

Brown. Well, probably I had quite a different idea. I do not know that I ought to reveal my plans. I am here a prisoner and wounded, because I foolishly allowed myself to be so. You overrate your strength in supposing I could have been taken if I had not allowed it. I was too tardy after commencing the open attack—in delaying my movements through Monday night, and up to the time I was attacked by the Government troops. It was all occasioned by my desire to spare the feelings of my prisoners and their families and the community at large. I had no knowledge of the shooting of the negro Heywood.

Vallandigham. What time did you commence your organization in Canada?

Brown. That occurred about two years ago; in 1858.

Vallandigham. Who was the secretary?

Brown. That I would not tell if I recollected; but I do not recollect. I think the officers were elected in May, 1858. I may answer incorrectly, but not intentionally. My head is a little confused by wounds, and my memory obscure on dates, etc.

Dr. Biggs. Were you in the party at Dr. Kennedy's house?

Brown. I was the head of that party. I occupied the house to mature my plans. I have not been in Baltimore to purchase caps.

Dr. Biggs. What was the number of men at Kennedy's?

Brown. I decline to answer that.

Dr. Biggs. Who lanced that woman's neck on the hill?

Brown. I did. I have sometimes practised in surgery when I thought it a matter of humanity and necessity, and there was no one else to do it; but I have not studied surgery.

Dr. Biggs. It was done very well and scientifically. They have been very clever to the neighbors, I have been told, and we had no reason to suspect them, except that we could not understand their movements. They were represented as eight or nine persons; on Friday there were thirteen.

Brown. There were more than that.

Q. Where did you get arms? A. I bought them.

Q. In what State? A. That I will not state.

Q. How many guns? A. Two hundred Sharpe's rifles and two hundred revolvers,—what is called the Massachusetts Arms Company's revolvers, a little under navy size.

Q. Why did you not take that swivel you left in the house? A. I had no occasion for it. It was given to me a year or two ago.

Q. In Kansas? A. No, I had nothing given to me in Kansas.

Q. By whom, and in what State? A. I decline to answer. It is not properly a swivel; it is a very large rifle with a pivot. The ball is larger than a musket ball; it is intended for a slug.

Reporter. I do not wish to annoy you; but if you have anything further you would like to say, I will report it.

Brown. I have nothing to say, only that I claim to be here in carrying out a measure I believe perfectly justifiable, and not to act the part of an incendiary or ruffian, but to aid those suffering great wrong. I wish to say, furthermore, that you had better—all you people at the South—prepare yourselves for a settlement of this question, that must come up for settlement sooner than you are prepared for it. The sooner you are prepared the better. You may dispose of me very easily,—I am nearly disposed of now; but this question is still to be settled,—this negro question I mean; the end of that is not yet. These wounds were inflicted upon me—both sabre cuts on my head and bayonet stabs in different parts of my body— some minutes after I had ceased fighting and had consented to surrender, for the benefit of others, not for my own.[25] I believe the Major would not have been alive; I could have killed him just as easy as a mosquito when he came in, but I supposed he only came in to receive our surrender. There had been loud and long calls of "surrender" from us,—as loud as men could yell; but in the confusion and excitement I suppose we were not heard. I do not think the Major, or any one, meant to butcher us after we had surrendered.

An Officer. Why did you not surrender before the attack?

Brown. I did not think it was my duty or interest to do so. We

---

[25] At the trial of Copeland the following evidence was given:—[This note is Sanborn's]

Mr. Sennott. You say that when Brown was down you struck him in the face with your sabre?
Lieutenant Green. Yes.
Q. This was after he was down? A. Yes; he was down.
Q. How many times, Lieutenant Green, did you strike Brown in the face with your sabre after he was down? A. Why, sir, he was defending himself with his gun.
Mr. Hunter. I hope the counsel for the defence will not press such questions as these.

assured the prisoners that we did not wish to harm them, and they should be set at liberty. I exercised my best judgment, not believing the people would wantonly sacrifice their own fellow-citizens, when we offered to let them go on condition of being allowed to change our position about a quarter of a mile. The prisoners agreed by a vote among themselves to pass across the bridge with us. We wanted them only as a sort of guarantee of our own safety,—that we should not be fired into. We took them, in the first place, as hostages and to keep them from doing any harm. We did kill some men in defending ourselves, but I saw no one fire except directly in self-defence. Our orders were strict not to harm any one not in arms against us.

Q. Brown, suppose you had every nigger in the United States, what would you do with them? A. Set them free.

Q. Your intention was to carry them off and free them? A. Not at all.

A Bystander. To set them free would sacrifice the life of every man in this community.

Brown. I do not think so.

Bystander. I know it. I think you are fanatical.

Brown. And I think you are fanatical. "Whom the gods would destroy they first make mad," and you are mad.

Q. Was it your only object to free the negroes? A. Absolutely our only object.

Q. But you demanded and took Colonel Washington's silver and watch? A. Yes; we intended freely to appropriate the property of slaveholders to carry out our object. It was for that, and only that, and with no design to enrich ourselves with any plunder whatever.

Bystander. Did you know Sherrod[26] in Kansas? I understand you killed him.

Brown. I killed no man except in fair fight. I fought at Black Jack Point and at Osawatomie; and if I killed anybody, it was at one of these places.

John Brown's last speech to the Court, November 2, 1859.

I have, may it please the Court, a few words to say.

In the first place, I deny everything but what I have all along admitted,—the design on my part to free the slaves. I intended cer-

[26] William T. Sherrard, formerly of Harpers Ferry and Winchester. He was mortally wounded in a shooting affray in the court room at Lecompton, Kansas, on February 18, 1857. John Brown was in Boston, Mass., on that date, and thus had nothing to do with that affair.

tainly to have made a clean thing of that matter, as I did last winter, when I went into Missouri and there took slaves without the snapping of a gun on either side, moved them through the country, and finally left them in Canada. I designed to have done the same thing again, on a larger scale. That was all I intended. I never did intend murder, or treason, or the destruction of property, or to excite or incite slaves to rebellion, or to make insurrection.

I have another objection; and that is, it is unjust that I should suffer such a penalty. Had I interfered in the manner which I admit, and which I admit has been fairly proved (for I admire the truthfulness and candor of the greater portion of the witnesses who have testified in this case),—had I so interfered in behalf of the rich, the powerful, the intelligent, the so-called great, or in behalf of any of their friends,—either father, mother, brother, sister, wife, or children, or any of that class,—and suffered and sacrificed what I have in this interference, it would have been all right; and every man in this court would have deemed it an act worthy of reward rather than punishment.

This court acknowledges, as I suppose, the validity of the law of God. I see a book kissed here which I suppose to be the Bible, or at least the New Testament. That teaches me that all things whatsoever I would that men should do to me, I should do even so to them. It teaches me, further, to " remember them that are in bonds, as bound with them." I endeavored to act up to that instruction. I say, I am yet too young to understand that God is any respecter of persons. I believe that to have interfered as I have done—as I have always freely admitted I have done—in behalf of His despised poor, was not wrong, but right. Now, if it is deemed necessary that I should forfeit my life for the furtherance of the ends of justice, and mingle my blood further with the blood of my children and with the blood of millions in this slave country whose rights are disregarded by wicked, cruel, and unjust enactments,—I submit; so let it be done!

Let me say one word further.

I feel entirely satisfied with the treatment I have received on my trial. Considering all the circumstances, it has been more generous than I expected. But I feel no consciousness of guilt. I have stated from the first what was my intention, and what was not. I never have had any design against the life of any person, nor any disposition to commit treason, or excite slaves to rebel, or make any general insurrection. I never encouraged any man to do so, but always discouraged any idea of that kind.

134

Let me say, also, a word in regard to the statements made by some of those connected with me. I hear it has been stated by some of them that I have induced them to join me. But the contrary is true. I do not say this to injure them, but as regretting their weakness. There is not one of them but joined me of his own accord, and the greater part of them at their own expense. A number of them I never saw, and never had a word of conversation with, till the day they came to me; and that was for the purpose I have stated.

Now I have done.

PRISON LETTERS

To Judge Thomas Russell, of Boston. Copies of this letter were also sent to Reuben A. Chapman, of Springfield, Mass., and Daniel R. Tilden, of Ohio.

Charlestown Jefferson County Va Oct. 21, 1859

Hon. Thos. Russell

Dear Sir

I am here a prisoner with several sabre cuts in my head, & bayonet stabs in my body. My object in writing to you is to obtain able, & faithful counsel for my-

5

self; & fellow prisoners five in all, as we have the faith of Virginia, pledged through her Governor and numerous other prominent citizens, to give us a fair trial. Without we can obtain such counsel from without the slave states : neither the facts in our case can come before the world : nor can we have the benefit of such facts (as might be considered mitigating in the view of others) upon our trial. I have money on hand *here* to the amount of $250. and personal property sufficient to pay a most liberal fee to yourself; or to any suitable man who will undertake our defence, if I can be allowed the benefit of said property. Can you or some other good man come in immediately for the sake of the young men prisoners at least? My wounds are doing well. Do not send an ultra Abolitionist.

Very respectfully yours,

John Brown

The trial is set for Wednesday next the 25th inst.

J. W. Campbell
Sheriff Jeff. County

135

Charlestown, Jefferson Co., Va., 31st. Oct. 1859.

My dear Wife, and Children every one

I suppose you have learned before this by the newspapers that two weeks ago today we were fighting for our lives at Harpers ferry: that during the fight Watson was mortally wounded; Oliver killed, Wm Thompson killed, & Dauphin slightly wounded. That on the following day I was taken prisoner immediately after which I received several Sabre cuts in my head; & Bayonet stabs in my body. As nearly as I can learn Watson died of his wound on Wednesday the 2d or on Thursday the 3d day after I was taken. Dauphin was killed when I was taken; & Anderson I suppose also. I have since been tried, & found guilty of treason, &c; and of murder in the first degree. I have not yet received my sentence. No others of the company with whom you were acquainted were so far as *I can learn* either killed or taken. Under all these terible calamities; I feel quite cheerful in the assurance that God reigns; & will overrule all for his glory; & the best possible good. I feel *no* con[s]ciou[s]ness of *guilt* in the matter: nor even mortifycation on account of my imprisonment; & irons; & I feel perfectly assured that very soon no member of my family will feel any possible disposition to "blush on my account." Already dear friends at a distance with kindest sympathy are cheering me with the assurance that *posterity* at least: will do me justice. I shall commend you all together with my beloved; but bereaved daughters in law to their sympathies which I have no doubt will soon reach you. I also commend you all to him "whose mercy endureth forever": to the God of my *fathers* "whose I am; & whom I serve." "He will never leave you nor forsake you" unless you forsake him. Finally my dearly beloved be of good comfort. Be sure to remember & *to follow my advice* & my example *too*: so far as it has been consistent with the holy religion of Jesus Christ in which I remain a most firm, & humble believer. Never forget the poor nor think any thing you bestow on them to be lost, to you even though they may be as *black* as Ebedmelch, the Ethiopian eunuch who cared for Jeremiah in the pit of the dungeon; or as *black* as the one to whom Phillip preached Christ. Be sure to entertain strangers for thereby some have—"Remember them that are in bonds as bound with them." I am in the charge of a jailor *like* the one who took charge of "Paul & Silas;" & you may rest assured that both *kind hearts* and *kind faces* are more or less about me: whilst thousands are thirsting for my blood. "These *light* afflictions which are

but *for a moment* shall work out for us a far *more exceeding &
eternal* weight of glory." I hope to be able to write you again. My
wounds are doing well. Copy this & send it to your sorrow stricken
brothers, *Ruth*; to comfort them. Write me a few words in regard to
the welfare of all. God Allmighty bless you all: & make you "joyful in the midst of all your tribulations." Write to John Brown,
Charlestown, Jefferson Co, Va, care of Capt John Avis
Your Affectionate Husband, & Father.

John Brown

Nov. 3d 1859

P. S. Yesterday Nov 2d I was sentenced to be hanged on 2 Decem
next. Do not grieve on my account. I am still quite cheerful.
 Go[d] bless you all Your Ever

J Brown

Charlestown, Jefferson County, Va., Nov. 1, 1859.
My Dear Friend E. B. of R. I.,—Your most cheering letter of the 27th
of October is received; and may the Lord reward you a thousandfold
for the kind feeling you express toward me; but more especially for
your fidelity to the "poor that cry, and those that have no help."
For this I am a prisoner in bonds. It is solely my own fault, in a
military point of view, that we met with our disaster. I mean that I
mingled with our prisoners and so far sympathized with them and
their families that I neglected my duty in other respects. But God's
will, not mine, be done.

 You know that Christ once armed Peter. So also in my case I think
he put a sword into my hand, and there continued it so long as he
saw best, and then kindly took it from me. I mean when I first went
to Kansas. I wish you could know with what cheerfulness I am now
wielding the "sword of the Spirit" on the right hand and on the left.
I bless God that it proves "mighty to the pulling down of strong-
holds." I always loved my Quaker friends, and I commend to their
kind regard my poor bereaved widowed wife and my daughters and
daughters-in-law, whose husbands fell at my side. One is a mother
and the other likely to become so soon. They, as well as my own
sorrow-stricken daughters, are left very poor, and have much greater
need of sympathy than I, who, through Infinite Grace and the kindness of strangers, am "joyful in all my tribulations."

 Dear sister, write them at North Elba, Essex County, N. Y., to comfort their sad hearts. Direct to Mary A. Brown, wife of John Brown. There is also another—a widow, wife of Thompson, who fell with my poor boys in the affair at Harper's Ferry—at the same place.

I do not feel conscious of guilt in taking up arms; and had it been in behalf of the rich and powerful, the intelligent, the great (as men count greatness), or those who form enactments to suit themselves and corrupt others, or some of their friends, that I interfered, suffered, sacrificed, and fell, it would have been doing very well. But enough of this. These light afflictions, which endure for a moment, shall but work for me " a far more exceeding and eternal weight of glory." I would be very grateful for another letter from you. My wounds are healing. Farewell. God will surely attend to his own cause in the best possible way and time, and he will not forget the work of his own hands.

Your friend,
John Brown.

To Thomas Wentworth Higginson, of Worcester, Mass.

Charlestown, Jefferson Co. Va. 4th. Nov. 1859.
Rev. T. W. Higginson
Dear Friend-
If my Wife were to come here just now it would *only tend* to distract *her mind, ten fold*; & would *only add* to my affliction; & *cannot possibly* do me *any good*. It will also use up the scanty means she has to supply Bread & cheap but comfortable clothing, fuel &C) for herself, and Children *through the Winter*. DO PERSUADE her to remain *at home for a time (at least)* till she can learn further from me. She will secure a Thousand times the consolation AT HOME that she can possibly find elsewhere. I have just *written her there & will* write her CONSTANTLY. Her presence *here* will deepen my affliction a thousand fold. I beg of her to be *calm*, & *submissive*; & not to go *wild* on my account. I lack *for nothing* & was feeling quite cheerful before I learned she talked *of coming on*. *I ask her to compose her mind* & *to remain quiet* till the last of *this month*; out of pity to me. I can certainly judge better in this matter than *any one else*. My warmest thanks to yourself; & *all other* kind friends. *God bless you all. Please send this line to my afflicted Wife*, by first possible conveyance.

Your friend in truth   John Brown

To Mrs. Lydia Maria Child, author and abolitionist.

Charlestown, Jefferson Co. Va. 4th. Nov. 1859.

Mrs L Maria Child
    Wayland
        Mass   My Dear friend

(Such you prove to be though an entire stranger)　Your most kind letter has reached me; with your kind offer to come here & take care of me. Allow me to express my gratitude for your great sympathy : & at the same time to propose to you a different course; together with my reasons for wishing it. I should certainly be greatly pleased to become personally acquainted with one so gifted; & so kind; but I cannot avoid seeing some objections to it under present circumstances. First I am in charge of a most humane gentleman who with his family have rendered me every possible attention I have desired or that could be of the least advantage : and I am so far recovered from my wounds as no longer to require nursing. Then again it would subject you to great personal inconvenience, & quite a heavy expence; without doing me any good. Now allow me to name to you another channel through which you may reach me with your sympathies much more effectually. I have at home a Wife & three young daughters. The youngest of whom is but a little over Five years old; the oldest is nearly Sixteen. I have also two daughters in law whose Husbands have both fallen near me here. One of these is a Mother & the other like to become so. There is also another Widow a Mrs. Thompson whose Husband also fell here. Whether she is a Mother or not I cannot say. They all (my Wife included) live at North Elba, Essex Co. New York. I have or suppose I have a middle aged Son who has been in some degree a cripple from childhood who would have as much as he could well do to earn a living. He was a most dreadful sufferer in Kansas; & lost all he had laid up : & has not enough to clothe himself for the Winter comfortably. I have *no Son or Son in law living*; who did not suffer terribly in Kansas. Now dear friend would you not as soon contribute Fifty Cents now : & a like sum *yearly* for the relief of those very poor; & deeply afflicted persons to enable them to supply themselves, & Children with Bread : & very plain clothing; & to enable the children to receive a common English education : & also to devote your own energies to induce others to join you in giving a like or other amount to constitute a little fund for the purpose named? I cannot see how your coming here can

139

possibly do me the least good : & I feel quite certain you can do me *immence good* where you are. I am quite cheerful under all my afflicting circumstances; & prospects, having as I humbly trust "the peace of God which passeth all understanding, to rule in my heart." You may make just such use of this as you see fit. Yours *in sincerity*; & *truth*, (God Allmighty bless; and reward you a thousand fold.)

John Brown

Charlestown, Jefferson County, Va., Nov. 8, 1859.
Dear Wife and Children, Every One,—I will begin by saying that I have in some degree recovered from my wounds, but that I am quite weak in my back and sore about my left kidney. My appetite has been quite good for most of the time since I was hurt. I am supplied with almost everything I could desire to make me comfortable, and the little I do lack (some articles of clothing which I lost) I may perhaps soon get again. I am, besides, quite cheerful, having (as I trust) "the peace of God, which passeth all understanding," to "rule in my heart," and the testimony (in some degree) of a good conscience that I have not lived altogether in vain. I can trust God with both the time and the manner of my death, believing, as I now do, that for me at this time to seal my testimony for God and humanity with my blood will do vastly more toward advancing the cause I have earnestly endeavored to promote, than all I have done in my life before. I beg of you all meekly and quietly to submit to this, not feeling yourselves in the least *degraded* on that account. Remember, dear wife and children all, that Jesus of Nazareth suffered a most excruciating death on the cross as a felon, under the most aggravating circumstances. Think also of the prophets and apostles and Christians of former days, who went through greater tribulations than you or I, and try to be reconciled. May God Almighty comfort all your hearts, and soon wipe away all tears from your eyes! To him be endless praise! Think, too, of the crushed millions who "have no comforter." I charge you all never in your trials to forget the griefs "of the poor that cry, and of those that have none to help them." I wrote most earnestly to my dear and afflicted wife not to come on for the present, at any rate. I will now give her my reasons for doing so. First, it would use up all the

scanty means she has, or is at all likely to have, to make herself and children comfortable hereafter. For let me tell you that the sympathy that is now aroused in your behalf may not always follow you. There is but little more of the romantic about helping poor widows and their children than there is about trying to relieve poor "niggers." Again, the little comfort it might afford us to meet again would be dearly bought by the pains of a final separation. We must part; and I feel assured for us to meet under such dreadful circumstances would only add to our distress. If she comes on here, she must be only a gazing-stock throughout the whole journey, to be remarked upon in every look, word, and action, and by all sorts of creatures, and by all sorts of papers, throughout the whole country. Again, it is my most decided judgment that in quietly and submissively staying at home vastly more of generous sympathy will reach her, without such dreadful sacrifice of feeling as she must put up with if she comes on. The visits of one or two female friends that have come on here have produced great excitement, which is very annoying; and they cannot possibly do me any good. Oh, Mary! do not come, but patiently wait for the meeting of those who love God and their fellow-men, where no separation must follow. "They shall go no more out forever." I greatly long to hear from some one of you, and to learn anything that in any way affects your welfare. I sent you ten dollars the other day; did you get it? I have also endeavored to stir up Christian friends to visit and write to you in your deep affliction. I have no doubt that some of them, at least, will heed the call. Write to me, care of Captain John Avis, Charlestown, Jefferson County, Virginia.

"Finally, my beloved, be of good comfort." May all your names be "written in the Lamb's book of life! "—may you all have the purifying and sustaining influence of the Christian religion!—is the earnest prayer of

Your affectionate husband and father,

John Brown

P. S. I cannot remember a night so dark as to have hindered the coming day, nor a storm so furious and dreadful as to prevent the return of warm sunshine and a cloudless sky. But, beloved ones, do remember that this is not your rest,—that in this world you have no abiding place or continuing city. To God and his infinite mercy I always commend you.

J. B.

Charlestown, Jefferson County, Va., Nov. 12, 1859.
Dear Brother Jeremiah,—Your kind letter of the 9th inst. is received, and also one from Mr. Tilden; for both of which I am greatly obliged. You inquire, "Can I do anything for you or your family?" I would answer that my sons, as well as my wife and daughters, are all very poor; and that anything that may hereafter be due me from my father's estate I wish paid to them, as I will endeavor hereafter to describe, without legal formalities to consume it all. One of my boys has been so entirely used up as very likely to be in want of comfortable clothing for the winter. I have, through the kindness of friends, fifteen dollars to send him, which I will remit shortly. If you know where to reach him, please send him that amount at once, as I shall remit the same to you by a safe conveyance. If I had a plain statement from Mr. Thompson of the state of my accounts with the estate of my father, I should then better know what to say about that matter. As it is, I have not the least memorandum left me to refer to. If Mr. Thompson will make me a statement, and charge my dividend fully for his trouble, I would be greatly obliged to him. In that case you can send me any remarks of your own. I am gaining in health slowly, and am quite cheerful in view of my approaching end,—being fully persuaded that I am worth inconceivably more to hang than for any other purpose. God Almighty bless and save you all!

Your affectionate brother,
John Brown.

November 13.

P.S. Say to my poor boys never to grieve for one moment on my account; and should many of you live to see the time when you will not blush to own your relation to Old John Brown, it will not be more strange than many things that have happened. I feel a thousand times more on account of my sorrowing friends than on my own account. So far as I am concerned, I "count it all joy." "I have fought the good fight," and have, as I trust, "finished my course." Please show this to any of my family that you may see. My love to all; and may God, in his infinite mercy, for Christ's sake, bless and save you all!

Your affectionate brother,
J. Brown.

Charlestown, Jefferson Co. Va, 15th. Nov. 1859.

Rev H L Vaill[27]

My Dear stedfast Friend

Your *most kind & most*
welcome letter of the 8th inst reached me in due time. *I am very*
grateful for all the good feeling you express & also for the kind
counsels you give together-with your prayers in my behalf. Allow
me here to say that notwithstanding "my soul is amongst lions," still
I believe that "God in very deed is with me." You will not therefore
feel surprised when I tell you that I am "joyful in all my tribulations": that I do not feel condemned of Him whose judgment is
just; nor of my own conscience. Nor do I feel degraded by my
imprisonment, my chains or prospect of the Gallows. I have not
only been (*though utterly unworthy*) permitted to suffer affliction
with God's people," but have also had *a great many rare* opportunities for "preaching *righteousness* in the great congregation."
I trust it will not all be lost. *The jailor* (in whose charge I am) & *his*
family; & *assistants* have all been most kind: & notwithstanding he
was one of the bravest of all who *fought me*: he is *now* being
abused for his humanity. So far as my observation goes; *none but*
brave men: are likely to be *humane*; to a fallen foe. "Cowards
prove their *courage* by their *ferocity*." It may be done in that way
with but little risk. I wish I could write you about a few only of the
interesting times, I here experience with different classes of men;
clergymen among others. Christ the great Captain of *liberty*; as well
as of salvation; & who began his mission, as foretold of him; by
proclaiming it, *saw fit* to take from me a sword of steel after I had
carried it for a time but he has put another in my hand: ("The
sword of the Spirit;") & I pray God to make me a faithful soldier
wherever he may send me, not less on the scaffold, then when surrounded by my warmest sympathizers. My dear old friend I do
assure you I have not forgotten our last meeting nor our retrospec-
tive look over the route by which God had then led us; & I bless
his name that he has again enabled me to hear your words of cheering; & comfort, at a time when I at least am on the "brink of
Jordan." See Bunyan's Pilgrim. God in Infinite mercy grant us *soon*
another meeting on the opposite shore. I have often passed under
the rod of him whom I *call my* Father; & certainly no son ever
needed it oftener; & yet I have enjoyed much of life, as I was

[27] John Brown's teacher in 1817, at the Morris Academy in Litchfield, Conn.

enabled to discover the secret of this; somewhat early. It has been in making the prosperity, & the happiness of others *my own*: so that really I have had a great deal of prosperity. I am very prosperous still; & looking forward to a time when "peace on Earth & good will to *men* shall every where prevail." I have no murmuring thoughts or *envyous* feelings to fret my mind. "I'll praise my *maker* with my *breath*." I am *an unworthy* nephew of Deacon John; & I loved him much; & in view of the many choice friends *I have had* here: I am led the more earnestly to pray; "gather *not* my soul with the *unrighteous*." Your assurance of the earnest sympathy of the friends in my native land is very greatful to my feelings; & allow me to say a word of comfort to them. As I believe most firmly that God reigns; I cannot believe that any thing I have *done suffered or may yet suffer will be lost*; to the *cause of God or of humanity*: & before I began my work at Harpers Ferry; I felt assured that in the *worst event*; it would certainly PAY. I often expressed that belief; & I can now see no possible cause to alter my mind. I am not as yet in the *maine* at all disappointed. I have been *a good deal* disappointed as it regards *myself* in not keeping up *to my own plans*; but I now feel entirely reconciled to that even: for Gods plan, was Infinitely better; *no doubt*; or I should have kept to my own. Had Samson kept to his *determination* of not telling Delilah wherein his great strength lay; he would probably have never overturned the house. I did not tell Delilah; but I was induced to act very *contrary* to my *better judgment*; & I have lost my two noble boys; & *other friends, if not my two eyes*.

But "Gods will *not mine* be done." I feel a comfortable hope that like that *erring servant* of whom I have just been writing *even I* may (through Infinite mercy in Christ Jesus) yet "*die in faith*." As to both the time, & manner of my death: I have but very little trouble on that score; & *am able* to be (as you exhort) "of good cheer." I send through you my best wishes to Mrs. Woodruff & her son George; & to all dear friends. May the God of the *poor* and *oppressed*; be the God & Saveior of you all.

Farewell till we "*meet again*."

Your friend in truth
John Brown

Charlestown, Jefferson Co., Va., 16th Nov., 1859.

My Dear Wife:—I write you in answer to a most kind letter, of Nov. 13, from dear Mrs. Spring. I owe her ten thousand thanks; for her kindness to *you particularly and more especially* than for what she has done, and is doing, in a more direct way for me personally. Although I feel grateful for every expression of kindness or sympathy towards me, yet nothing can so effectually minister to my comfort as acts of kindness done to relieve the wants, or mitigate the sufferings of my poor distressed family. May *God Almighty* and *their own consciousness* be their eternal rewarders. I am exceedingly rejoiced to have you make the acquaintance and be surrounded by such choice friends, as I have *long known* some of those to be, with whom you are staying, by reputation. I am most glad to have you meet with one *of a family* (or I would rather say of two families) *most beloved and never to be forgotten by me.* I mean *dear gentle* Sarah Wattles. *Many and many* a time has *she, her father, mother, brothers, sisters, uncle and aunt,* (like angels of mercy) ministered to the wants of myself and of my poor sons, both in sickness and in health. Only last year I lay sick for quite a number of weeks with them, and was cared for *by all,* as though I had been a most affectionate brother or father. *Tell her* that I ask God to bless and reward them *all* forever. "I *was* a stranger, and they took me in." It may possibly be that Sarah would like to copy this letter, and send it to her home. If so, by all means, let her do so. *I would write them* if I had the power.

Now let me say a word about the effort to educate our daughters. I am no longer able to provide means to help towards that object, and it therefore becomes me not to dictate in the matter. I shall gratefully submit the direction of the whole thing to those whose generosity may lead them to undertake in their behalf, while I give *anew* a little expression of my own choice respecting it. You, my wife, *perfectly well* know that I have always expressed a decided preference for a very *plain but perfectly practical* education for both *sons and daughters.* I do not mean an education so very miserable as that *you* and *I* received in early life; nor as some of our children enjoyed. When I say plain but practical, I mean enough of the learning of the schools to enable them to transact the common business of life, comfortably and respectably, together with that thorough training to good business habits which prepares both men and women to be *useful though poor,* and to meet the *stern* Realities of life with a *good* grace. You well know that I always claimed that the *music* of the broom, washtub, needle, spindle, loom, axe, scythe, hoe, flail, etc., should first be learned, at all events, and that of the piano, etc., Afterwards. I put them in that order as most conducive to health of body and mind; and for the obvious reason, that after a life of some *experience and of much observation*, I have found *ten women* as well as *ten men* who have made their mark in life *Right*, whose early training was of that *plain, practical* kind, to *one* who had a more popular and fashionable *early* training. But enough of that.

Now, in regard to your coming here; If you feel sure that you can endure the trials and the shock, which will be *unavoidable* (if you come), I should be most glad to see you *once more*; but when I think of your being insulted on the road, and perhaps *while here*, and of only seeing your wretchedness made complete, I *shrink* from it. Your composure and fortitude of mind may be *quite equal to it all*; but I am in *dreadful* doubt of it. *If you do come*, defer your journey till about the 27th or 28th of this month. The scenes which you will have to pass through on coming here will be *anything but those* you now pass, with tender, kind-hearted friends, and kind faces to meet you everywhere. *Do consider the matter well* before you make the *plunge*. I think I had better say *no more* on this *most painful* subject. My health improves a little; my mind is very tranquil, I may say joyous, and I continue to receive every kind attention that I have any possible need of. I wish you to send copies of all my letters to all our poor children. What I write to one must answer for all, till I have more strength. I get numerous kind letters from friends in almost all directions, to encourage me to " be of good cheer," and I still have, *as I trust*, " the peace of God to rule in my heart." May God, for Christ's sake, ever make his face to shine on you all.

Your affectionate husband,
John Brown

To Thomas B. Musgrave, Jr., the son of a business friend of John Brown, then living in Northampton, Massachusetts.

Charlestown, Jefferson Co. Va. 17th Nov. 1859

J B Musgrave Esqr

My Dear Young Friend

I have just received your most kind; & welcome letter of the 15th inst but did not get any other from you. I am under many obligations *to you & to your Father* for all the kindness you have shown me, especially since my disaster. *May God* & your own conciousness ever be your rewarders. Tell your Father that I am quite cheerful that I do not feel myself in the least degraded by my imprisonment, my chain, or the *near prospect* of the Gallows. *Men* cannot *imprison*, or *chain*; or *hang* the *soul*. I go joyfuly in behalf of Millions that "have no rights" that this "great, & glorious"; "*this Christian* Republic," "is bound to respect." Strange *change in morals political*; as well as *Christian*; since 1776. I look forward *to other changes* to take place *in* "*Gods good time*;" fully believeing that "the fashion of this world passeth away." (I am unable *now* to tell you where my friend is; that you inquire after. Perhaps my Wife who I suppose is still with Mrs. Spring, may have some information of him. I think it quite uncertain however.) Farewell; May God abundantly bless You all.

Your Friend
John Brown

To his cousin, Rev. Luther Humphrey, of Windham, Portage County, Ohio.

Charlestown, Jefferson Co. Va. 19th. Nov. 1859.

Rev. Luther Humphrey.

My dear friend,

Your kind letter of 12th inst. is now before me. So far as my knowledge goes as to our mutual kindred, I suppose *I am the first* since the landing of Peter Brown from the Mayflower that has *either been sentenced to imprisonment*; or to the Gallows. But my dear old friend, let not that fact *alone* grieve you. You cannot have forgotten *how; & where our Grandfather* (Capt. John Brown) fell in 1776; & *that he too* might have perished on the scaffold had circumstances been but *very little* different. *The fact* that a man dies under the hand of an executioner (or other wise) has but little to do with his true character, as I suppose. John Rogers perished at the stake *a great & good* man as I suppose : but *his being so* does *not prove* that any other man who has died in the same way was *good or otherwise*. Whether I have any reason to " be of good cheer " (or not) in view of my end; I can assure you that *I feel so*; & that I am totally *blinded* if I do not really *experience* that *strengthening*; & *consolation* you so faithfully implore in my behalf. God of *our Fathers*; reward your fidelity. I neither feel *mortified, degraded, nor in the least ashamed* of my imprisonment, my chain, or my near prospect *of death by hanging*. I feel assured " that not one hair shall fall from my head without my heavenly Father." I also feel that I have *long been endeavouring* to hold exactly " such a *fast* as God has chosen." See the passage in Isaiah which you have quoted. No part of my life has been more hapily spent; than that I have spent here; & I humbly *trust* that no past has been spent to better purpose. *I would not say boastingly* : but " thanks be unto God who giveth us the victory: *through infinite grace*." I should be sixty years old were I to live till May 9th 1860. I have enjoyed much of life as it is: & have been remarkably prosperous; having *early learned* to regard the welfare & prosperity of others as *my own*. I have never since I can remember required a great amount of sleep : so that I conclude that I have already enjoyed *full an average* number of waking hours with those who reach their " Three Score years, & ten." I have not as yet been driven to the use of glasses; but can still see to read, & write quite comfortably. But more than that I have *generally* enjoyed remarkably good health. I might go on to recount unnumbered & *unmerited* blessings among which would be some very severe afflictions : & those the most needed blessings of all. And now when I think how easily I might *be left to spoil* all I have done, or suffered in the cause of freedom; I hardly dare risk another voyage; if I even had the opportunity. It is a long time since we met; but we shall now soon come together in our " Fathers House," *I trust*. " Let us hold fast that we already have." " remembering that we shall reap in due time if we faint not." " Thanks be *ever* unto God; who giveth us the victory through Jesus Christ our Lord." And now my old warmhearted friend, " Good bye."

Your Affectionate Cousin
John Brown

Charlestown, Jefferson County, Va., Nov. 21, 1859.

My Dear Wife,—Your most welcome letter of the 13th instant I got yesterday. I am very glad to learn from yourself that you feel so much resigned to your circumstances, so much confidence in a wise and good Providence, and such composure of mind in the midst of all your deep afflictions. This is just as it should be; and let me still say, "Be of good cheer," for we shall soon "come out of all our great tribulations;" and very soon, if we trust in him, "God shall wipe away all tears from our eyes." Soon "we shall be satisfied when we are awake in His likeness." There is now here a source of disquietude to me,—namely, the fires which are almost of daily and nightly occurrence in this immediate neighborhood. While I well know that no one of them is the work of our friends, I know at the same time that by more or less of the inhabitants we shall be charged with them,—the same as with the ominous and threatening letters to Governor Wise. In the existing state of public feeling I can easily see a further objection to your coming here at present; but I did not intend saying another word to you on that subject.

Why will you not say to me whether you had any crops mature this season? If so, what ones? Although I may nevermore intermeddle with your worldly affairs, I have not yet lost all interest in them. A little history of your failures I should very much prize; and I would gratify you and other friends some way were it in my power. I am still quite cheerful, and by no means cast down. I "remember that the time is short." The little trunk and all its contents, so far as I can judge, reached me safe. May God reward all the contributors! I wrote you under cover to our excellent friend Mrs. Spring on the 16th instant. I presume you have it before now. When you return, it is most likely the lake will not be open; so you must get your ticket at Troy for Moreau Station or Glens Falls (for Glens Falls, if you can get one), or get one for Vergennes in Vermont, and take your chance of crossing over on the ice to Westport. If you go soon, the route by Glens Falls to Elizabethtown will probably be the best.

I have just learned that our poor Watson lingered until Wednesday about noon of the 19th of October. Oliver died near my side in a few moments after he was shot. Dauphin died the next morning after Oliver and William were killed,—namely, Monday. He died almost instantly; was by my side. William was shot by several persons. Anderson was killed with Dauphin.

149

Keep this letter to refer to. God Almighty bless and keep you all!
Your affectionate husband,
John Brown.

Dear Mrs. Spring,—I send this to your care, because I am at a loss where it will reach my wife.
Your friend in truth,
John Brown.

To his children at North Elba.

Charlestown, Jefferson County, Va., Nov. 22, 1859.
Dear Children, All,—I address this letter to you, supposing that your mother is not yet with you. She has not yet come here, as I have requested her not to do at present, if at all. She may think it best for her not to come at all. She has (or will), I presume, written you before this. Annie's letter to us both, of the 9th, has but just reached me. I am very glad to get it, and to learn that you are in any measure cheerful. This is the greatest comfort I can have, except it would be to know that you are all Christians. God in mercy grant you all may be so! That is what you all will certainly need. When and in what form death may come is but of small moment. I feel just as content to die for God's eternal truth and for suffering humanity on the scaffold as in any other way; and I do not say this from any disposition to "brave it out." No; I would readily own my wrong were I in the least convinced of it. I have now been confined over a month, with a good opportunity to look the whole thing as "fair in the face" as I am capable of doing; and I now feel it most grateful that I am counted in the least possible degree worthy to suffer for the truth. I want you all to "be of good cheer." This life is intended as a season of training, chastisement, temptation, affliction, and trial; and the "righteous shall come out of" it all. Oh, my dear children, let me again entreat you all to "forsake the foolish, and live." What can you possibly lose by such a course? "Godliness with contentment is great gain, having the promise of the life that now is, and of that which is to come." "Trust in the Lord and do good, so shalt thou dwell in the land; and verily thou shalt be fed." I have enjoyed life much; why should I complain on leaving it? I want some of you to write me a little more particularly about all

that concerns your welfare. I intend to write you as often as I can. "To God and the word of his grace I commend you all."

Your affectionate father,

John Brown.

To his older children living in Ohio.

Charlestown, Jefferson County, Va., Nov. 22, 1859.

Dear Children,—Your most welcome letters of the 16th inst. I have just received, and I bless God that he has enabled you to bear the heavy tidings of our disaster with so much seeming resignation and composure of mind. That is exactly the thing I have wished you all to do for me,—to be cheerful and perfectly resigned to the holy will of a wise and good God. I bless his most holy name that I am, I trust, in some good measure able to do the same. I am even "joyful in all my tribulations" ever since my confinement, and I humbly trust that "I know in whom I have trusted." A calm peace, perhaps like that which your own dear mother felt in view of her last change, seems to fill my mind by day and by night. Of this neither the powers of "earth or hell" can deprive me. Do not, my dear children, any of you grieve for a single moment on my account. As I trust my life has not been thrown away, so I also humbly trust that my death will not be in vain. God can make it to be a thousand times more valuable to his own cause than all the miserable service (at best) that I have rendered it during my life. When I was first taken, I was too feeble to write much; so I wrote what I could to North Elba, requesting Ruth and Anne to send you copies of all my letters to them. I hope they have done so, and that you, Ellen,[28] will do the same with what I may send to you, as it is still quite a labor for me to write all that I need to. I want your brothers to know what I write, if you know where to reach them. I wrote Jeremiah a few days since to supply a trifling assistance, fifteen dollars, to such of you as might be most destitute. I got his letter, but do not know as he got mine. I hope to get another letter from him soon. I also asked him to show you my letter. I know of nothing you can any of you now do for me, unless it is to comfort your own hearts, and cheer and encourage each other to trust in God and Jesus Christ whom he hath sent. If you will keep his sayings, you shall certainly

---

[28] Mrs. Jason Brown.

151

"know of his doctrine, whether it be of God or no." Nothing can be more grateful to me than your earnest sympathy, except it be to know that you are fully persuaded to be Christians. And now, dear children, farewell for this time. I hope to be able to write you again. The God of my fathers take you for his children.

Your affectionate father,
John Brown.

To Andrew Hunter, the special prosecutor of John Brown's case on behalf of the State of Virginia.

Charlestown, Jefferson County, Va.,
November 22, 1859

Dear Sir: I have just had my attention called to a seeming confliction between the statement I at first made to Governor Wise and that which I made at the time I received my sentence, regarding my intentions respecting the slaves we took *about the Ferry*. There need be no such confliction, and a few words of explanation will, I think, be quite sufficient. I had given Governor Wise a *full and particular* account of that, and when called in court to say whether I had anything further to urge, I was taken wholly by surprise, as I did not expect my sentence before the others. In the hurry of the moment, I forgot much that I had before *intended to say*, and did *not* consider the full bearing of what *I then said*. I intended to convey this idea, that it was my object to place the slaves in a condition to defend their liberties, if they would, *without any bloodshed, but not* that I intended *to run them out of the slave States*. I was not *aware* of any such apparent confliction until my attention *was called* to it, and I do not suppose that a man in *my then circumstances* should be *superhuman* in respect to the *exact purport* of every word he might utter. What I said to Governor Wise was spoken with all the deliberation I was master of, *and was intended for truth*; and what I said in court was *equally intended for truth*, but required a more full explanation *than I then gave*. Please make such use of this as you think calculated to correct any *wrong* impressions I may have given.

Very respectfully, yours,

JOHN BROWN

ANDREW HUNTER, Esq., *Present*.

Charlestown, Jefferson Co. Va. 22d, Nov. 1859.
Rev T W Higginson
           Dear Sir
                        I write you a few lines to express to you my
deep feeling of gratitude for your journey to visit & comfort my
family as well as myself in different ways & at different times; since
my imprisonment here. Truly you have proved yourself to be " a
friend in need;" & I feel my many obligations for all your kind
attentions, none the less: for my wishing my Wife not to come on
when she first set out. I would it were in my power to make to all
my kind friends: some other acknowledgements than a mere tender
of our & my thanks. I can assure all: Mrs. Stearns, my young friend
Hoyt; & many others I have been unable to write as yet: that I
certainly do not forget; their love, & kindness. God Allmighty bless;
& save them all; & grant them to see; a fulfilment of all their reasonable desires. My Daughter writes me that you have sent $25.
Twenty Five Dollars in a letter with a bundle of papers. I wish to
thank you in particular for sending them papers; & hope you will
continue this kindness. Friends in the cities who get more papers
than they can read; cannot think how much it may add to the comfort of a bereaved family to receive a good paper from time to time
from distant friends even though those friends may be entire
strangers. I am getting much better of my wounds; but am yet
rather lame. Am very cheerful & trust I may continue so " to the
end." My Love to all dear friends.   Yours for God & the right.
                                        John Brown

To Reverend James W. McFarland of Wooster, Ohio.

                    Jail, Charlestown, Wednesday, Nov. 23, 1859
Rev. McFarland.
Dear Friend: Although you write to me as a stranger, the spirit you
show towards me and the cause for which I am in bonds, makes me
feel towards you as a dear friend. I would be glad to have you, or
any of my liberty-loving ministerial friends here, to talk and pray
with me. I am not a stranger to the way of salvation by Christ.
From my youth I have studied much on that subject, and at one
time hoped to be a minister myself; but God had another work for

153

me to do. To me it is given in behalf of Christ, not only to believe on him, but also to *suffer* for his sake. But while I trust that I have some experimental and saving knowledge of religion, it would be a great pleasure to me to have some one better qualified than myself to lead my mind in prayer and meditation, now that my time is so near a close. You may wonder, are there no ministers of the gospel here? I answer, No. There are no ministers of *Christ* here. These ministers who profess to be Christian, and hold slaves or advocate slavery, I cannot abide them. My knees will not bend in prayer with them while their hands are stained with the blood of souls. The subject you mention as having been preaching on, the day before you wrote to me, is one which I have often thought of since my imprisonment. I think I feel as happy as Paul did when he lay in prison. He knew if they killed him it would greatly advance the cause of Christ; that was the reason he rejoiced so. On that same ground " I do rejoice, yea, and will rejoice." Let them hang me; I forgive them, and may God forgive them, for they know not what they do. I have no regret for the transaction for which I am condemned. I went against the laws of men, it is true; but " whether it be right to obey *God* or *men*, judge ye." Christ told me to remember them that are in bonds, as *bound with them*, to do towards them as I would wish them to do towards me in similar circumstances. My conscience bade me do that. I tried to do it, but failed. Therefore I have no regret on that score. I have no sorrow either as to the result, only for my poor wife and children. They have suffered much, and it is hard to leave them uncared for. But God will be a husband to the widow, and a father to the fatherless.

I have frequently been in Wooster; and if any of my old friends from Akron are there, you can show them this letter. I have but a few more days, and I feel anxious to be away, "where the wicked cease from troubling, and the weary are at rest." Farewell.

Your friend, and the friend of all friends of liberty,

John Brown.

Charlestown, Jefferson County, Va., Nov. 24, 1859.
My Dear Mrs. Spring,—Your ever welcome letter of the 19th inst., together with the one now enclosed, were received by me last night too late for any reply. I am always grateful for anything you either do or write. I would most gladly express my gratitude to you and

yours by something more than words; but it has come to that, I now have but little else to deal in, and sometimes they are not so kind as they should be. You have laid me and my family under many and great obligations. I hope they may not soon be forgotten. The same is also true of a vast many others, that I shall never be able even to thank. I feel disposed to leave the education of my dear children to their mother, and to those dear friends who bear the burden of it; only expressing my earnest hope that they may all become strong, intelligent, expert, industrious, Christian housekeepers. I would wish that, together with other studies, they may thoroughly study Dr. Franklin's "Poor Richard." I want them to become matter-of-fact women. Perhaps I have said too much about this already; I would not allude to this subject now but for the fact that you had most kindly expressed your generous feelings with regard to it.

I sent the letter to my wife to your care, because the address she sent me from Philadelphia was not sufficiently plain, and left me quite at a loss. I am still in the same predicament, and were I not ashamed to trouble you further, would ask you either to send this to her or a copy of it, in order that she may see something from me often.

I have very many interesting visits from proslavery persons almost daily, and I endeavor to improve them faithfully, plainly, and kindly. I do not think that I ever enjoyed life better than since my confinement here. For this I am indebted to Infinite Grace, and the kind letters of friends from different quarters. I wish I could only know that all my poor family were as much composed and happy as I. I think that nothing but the Christian religion can ever make any one so much composed.

> "My willing soul would stay
> In such a frame as this."

There are objections to my writing many things while here that I might be disposed to write were I under different circumstances. I do not know that my wife yet understands that prison rules require that all I write or receive should first be examined by the sheriff or State's attorney, and that all company I see should be attended by the jailer or some of his assistants. Yet such is the case; and did she know this, it might influence her mind somewhat about the opportunity she would have on coming here. We cannot expect the jailer to devote very much time to us, as he has now a very hard task on his hands. I have just learned how to send letters to my wife near Philadelphia.

I have a son at Akron, Ohio, that I greatly desire to have located in such a neighborhood as yours; and you will pardon me for giving you some account of him, making all needful allowance for the source the account comes from. His name is Jason; he is about thirty-six years old; has a wife and one little boy. He is a very laborious, ingenious, temperate, honest, and truthful man. He is very expert as a gardener, vine-dresser, and manager of fruit-trees, but does not pride himself on account of his skill in anything; always has underrated himself; is bashful and retiring in his habits; is not (like his father) too much inclined to assume and dictate; is too conscientious in his dealings and too tender of people's feelings to get from them his just deserts, and is very poor. He suffered almost everything on the way to and while in Kansas but death, and returned to Ohio not a spoiled but next to a ruined man. He never quarrels, and yet I know that he is both morally and physically brave. He will not deny his principles to save his life, and he " turned not back in the day of battle." At the battle of Osawatomie he fought by my side. He is a most tender, loving, and steadfast friend, and on the right side of things in general, a practical Samaritan (if not Christian); and could I know that he was located with a population who were disposed to encourage him, without expecting him to pay too dearly in the end for it, I should feel greatly relieved. His wife is a very neat, industrious, prudent woman, who has undergone a severe trial in " the school of affliction."

You make one request of me that I shall not be able to comply with. Am sorry that I cannot at least explain. Your own account of my plans is very well. The son I mentioned has now a small stock of choice vines and fruit-trees, and in them consists his worldly store mostly. I would give you some account of others, but I suppose my wife may have done so.

Your friend,
John Brown.

Charlestown, Jefferson County, Va., Nov. 25, 1859.

Rev. Heman Humphrey, D.D.

My Dear and Honored Kinsman,—Your very sorrowful, kind, and faithful letter of the 20th instant is now before me. I accept it with all kindness. I have honestly endeavored to profit by the faithful advice it contains. Indeed, such advice could never come amiss. You will allow me to say that I deeply sympathize with you and all my sorrowing friends in their grief and terrible mortification. I feel ten times more afflicted on their account than on account of my own circumstances. But I must say that I am neither conscious of being "infatuated" nor "mad." You will doubtless agree with me in this, —that neither imprisonment, irons, nor the gallows falling to one's lot are of themselves evidence of either guilt, "infatuation, or madness."

I discover that you labor under a mistaken impression as to some important facts, which my peculiar circumstances will in all probability prevent the possibility of my removing; and I do not propose to take up any argument to prove that any motion or act of my life is right. But I will here state that I know it to be wholly my own fault as a leader that caused our disaster. Of this you have no proper means of judging, not being on the ground, or a practical soldier. I will only add, that it was in yielding to my feelings of humanity (if I ever exercised such a feeling), in leaving my proper place and mingling with my prisoners to quiet their fears, that occasioned our being caught. I firmly believe that God reigns, and that he overrules all things in the best possible manner; and in that view of the subject I try to be in some degree reconciled to my own weaknesses and follies even.

If you were here on the spot, and could be with me by day and by night, and know the facts and how my time is spent here, I think you would find much to reconcile your own mind to the ignominious death I am about to suffer, and to mitigate your sorrow. I am, to say the least, quite cheerful. "He shall begin to deliver Israel out of the hand of the Philistines." This was said of a poor erring servant many years ago; and for many years I have felt a strong impression that God had given me powers and faculties, unworthy as I was, that he intended to use for a similar purpose. This most unmerited honor He has seen fit to bestow; and whether, like the same poor frail man to whom I allude, my death may not be of vastly more value than my life is, I think quite beyond all

157

human foresight. I really have strong hopes that notwithstanding all my many sins, I too may yet die "in faith."

If you do not believe I had a murderous intention (while I *know* I had not), why grieve so terribly on my account? The scaffold has but few terrors for me. God has often covered my head in the day of battle, and granted me many times deliverances that were almost so miraculous that I can scarce realize their truth; and now, when it seems quite certain that he intends to use me in a different way, shall I not most cheerfully go? I may be deceived, but I humbly trust that he will not forsake me "till I have showed his favor to this generation and his strength to every one that is to come." Your letter is most faithfully and kindly written, and I mean to profit by it. I am certainly quite grateful for it. I feel that a great responsibility rests upon me as regards the lives of those who have fallen and may yet fall. I must in that view cast myself on the care of Him "whose mercy endureth forever." If the cause in which I engaged in any possible degree approximated to be "infinitely better" than the one which Saul of Tarsus undertook, I have no reason to be ashamed of it; and indeed I cannot now, after more than a month for reflection, find in my heart (before God in whose presence I expect to stand within another week) any cause for shame.

.   .   .   .

I got a long and most kind letter from your pure-hearted brother Luther, to which I replied at some length. The statement that seems to be going around in the newspapers that I told Governor Wise that I came on here to seek revenge for the wrongs of either myself or my family, is utterly false. I never intended to convey such an idea, and I bless God that I am able even now to say that I have never yet harbored such a feeling. See testimony of witnesses who were with me while I had one son lying dead by my side, and another mortally wounded and dying on my other side. I do not believe that Governor Wise so understood, and I think he ought to correct that impression. The impression that we intended a general insurrection is equally untrue.

Now, my much beloved and much respected kinsman, farewell. May the God of our fathers save and abundantly bless you and yours!

John Brown.

Charlestown, Jefferson Co. Va. 26th Nov. 1859
(Nov. 27th I mean to write again to some care

My dear Wife

I wrote our dear friend McKim a few lines yesterday saying I had got his kind letter informing me of where you then were; & how to direct to you while in his neighbourhood. I also said to him that I would be glad to have you rem[a]in about there; until I was disposed of: *or untill*; I could send you a few little articles by Express: & also write you further; if that (could be) without your becoming burdensome to friends. Our friend McKim wrote me you had gone; *or was going* to stay a while with *Lucretia Mott*. I remember the faithful old Lady well; but presume she has no recollection of me. I once set myself to oppose a *mob* at Boston; where she was. After I interfered the police immediately took up the matter; & soon put a stop to mob proceedings. The meeting was I think in *Marlboro Street* Church, or *Hotel perhaps*. I am glad to have you make the acquaintance of such old "Pioneers" in the cause. I have just received from Mr. John Jay of New York a draft for $50, Fifty Dollars for the benefit of my family; & will enclose *it*; made payable to your order. I have also $15, Fifteen Dollars to send to our *cripled*, & *destitute* unmarried son; when I can I intend to send you by Express Care of Mr. McKim Two or Three little articles to carry home. Should you happen to meet with Mr. Jay say to him that I fully appreciate his great kindness both to *me*; & *my family*. God bless *all* such friends. It is out of my power to reply to *all* the kind, & encourageing letters *I get*; *Wish* I could do so. I have been so much relieved from my lameness for the last Three or Four days as to be able to sit up to read; & write pretty much all day: as well as part of the Night; & I do assure you & *all other* friends that I am quite busy; & *none the less hapy* on that account. The time passes *quite pleasantly*; & the near aproach of my great change is not the occasion of any particular dread. I trust that *God* who has sustained me *so long*; will not *forsake* me when I most feel my need of *Fatherly aid*; & *support*. Should he hide his face; my spirit will droop, & die: *but not otherwise*: *be assured*. My only anxiety is to be properly assured of my *fitness* for the company of those who are "washed from *all filthiness*:" & *for the presence of Him who is Infinitely pure*. I certainly *think* I do have *some* "hunger, & *thirst* after righteousness." If it be only *genuine* I make *no doubt I* "*shall be filled*." Please let all our friends read my letters when you can;

& ask them to accept of it *as in part for them*. I am inclined to think you will not be likely to succeed well about getting away the bodies of your family; but should that *be so* : *do not let that grieve you*. It can make but little difference *what is done with them*. I would advise that you take any little funds you may have to carry home in Gold (smallish sized) *in good part*; which some kind friend will obtain at a Bank for you. You can continue to carry (*the most of it*) about your person in some *safe way* : & it will not be best for me to advise you about making the little you now get; reach as far as you consistently can. You can well remember the changes you have passed through. Life is made up of a series of changes : & let us try to meet them in the best maner [sic] possible. You will not wish to make yourself & children any more burdensome to friends than you are really compelled to do. *I would not.*

I will close this by saying that if you *now feel* that you are *equal* to the undertaking do *exactly as you* FEEL *disposed to do* about coming to see me before I suffer. *I am entirely willing.*

Your Affectionate Husband

John Brown

Charlestown, Jefferson Co. Va. 27th Nov. 1859. Sabbath
My dearly beloved Sisters *Mary A, & Martha.*

I am obliged to occupy a part of what is probably (my last) Sabbath on Earth in answering the *very kind* & *very comforting* letters of Sister Hand & Son of the 23d inst or I must fail to do so at all. I do not think it any violation of the day that "God made for man. [quote missing.] Nothing could be more grateful to my feelings than to learn that you do *not* feel *dreadfully mortified* & *even disgraced* on account of your relation to one who is to *die on the Scaffold* I have really suffered *more* by Ten fold since my confinement here; on account of what I feared would be the *terible feelings of my kindred* on my account than from *all other* causes. I am most glad to learn *from you* that my fears on *your own* account were ill founded I was afraid that a little *seeming present* prosperity might have carried you away from realities so that the honor that comes from men might lead you in *some measure* to undervalue that which " cometh from God." I bless God who has *most abundantly supported & com-*

forted me; all along to find you are not ensnared. Dr Heman Humphrey has just sent me a *most doleful Lamentation* over my "*infatuation*" & "*madness*" (very kindly expressed:) in which I cannot doubt he has given expression to the *extreme grief* of others of our kindred. I have endeavoured to answer him kindly *also*: & at the same time to deal faithfully with my old friend. I think I will send you his letter; & if you deem it worth the trouble you can probably get my reply or a copy of it. Suffise it for me to say none of these things move me." I here experienced a consolation; & peace which I fear he has not yet known. Luther Humphrey wrote me a very comforting letter There are "things dear Sisters that God hides *even* from the wise & prudent" I feel astonished that one *so exceedingly vile & unworthy* as *I am* would even be suffered to have a place *anyhow or any where* amongst the *very least of All* who when they came to die (as all must:) *were permitted* to pay the debt of nature" in defence of the *right*: & of Gods *eternal* & *immutable truth*. Oh my dear friends can you believe *it possible* that the Scaffold *has no terrors* for your *own* poor, old, unworthy brother? *I thank God* through Jesus Christ *my Lord*: *it is even so* I am now sheding tears: but they *are no longer* tears of *grief or sorrow*. I trust I have nearly DONE with those. I am weeping for *joy*: & *gratitude* that I can *in no other way* express. I get many *very kind* & *comforting* letters that I cannot possibly reply to. Wish I had time & strength to answer all. I am obliged to ask those to whom I do write to let friends read what I send as much as they well can. *Do write* my deeply & oft afflicted Wife: It will greatly comfort her to have you write her freely. She has born up *manfully* under accumulated trials. She will be most glad to know that she has not been entirely forgotten by relatives and say to all my friends that I am "waiting cheerfully" & "patiently the days of my appointed time": fully believing that for me now "to die will be to me an Infinite gain;" & of *untold* benefit to the cause *we love*. Wherefore "be of good cheer" & "let not your hearts be troubled." "To him that overcometh will I grant to sit with me;" in my throne even as I also overcame; & am set down with my Father in his throne." I wish my friends could know but a little of the same opportunities I now get for *Kind* & *faithful* labour in *Gods cause*. I hope they have not been entirely lost. Now dear friends I have done "May the God of peace bring us all again from the dead."

Your Affectionate Brother
John Brown

Charlestown, Jefferson Co., Va., Monday, Nov. 28, 1859.
Hon. D. R. Tilden.

My Dear Sir,—Your *most kind and comforting* letter of the 23d inst. is received.

I have no language to express the feelings of gratitude and obligation I am under for your kind interest in my behalf ever since my disaster.

The great bulk of mankind estimate each other's actions *and motives* by the measure of success or *otherwise* that attends them through life. By that rule I have been one of the *worst* and one of the *best* of men. I *do* not claim to have been one of the *latter*; and I leave it to an impartial tribunal to decide whether the world has been the *worse* or the better of my *living* and *dying* in it. My present great anxiety is to get as near in readiness for a different field of action as I well *can* since being in a good measure *relieved from the fear* that my poor, *broken-hearted wife and children* would come to immediate want. May God reward, *a thousand fold*, all the kind efforts made in their behalf. I have enjoyed *remarkable cheerfulness and composure of mind* ever since my confinement; and it is a great comfort to *feel assured* that I *am permitted* to die (for a *cause*) not *merely* to pay the debt of nature, (as all must.) I feel myself to be *most* unworthy of *so great* distinction. The particular manner of dying *assigned* to me, gives me but very little *uneasiness*. I wish I had the time and the ability to give you (my dear friend) some little idea of what is *daily, and, I might almost say*, hourly, passing within my *prison walls*; and could my friends but witness only a few of those scenes just as they occur, I think they would feel very well reconciled to my being here *just what I am, and just as I am*. My *whole* life *before* had not afforded me one half the opportunity to plead *for the right. In this*, also, *I find* much to reconcile me to both my present condition and my immediate prospect. I may be *very insane*, (and I *am so*, if insane at all.) But if that be so, *insanity* is like a very pleasant dream to me. I am not in the least degree conscious of my *ravings*, of my fears, or of any terrible visions whatever; but *fancy* myself entirely composed, and that my *sleep, in particular*, is as sweet as that of a healthy, joyous little infant. I pray God that he will grant me a continuance of the same calm, but delightful, *dream*, until I come to know of those realities which "eyes have not seen, and which ears have not heard." I have scarce realized that I am in prison, or in irons, at all. I certainly think I was never more cheerful in my life. I intend to take the liberty of sending, by express, to your care, some trifling articles for those of my family who may be in Ohio, which you can hand to my brother JEREMIAH, when you may see him, together with fifteen dollars I have asked him to advance to them. Please excuse me so often troubling you with my letters, or any of my matters. Please also remember me *most* kindly to Mr. GRISWOLD,[29] and to all others who love their neighbors. I write JEREMIAH to your care.

Your friend, in truth,
John Brown.

Charlestown, Jefferson Co Va. 29th Nov. 1859.

Mrs George L Stearns
    Boston Mass
My Dear Friend

No letter I have received since my imprisonment here, has given me more satisfaction, or comfort; then yours of the 8th inst. I am quite cheerful: & was never more happy. Have only time [to] write you a word. May God forever reward you & *all yours. My love to All* who love their neighbors. I have asked to be *spared* from having any *mock; or hypocritical prayers made over me*, when I am publicly *murdered*: & that my only *religious attendants* be poor *little, dirty, ragged, bare headed, & barefooted Slave boys*; & *Girls*; led by some old *grey headed Slave Mother*.

Farewell. Farewell.

Your Friend
John Brown.

Charlestown, Jefferson Co., Va., Nov. 29, 1859.

S. E. Sewall, Esq.
My dear Sir: Your most kind letter of the 24th inst. is received. It does, indeed, give me "pleasure," and the greatest encouragement to know of any efforts that have been made in behalf of my poor and deeply afflicted family. It takes from my mind the greatest cause of sadness I have experienced during my imprisonment here. I feel quite cheerful, and ready to die. I can only say, for want of time, may the *God of the oppressed* and the poor, *in great mercy*, *remember* all those to whom we are so deeply indebted!

Farewell!   Your friend,   John Brown.

<hr>

[29] Hiram Griswold, of Cleveland, who was one of Brown's attorneys at his trial.

Charlestown, Prison, Jefferson Co. Va. 30th Nov 1859.
My Dearly beloved Wife, Sons : & Daughters, *every one*

As I now begin what is probably the last letter I shall ever write to any of you; I conclude to write you all at the same time. I will mention some little matters particularly applicable to little property concerns in another place. I yesterday received a letter from my wife from near Philadelphia : dated Nov 27th, by which it would seem that she has about given up the idea of seeing me again. I had written her to come on; if *she* felt equal to the undertaking : but I do not know as she will get my letter in time. It was on her *own account chiefly* that I asked her to stay *back* at first. I had a most strong desire to see her again; but there appeared to be very serious objections; & should we never meet in *this life*; I trust she will in the end be satisfied it was *for the best at least*; if not most for her comfort. I enclosed in my last letter to her a Draft of $50, Fifty Dollars from John Jay made payable to her order. I have now another to send her from my excellent old friend Edward Harris of Woonsocket Rhode Island for $100, One Hundred Dollars; which I shall *also make payable* to *her* order. I am waiting the hour of my public *murder* with great composure of mind, & cheerfulness : feeling the strongest assurance that in no other possible way could I be used to so much advance the cause of God; & of humanity : & that nothing that either I or all my family have sacrificed or suffered : *will be lost.* The reflection that a *wise,* & *merciful, as well as Just,* & *holy* God : rules not only the affairs of *this world*; but of all worlds; is a rock to set our feet upon; under all circumstances : *even* those more severely *trying ones* : into which our own follies; & [w]rongs have placed us. I have now no doubt but that our seeming *disaster* : will ultimately result in the most *glorious success.* So my dear *shattered;* & *broken* family; be of good cheer; & believe & trust in God; " *with all your heart: & with all your soul;* " for *he* doeth *All things well.*" Do not feel ashamed on my account; nor *for one moment* despair of the cause; or grow *weary* of *well doing.* I bless God; I never felt stronger confidence in the certain & near approach of a *bright Morning*; & a *glorious day* : than I have felt; & do now feel; since my confinement here. I am endeavouring to " return " like a " poor Prodigal " *as I am*; to my Father : against whom I have *always* sined : *in the hope*; that he may kindly, & forgivingly " meet me : though; *a verry great way off*." Oh my dear Wife & Children would " to God " you could know how I have been " traveling in birth for

164

you " all; that no one of you " may fail of the grace of God, through Jesus Christ: " that no one of you may be blind to the truth : & glorious " light of *his* word;" in which Life; & Immortality; are brought to light." I beseech you *every one* to make the bible your *dayly & Nightly study*; with a *childlike honest, candid, teachable spirit* : out of love and respect for your Husband; & Father : & I beseech *the God* of *my Fathers*; to open all your eyes to a discovery of *the truth.* You *cannot immagine* how much *you* may *soon need* the consolations of the Christian religion.

Circumstances like my own; for more than a month past; convince me beyound *all doubt* : of our great need : of something more to rest our hopes on; than merely our own vague theories framed up, while our *prejudices* are excited; *or* our *Vanity* worked up to its highest pitch. Oh do not trust your eternal all uppon the boisterous Ocean, without *even* a *Helm*; or *Compass* to *aid* you in steering. I do *not ask any* of you; to throw *away your reason* : I only *ask* you, to make a candid, & sober *use of your reason* : My dear younger children will you listen to this last poor admonition of one who can *only* love you? Oh be determined at once to give your whole hearts to God; & let *nothing* shake; *or alter*; that resolution. You need have no fear *of* REGRETING *it.* Do not be vain; and thoughtless : but *sober minded.* And let me entreat you all to love *the whole remnant* of our once great family : " with a pure *heart fervently*." Try to *build again* : your broken walls : & to make *the utmost* of every *stone* that is left. Nothing can so tend to make life a blessing as the consciousness that you *love: & are beloved* : & " love ye the stranger " *still.* It is ground of the utmost comfort to *my mind:* to know that so many of you as have had *the opportunity*; have given full proof of your fidelity to the great family of man. *Be faithful* until *death.* From the exercise of habitual love to man : *it cannot* be very *hard* : to *learn to love* his *maker.* I must *yet* insert a reason for my firm belief in the Divine inspiration of the Bible : notwithstanding I am (perhaps naturally) skeptical. (certainly not, *credulous*.) I wish you all to consider *it most thoroughly*; when you read that blessed book; & see whether you *can not* discover such evidence yourselves. It is the purity of *heart, feeling, or motive* : as well as *word, & action* which is every where insisted on; that distinguish it from *all other teachings*; that *commends it* to *my conscience* : whether *my heart* be " willing, & obedient " *or not.* The inducements that it holds out; are another reason *of my conviction* of its *truth: & genuineness*; that I cannot here *omit*; in this my *last argument*, for the Bible

Eternal life: is that my soul *is* " *panting after* " *this moment.* I mention this; as reason for endeavouring to leave a valuable copy of the Bible to be carefully *preserved* in remembrance of *me* : to so many of my posterity; *instead* of some *other* thing : of equal *cost.* I beseech you all to live in habitual contentment with verry *moderate* circumstances : & gains, of *worldly store* : & most earnestly to teach this : to your *children*; & *Childrens, Children*; after you : by *example: as well*; as precept. Be determined to know by experience *as soon as may be* : whether bible instruction is of *Divine origin* or not; *which says;* " *Owe no man anything but* to love one another." John Rogers wrote to his children, " Abhor that arrant whore of Rome." John Brown writes to his children to abhor with *undiing hatred,* also : that " sum of all vilanies;" Slavery. *Remember* that " he that is *slow* to *anger* is *better* than the mighty : and he that ruleth his *spirit*; than he that taketh a city." Remember also : *that* " they that be *wise* shall *shine* : and they that *turn* many to *righteousness:* as the stars forever; & ever." And now dearly beloved *Farewell* To God & the word of his grace I comme[n]d you all.

Your Affectionate Husband & Father
John Brown

John Brown's last letter, written an hour before his execution, to Mr. Lora Case, of Hudson, Ohio.

Charlestown, Jefferson, Co Va, 2d, Dec. 1859.

Lora Case Esqr

My Dear Sir

Your most kind & cheering letter of the 28th Nov is received Such an outburst of warm hearted sympathy not only for myself; but also for those who " *have no helper* " compells me to steal a moment from those allowe[d] me; in which to prepare for my last great change to send you a few words. Such a feeling as you manifest makes you to " *shine* (in my estimation) in the midst of this wicked; & perverse generation as a light in the world" May you ever prove yourself equal to the high estimate I have placed on you. Pure & undefiled religion befor God & the Father is as I understand it : an *active* (not a dormant) *principle.* I do not undertake to direct any more about my Children. I leave that now entirely to their excellent Mother from whom I have

just parted. I send you my "salutation with my own hand."
Remember me to all *yours*, & *my dear friends*. Your Friend
John Brown

This sentence was handed by Brown to one of his guards on the morning
of his execution.

Charlestown, Va, 2d, December, 1859.
I John Brown am now quite *certain* that the crimes of this *guilty*,
land: will never be purged *away*; but with Blood. I had *as I now*
think: vainly flattered myself that without *verry much* bloodshed;
it might be done.

PART TWO

IN THE WORDS OF THOSE
WHO KNEW HIM

THIS SECTION IS DEVOTED
TO THE REMINISCENCES OF THOSE
WHO EITHER KNEW JOHN BROWN
INTIMATELY, OR IF THEY
KNEW HIM ONLY CASUALLY
YET HAD OPPORTUNITY
IN DIRECT CONTACT WITH HIM
TO LEARN OF SOME IMPORTANT
ASPECT OF HIS LIFE
AND WORK

JAMES FOREMAN, an employee of John Brown in 1820, writes about his former employer to James Redpath, Brown's first biographer.

Youngsville Warren Co Pa
Dec 28th 1859

Mr James Redpath

Sir your letter of Dec 21st asking me to relate what I might know of Capt John Brown has been received I have already mentioned so many things of him which have found their way into the papers that it seems to me that they must have become almost stale, yet for your benefit and the benefit of others I will relate some of his habits peculiar to his character

John Brown was born as you already know in the year 1800 in the State of Ct came with his father when a boy and settled in Hudson Portage county Ohio. He was a man of liberal education and a first rate surveyor and a Tanner & Currier by trade which he seems to have learnt of his father in consequence of his eyes rather failing so that he could not pursue his studies   I went to live with him about the year 1820 in Hudson Ohio at which time he was a rigid member of the Presbyterian church and one of his standing rules was that his apprentices and journeymen must under all circumstances attend church every Sabbath and family worship every morning and I do not believe he ever eat a meal of even Potatoes & Salt but he asked a blessing and returned thanks

In the summer of 1824 a Journeyman of his stole from him a very choice calf skin and the journeyman was suspected by Brown for the theft from the fact that he was rather opposed to good order and religious habits. About a week after the theft a brother of the journeyman came to the Tanery on business and shortly before he started home Brown sent two men ahead of the brother to secrete themselves and see if the brother was not carying the calf skin home with him   Such proved to be the fact They took the skin from him and brought it back and gave it to Brown who took the Skin in his hand called the journeyman one Side and he owned up to the theft cryed like a child under the lecture Brown gave him and told him he would not prossecute him unless he left but if he did he would prossecute to the end of the law   The jour Staid about two months through fear of prossecution and in the meantime all hands about the Tanery & in the House were Strictly forbiden Speaking to him not even to ask a question and I think a worse punishment could not have been Set upon a poor human being than that was to him, but it reformed him and he afterwards became a useful man.

I relate this to Show his Sigacity in detecting crime and his manner of punishing

In the fall of the Same year his wife was taken Sick under peculiar circumstances & Brown Started for the Dr and Some Lady friends from his residence   One and half miles to the center of Hudson   On his way he espied two men tying up two bags of apples and making ready to put them on their Horses   Brown immediately tied his own Horse went to the men and made them empty their apples own up to the theft and Settle up the matter before he attended to the case of his wife   Such was his Strict integrity for honesty and justice.

In May 1825[1] he mooved from Hudson O to Randolph township Crawford county Penn and built a fine Tanery Sunk vats and had leather in vats taning on the 1st of Oct besides clearing off 25 acres of new heavy timbered land   Such was his perseverance in business matters and So Strict was he that his leather Should be perfectly dry before Sold that a man might come ten miles for five pounds of Sole leather and if the least particle of moisture could be detected in it he must go home without it   no compromise as to amount of dampness could be effected

In December 1829 a man living about 16 miles North east from Meadville Stole a cow in Meadville and Started home with her about 6 miles was followed and brot back on a warrant to Meadville when the owner of the cow learning the fact of the man being very poor took his cow and dismissed the man & Started him home, but Brown being in Meadville next day & hearing the facts Sent the Const & had the man rearrested and committed to jail where he was confined for Some time and while he was in jail Brown Supplied his family with abundance of provisions regularly once a week until his release, and the principle he took was the man had committed a crime and must be punished but the family was innocent and must not Suffer for the mans wrongs   It was always a Standing principle with him that crime must not go unpunished nor honesty unrewarded

In the year 1832 to the best of my recollection his first wife whoes

1 Documentary evidence recently discovered strongly indicates that Brown moved to Pennsylvania in May, 1826.

maiden name was Diantha Lusk Died at his residence in Crawford
Co Pa a very worthy and exemplary woman After this Brown and
his children came and boarded with me I having just been married
On one cold Snowey Sabbath the Snow 1½ feet deep Brown took it
in his head that a family about 4 miles distant were destitute of any
thing to eat or ware and that the man being high Spirited might let
his family Suffer before he would make his wants Known So the
next day he dispatched [word crossed over] my Self & wife as Spies
to find out their condition and if needy to propose to the man to
come to Brown get provision and promise labor for it the next
Summer and Brown Says if I can only manage to get the provision
on to him without his Knowing my object I will never take one
cent from him and the ends of charity will be answered

The man & family we found destitute proposed to him to come to
Brown and get what was needed & pay in work next Summer he
came got the provision & Some clothing, but Brown uterly refused
ever to receive any remuneration therefor

Brown was always a strong predestinarian & a firm believer in
fore ordination and decrees and it so hapened that he met one evening with a Methodist Clergyman at the House of a neighbor and the
conversation turned on that question and the Clergyman being
pretty flipant with the tongue Kept talking about all the time, which
gave Brown who was rather Slow of Speech but little chance to
reply and the consequence was that the impression went abroad that
Brown was used up on his favorite doctrine Brown in reply Said he
had not been treated gentlemanly and would like another debate
which Should be in public

The Clergyman called one morning at the Tanery to Know if Such
was the fact that he wanted another debate which he would be
happy to grattify also that he had misunderstood, that Brown had
Said he the Clergyman was no gentleman let alone being a Clergyman Brown fixed his Lyon eye on the Minister and replied " I did
Say you were no gentleman, I said more than that Sir, What did you
Say Sir enquired the Preacher "I said Sir, replied Brown "that it
would take as many men like you to make a Gentleman as it would
Wrens to make a cock Turkey " The Clergyman was confounded but
arranged for the debate which was to be conducted in questions &
answers Brown to ask his, the Clergyman to answer, and then the
Clergyman to ask, & Brown to answer, The debate came off, Brown
asked his questions the Clergyman answered, and then the debate
Stoped the Clergyman having used himself up so in his answers that

he deemed it prudent to Stop the debate and own himself used up
I have the questions and answers some where in my House but I can
not lay my hands upon them, but the three first questions Brown
asked I well remember, and for your benefit will relate them
Browns first question was, what was the great end for which man
was created, The answer was, to Glorify God and enjoy him forever
2 Do man kind taken collectively answer the end for which they
were created, Answer I think not 3d Has God ever expressed dis-
apointment which was unanswered, These were the three first Questions and Answers and the balance 24 in number in which the
Clergyman confused him Self So much, that he gave up the debate
and although a Clergyman has amounted to little or nothing Since.
One of his other questions was this, Is Satan in his present State of
Sin and rebellion against God capable of doing good, The answer
was I think not, next question, Is Sattan become worthy therefore
for continuing in this State of Sin and rebellion Answer, unanswered

I mention what I remember of the questions and answers to Show
Browns thought and penetration of mind

John Brown as I have always understood was designed for the
ministry and went through an academy School and entered college
in Connectticut with a Mr Hallock, but his eyes became rather weak
So that he had to abandon his Studies, and with him it was one of
his principles never to yield a point or abandon anything he fixed
his purpose upon, but necessity compelled him and his father, to
give up the original design As a man he Seemed always partial to a
new country to improve and help Subdue it and grow up with the
improvements made & thus he was of great use in Pen in Surveying
out new Roads building School Houses procuring preaching and
encouraging every thing which would have a moral tendency to
improve the country, being then almost a wilderness and it became
almost a proverb that Speaking of an enterprising man that " He
was as enterprising and as honest as John Brown " and as " useful to
the country " Brown in his personal habits was one of the neatest
men I ever Knew and particular as to the cleanliness of his person,
but he would never wear expensive clothing for the reason that it
was useless waste of money which might better be given to the
poor, also he dispised every thing like foping watch chains, guards
Seals or any unnecessary finery and although a great man to talk for
information sake he dispised any man who would on all points coin-
cide with him in opinion, he must have Ideas of his own or Brown
could not bear him

In order to improve the country he brot into Crawford Co Pa the first blooded stock that was ever introduced there which he brot from Hudson Ohio about the Year 1828   Also he brought to Waterford Erie Co Pa a Bull for which an old citizen of Waterford paid $100.00 therefor and from this animal Sprang the first blooded Stock introduced in that section   I mention these facts to Show his general usefulness not as a matter of record in your history of him unless you See proper to use them together with the other incidents as I have mentioned them which if you use, please correct the gramatical language and speling & use what you See fit of them

In his habits he was jocuse and mirthful when the conversation did not turn on anything profane or vulgar and the Bible was almost at his tongues end from one end to the other   Upon the Subject of Slavery he was always of one mind and looked upon it as a great Sin against God and menous [menace] to the morals of the countrys where it existed, and he considered it as much his duty to help a negro to make his escape as it was to help catch a Horse thief and So always argued the question, and if a new Settler came the first enquiry of him was whether he was an observer of the Sabbath, opposed to Slavery and a Supporter of the Gospel and common Schools, if So all was right with him, if not he was looked upon by Brown with Suspicion

In politics he was originally an Adams man and after wards a whig and I believe a Strong one yet I do not believe the time ever was that he would have voted for Henry Clay for the reason that he had fought a duel and owned Slaves and I do not believe he ever was a Supporter of the Republican party in general for the reason that in the main they were not anti Slavery enough to Suit him

His food was always plain and Simple all luxuries being despensed with and not allowed in the family and in the year 1830 he rigidly adopted the tetotal temperance principles and I do not believe he ever tasted liquor of any kind from that time to his death   In conversation he Seemed always to have a text of Scripture at his tongues end that would exactly apply to his argument and Strengthen his position and I never Knew a man who could at all times quote a verse of the Bible with as much force and as applicable as he could

Hunting Gunning and fishing he had an abhorance of, as learning men & boys to idle away their time and learn them lazy habits and it was with the greatest reluctance he would trust a man with a piece of leather who came after it with a gun on his Shoulder although in after life he became a good marksman with the Rifle

With him the principle was "Six days thou Shalt labor and do all thy work but on the 7th day is the Sabbath" and Brown always considered it wrong and Sinful to waste the time on a week day as well as to work on the Sabbath   He took great pains to circulate general information among the people good moral books and papers, and to establish a reading community   He was always a man of nerve from his first Start in life and (with an) Iron will which no man could change until he was convinced and then he would yield the point with pleasure, and for courage and determination Naapoleon or Gen Jackson was never more than his equal I have wrote you so much I presume you will be tired of it and will draw to a close   I have had to write by [word crossed out] Spells and have not even copied the papers Sent you and no doubt you will be put to it to read the papers Sent, but if you can make any thing out of it by correcting the language you can do So also if you want any other information about him please to me and I will furnish any thing about him I Know as he was a Kind friend to me I would like the world should Know his true character   I received a letter from him written Some 8 or 10 hours before his execution which I will treasure up for the rest of my life

I have Said but little of his first wife whose Maiden name as I have before mentioned was Diantha Lusk a daughter of Capt Lusk who was on our frontiers during the late War of 1812 where he comtracted a disease which he died with on his return home

Brown by his first wife had Seven children John Jason & Owen were born in Hudson O and Ruth & Frederick were born in Crawford Co Pa and two with their mother lie burried Side by Side in Crawford County making Seven   Mrs Brown was one of the best women that ever lived Kind & charitable to the poor devoted in her religious habits and her mind absorbed in the welfare and happiness of her family   I must cease if you ever receive this please write me Also if you want any further information about him or his family you will please write me and I will cheerfully give you all in my power

Yours Sincly
James Foreman

George B. Delamater, whose family lived about four miles from the Brown homestead, which was in Randolph (later New Richmond), Crawford County, Pa., and who knew Brown from 1830 to 1845, offers his impressions of the man in an address delivered at Meadville, Pa., some time after Brown's death.

. . . . It was my fortune to be much under his [John Brown's] influence at the time of my life which retains impressions most thoroughly, namely from my 10th to my 25th year, and I shall therefore perhaps tell you rather more of his private and domestic [life] as it came under my observation than of his public life: though I cannot pass over in silence the latter. The period of Brown's life when I knew him personally [and] most intimately was from the year 1830, when he resided in this county, till 1845 when his home was in Ohio. My knowledge of his subsequent operations and experiences in Kansas and other wheres I have from the lips of his sons and others who co-operated with him, as well as from correspondence and published accounts undoubtedly authentic. An outline of a plan of operation similar to that adopted by him at Harper's Ferry had been given me by John Brown himself in 1842 - and the result as matured and attempted in action I learned not only through the newspapers at the time, but from the statements of Owen Brown and Charley P. Tidd, who were in the Harper's Ferry movement, but upon the defeat retired through the mountains and remained during the winter of 1859-60 at Townville, in this county, where I then resided. My wife could tell where they made their homes there.[2] As the sons of Brown slain at Harper's Ferry were also sons of a half-sister of my mother, and as the social relations of our families had been [good] I trust I will not be censured for not taking them back to Virginia and claiming the reward offered for their apprehension. It was clear it would be death for them to go to Virginia; they were thoroughly armed and prepared to *die here* rather than go there, and besides some of their friends took the same view, and they were not meddled with.

When John Brown came to Richmond township in this county he and my father became neighbors and friends. That section was at that time a wilderness sparsely settled. Deer, bears, wolves, turkeys and other game were abundant. I have listened both in my father's house and in the house of old John Brown to the 'long howl' of the wolf as he prowled about the sheepfolds and the barns in the dark-

[2] According to Mr. Boyd B. Stutler, this is Delamater's " left-handed way of saying that the fugitives lived with him."

ness of the night. [Says that there were hunters in the region but that John Brown never cared for such pursuits.]

His mind was rather intent upon his business pursuits, the education and improvement of his family and friends, with other projects of public interest or utility. He built a log house, framed barn, a stone and frame tannery, and engaged in tanning, at the same time clearing and improving his farm. One motive in locating there was founded on the fact that bark for tanning purposes was aboundant there; and hides could be taken there from abroad more economical than bark could be transported for the purpose of manufacturing leather. He appreciated fine stock and brought into the neighborhood some fine blooded horses, sheep, hogs and cattle at various times during his residence there. His house was located about 12 miles from the city on a rising ground about 15 rods from the road running from the State road toward Gray's and about 100 rods southeast of the State road - It was of logs divided into two large rooms in the first story, and was supplied at each end with large fireplaces. In the north end was the living or family room, which served for kitchen, dining room and other domestic purposes, while the other was used for sitting room, library and school room—and the sleeping apartments were above and at the tannery, which, by the bye, in that day and at that place so destitute of sawmills was regarded as quite an imposing structure. This was the home of John Brown; here with his family and those in his employ, usually from 10 to 15 persons, he resided for about ten years, carrying on his business operations and aiding in the improvement of the country. Through his agency New Richmond[3] [? Randolph] postoffice was established at that place, he being the first postmaster. Although my father lived about 4 miles away toward the city, John Brown and he agreed that as there was no school in that vicinity and as each had children they would between them maintain the school on the following plan - One of them should furnish a school in his house during one part of the year, taking charge of and boarding the children of the other, and the other should furnish a school and similar accomodations, & care for the children of the first another portion of the year. The summer terms were at my father's house, and the winter terms at Brown's for some four years, but few scholars attending from outside. John Brown's industrious habits and ideas of business induced

[3] According to Boyd B. Stutler: " Originally the post office designation of Brown's place in Crawford County, Pennsylvania, was Randolph, and so continued during the period of his residence there. The name was changed to *New Richmond* on November 9, 1835, and is so known today though the post office there was discontinued on May 31, 1909."

him to require his household to rise early and be promptly ready to engage in the occupations of the day. Things were generally done methodically. In the winter breakfast was usually had before daylight, immediately after which bibles were distributed—Brown requiring each one to read a given number of verses, himself leading; then he would stand up to pray, grasping the back of a chair at the top, and inclining slightly forward. After this members of the family dispersed to their respective pursuits. During these exercises of worship, which were generally held with great regularity, no one hesitated about taking part, for everything seemed fixed as fate by the inspiring presence of him whose every movement, however spontaneous, seemed to enforce conformity to his ideas of what must or must not be done. It would be a new thing for a person to whom Brown gave a bible to decline it without good reason, and he never required a thing of that kind but it seemed fit and becoming. He was no scold, did nothing petulantly, but seemed to be simply an inspired paternal ruler controlling and providing for the circle of which he was the head." . . . .

Though he maintained when circumstances permitted family worship and was a devoutly religious man, he was eminently practical in this as in everything. He abhorred all cant, and had great reverence for the Deity. He was shocked at the familiar, and what he deemed improper, manner with which He was sometimes addressed. His government of family was strict and his chastisements for disobedience or misconduct, while perhaps not seriously severe, were impressive. His manner of requiring the urchin whose exuberance of feeling led him to indulge in noise or other disorderly conduct, to come forward and receive a few words of admonition was like no other man's. Religious services were often held at his house, or in his tannery or barn, or in the school house which was afterwards built by Brown. Sometimes a preacher was present, but often Brown read sermons which he had selected. He held broad views of physical and mental culture, and I have witnessed contests of strength and skill, conducted not in a boisterous and rude but in a quiet and orderly manner, upon the floor of the house between various competitors during the long winter evenings. I was encouraged to try my hand at these sports or exercises, and have seen Mr. Brown do the same. He held that this was not mere amusement, but also a means of strengthening the muscles, and gaining physical power. For a man of his weight he was very strong; his resolute will gave him an advantage here as well as elsewhere. One process for mental improvement and social enjoyment occasionally introduced and encouraged by him was by organizing and carrying on debates in his household. While a magnificent fire of logs was kept up during the long winter evenings in the large fireplace, John Brown and his family and employees were seated around the room on chairs or benches engaged in the discussion of some question deemed worthy of investigation. During these discussions Brown was the leading spirit, and no matter whether the question of debate were religious, political or one involving a knowledge of a domestic, social or scientific subject, he seemed to be well informed on all and always had a decided opinion on the one side or the other. One mode of discussion to which he was accustomed was to propose a series of questions to the person who differed from him, concealing his design till the admission of obvious truths would compel a concession of the point for which he contended. In this he was skilfull. In theology he was a Calvinist, and in politics an Adams man; was outstanding in sentiment and seemed a philosopher as well as a Christian of high tone. In character [he was] above criticism. He used no tobacco or spirituous liquors. As I have before remarked Brown was well informed on most subjects and for a man who during his whole life had been so closely engaged in business affairs, he was very thoroughly read: particularly in those departments in which he took special interest. In his library, among other works I remember Edwards, Witherspoon, Franklin and Aesop's Fables. These latter were often read and the moral never overlooked. The maxims of Franklin lost nothing of their meaning when uttered by the lips of John Brown. He often repeated to us such maxims as these: "Diligence is the mother of good luck," or "God gives all things to industry - they plough deep while sluggards sleep, and you shall have corn to sell and keep," or again "One today is worth two tomorrows," "If you would have your business done, go; if not, send," "If you would have a faithful servant and one that you like, serve yourself," "What maintains one vice will set up two children," "A small leak will sink a great ship," "Buy what thou has no need of and ere long thou wilt have to sell thy necessaries," "A ploughman on his legs is higher than a gentlemen on his knees," "God helps those that help themselves." I have mentioned so many of these maxims to assure you that he was familiar with them, and accorded them in sentiment and cited them to influence conduct and character. He gave me a line of argument for my encouragement like this: "He that walks with wise men shall be wise also," "One valuable idea a day will give you seven in a week, and at the same rate 365 in a year - many persons do not get so many in a lifetime."

I was present on one occasion when he, hearing a neighbor recommending to some friends that they heap the measure when sending grain to mill as the toll for grinding would be the same as for scant measure, denounced such a practice as unjust and dishonest. He always laid great emphasis on justice.

I must however not delay in speaking of that subject which at that early time when Brown was our fellow citizen received no little attention from him and which afterwards engrossed his whole life: the question of slavery. Old citizens of Richmond and Randolph townships tell of his applications to them to furnish relief and homes for fugitives from slavery. If he had been a mere *dreamer* there would have been many to tell of a prospect to liberate slaves extensively and without bloodshed. But because he had formed within his own mind such a plan and because he contemplated on some future time acting in accordance with this plan he did not publish it broadcast, but submitted it merely to a select few that his future operations might not be thwarted. I was one of the few who had his confidence in the matter. In our discussion of the subject Brown held that any scheme for the liberation of the slaves in the South involved the possibility if not the probability of failure and under some circumstances involved the loss of those engaged in it. The objects of life, he enumerated and discussed their value. He said that the longest life was short, that it could be shortened but by a few years, that death for a good cause was glorious, and he deserves the co-operation and counsel of a limited number of such as could use to the performance of such service, if it should be deemed best. Having spent several days and nights with old John Brown at various times between 1840 and 1844, I enjoyed his society and was made acquainted with his views in regard to American slavery and its relation at that time from various standpoints and also with the schemes which he had under consideration for freeing persons held in bondage. I will only try to give you a brief statement of some of the views he presented in relation to these, passing over the reasons by which they were supported, and the manner in which objections were answered. He regarded slavery as a system of [here the manuscript breaks off]

John Brown, Jr., the eldest son of John Brown, born at Hudson, Ohio, on July 25, 1821, describes his earliest memories of Hudson and Randolph (New Richmond).

"Father had a rule not to threaten one of his children. He commanded, and there was obedience. Up to this time (1824) I had not heard a threat. I was playing round where the timbers for the new house were being hewed, and occasionally I picked up the tools belonging to Mr. Herman Peck the carpenter, who spoke up sharp to me and said, 'John, put them down, or I'll cut your ears off!' Believing he would do so, I scrambled under the timbers which were laid up on logs to be hewed (and in my hurry I bumped the back of my head on most of them as I went), and ran off to the tannery, in a room of which we were temporarily living; for the log-house in which I was born had been torn down to give place to the new one. Besides the sharpest recollection of this, I have heard father mention, when speaking of the matter of threatening children, how greatly alarmed I was on that occasion. I cannot say how old I was then,— probably less than three,—yet my memory of the event is clear. I don't know the year when we moved to Pennsylvania, though I remember the circumstances. Owen was then a baby.[4]

"My first apprenticeship to the tanning business consisted of a three years' course at grinding bark with a blind horse. This, after months and years, became slightly monotonous. While the other children were out at play in the sunshine, where the birds were singing, I used to be tempted to let the old horse have a rather long rest, especially when father was absent from home; and I would then join the others at their play. This subjected me to frequent admonitions and to some corrections for 'eye-service,' as father termed it. I did not fully appreciate the importance of a good supply of ground bark, and on general principles I think my occupation was not well calculated to promote a habit of faithful industry. The old blind horse, unless ordered to stop, would, like Tennyson's Brook, 'go on forever,' and thus keep up the appearance of business; but the creaking of the hungry mill would betray my neglect, and then father, hearing this from below, would come up and stealthily pounce upon me while at a window looking upon outside attractions. He finally grew tired of these frequent slight admonitions for my laziness and other shortcomings, and concluded to adopt with me a sort of book-account, something like this : —

4 Owen was born Nov. 4, 1824. Frederick, the next child, was born at Randolph (New Richmond), January 9, 1827.

182

John, Jr.,

For disobeying mother................8 lashes		
„ unfaithfulness at work.............3	„	
„ telling a lie.............................8	„	

This account he showed to me from time to time. On a certain Sunday morning he invited me to accompany him from the house to the tannery, saying that he had concluded it was time for a settlement. We went into the upper or finishing room, and after a long and tearful talk over my faults, he again showed me my account, which exhibited a fearful footing up of *debits*. I had no credits or off-sets, and was of course bankrupt. I then paid about *one-third* of the debt, reckoned in strokes from a nicely-prepared blue-beech switch, laid on 'masterly.' Then, to my utter astonishment, father stripped off his shirt, and, seating himself on a block, gave me the whip and bade me 'lay it on' to his bare back. I dared not refuse to obey, but at first I did not strike hard. 'Harder!' he said; 'harder, harder!' until he *received the balance of the account.* Small drops of blood showed on his back where the tip end of the tingling beech cut through. Thus ended the account and settlement, which was also my first practical illustration of the Doctrine of the Atonement. I was then too obtuse to perceive how Justice could be satisfied by inflicting penalty upon the back of the innocent instead of the guilty; but at that time I had not read the ponderous volumes of Jonathan Edwards's sermons which father owned."

Ruth Brown Thompson, the only daughter of John Brown's first marriage, who was born at Randolph (New Richmond), Pa., on February 18, 1829, and married Henry Thompson in 1850, wrote these reminiscences many years after her father's death.

"My mother, Dianthe Lusk Brown, died at Randolph, Pa., in August, 1832. The baptism of myself and my brother Fred must have been in the spring of 1832, when I was a little more than three years old, and while my own mother was living. The first housework that I remember is wiping some dishes for my new mother, perhaps when I was five years old. My father was married a second time to Mary Anne Day, July 11, 1833, and I continued to live at Randolph (now Richmond) until 1835, when we went back to Ohio, where my grandfather, Owen Brown, was living. While I was wiping the knives, at the time I mention, I cut my finger and was faint, so that father got some wine for me, and told me to drink it. The boys bothered me about that wine for a long time, but were very careful never to say anything about it before father, who was sometimes very stern and strict. He used to whip me quite often for telling lies, but I can't remember his ever punishing me but once when I thought I didn't deserve it, and then he looked at me so stern that I didn't dare to tell the truth. He had such a way of saying 'tut, tut!' if he saw the first sign of a lie in us, that he often frightened us children. When we were moving back from Pennsylvania to Ohio, father stopped at a house and asked for a pail of water and a cup to give us a drink; but when he handed the cup of water to mother he said, with a queer, disgusted look, 'This pail has sore ears.'

"When I first began to go to school, I found a piece of calico one day behind one of the benches,—it was not large, but seemed quite a treasure to me, and I did not show it to any one until I got home. Father heard me then telling about it, and said, 'Don't you know what girl lost it?' I told him I did not. 'Well, when you go to school to-morrow take it with you, and find out if you can who lost it. It is a trifling thing, but always remember that if you should lose anything *you* valued, no matter how small, you would want the person that found it to give it back to you.' The impression he made on me about that little piece of calico has never been forgotten. Before I had learned to write, the school-teacher wanted all the scholars to write a composition or read a piece. Father wanted me to read one of Aesop's fables,—I can't remember what fable. Brother John said he would write it for me. 'No,' I said, 'I had rather have one of the other boys write it, for if you do the whole school will soon know I did not write it.' My father spoke up quickly and said, 'Never appear to be what you are not,—honesty is the best policy.' When I was telling something done by another girl that I thought was wrong, he said, 'Who made you to differ?' He showed a great deal of tenderness to me; and one thing I always noticed was my father's peculiar tenderness and devotion to his father. In cold weather he always tucked the bedclothes around grandfather, when he went to bed, and would get up in the night to ask him if he slept warm,—always seeming so kind and loving to him that his example was beautiful to see. He used to tell us a story of a man whose old father lived with him, and broke a plate while he was eating; and then his son concluded to make him a trough to eat out of. While he

184

was digging the trough, his little boy asked him what he was making. 'I am making a trough for your grandfather to eat out of.' The little boy said, 'Father, shall I make a trough for you to eat out of when you are old?' This set the man thinking, and he concluded his father might still eat on a plate. He often told us when we were where old people were standing, always to offer them a seat if we had one, and used to quote this verse, 'Thou shalt rise up before the hoary head, and honor the face of the old man.' While we were living at Hudson, an old man, leading an old white ox, came to our house one rainy afternoon, asking for something to eat and to stay over night. Father and the older boys were gone from home, and mother and we younger children were afraid of him,—he acted so strangely, did not talk much, but looked down all the time, and talked strangely when he said anything. Mother gave him something to eat, and told him there was a tavern a half mile from there, where he could stay. He went on and we thought no more about him. The next Sunday father was talking to us about how we should treat strangers, and read this passage from the Bible, 'Forget not to entertain strangers, for thereby some have entertained angels unawares.' Mother then told about the old man. John said, 'I met that same old man as I was coming home from Franklin about midnight, riding his old white ox; it was raining and cold.' When father heard that he said, '*Oh dear!* no doubt he had no money, and they turned him off at the tavern, and he could get no place to stay, and was obliged to travel all night in the rain.' He seemed to feel really hurt about it. When his children were ill with scarlet fever, he took care of us himself, and if he saw persons coming to the house, would go to the gate and meet them, not wishing them to come in, for fear of spreading the disease. Some of his friends blamed him very much for not calling in a physician,—but he brought the whole family through nicely, and without any of the terrible effects afterward, which many experience. Right away he became famous as a doctor, and those who blamed him most were the first to call for him when they were taken with the same disease.

" As a shepherd, he showed the same watchful care over his sheep. I remember one spring a great many of his sheep had a disease called 'grub in the head,' and when the lambs came the ewes would not own them. For two weeks he did not go to bed, but sat up or slept an hour or two at a time in his chair, and then would take a lantern, go out and catch the ewes, and hold them while the lambs sucked. He would very often bring in a little dead-looking lamb, and put it in warm water and rub it until it showed signs of life, and then wrap it in a warm blanket, feed it warm milk with a tea-spoon, and work over it with such tenderness that in a few hours it would be capering around the room. One Monday morning I had just got my white clothes in a nice warm suds in the wash-tub, when he came in bringing a little dead-looking lamb. There seemed to be no sign of life about it. Said he, 'Take out your clothes quick, and let me put this lamb in the water.' I felt a little vexed to be hindered with my washing, and told him I didn't believe he could make it live; but in an hour or two he had it running around the room, and calling loudly for its mother. The next year he came in from the barn and said to me, 'Ruth, that lamb that I hindered you with when you were washing, I have just sold for one hundred dollars.' It was a pure-blooded Saxony lamb."

*　*　*　*　*

"Father used to hold all his children, while they were little, at night, and sing his favorite songs, one of which was, 'Blow ye the trumpet, blow!' One evening after he had been singing to me, he asked me how I would like to have some poor little black children that were slaves (explaining to me the meaning of slaves) come and live with us; and asked me if I would be willing to divide my food and clothes with them. He made such an impression on my sympathies, that the first colored person I ever saw (it was a man I met on the street in Meadville, Penn.,) I felt such pity for him that I wanted to ask him if he did not want to come and live at our house. When I was six or seven years old, a little incident took place in the church at Franklin, Ohio (of which all the older part of our family were members), which caused quite an excitement. Father hired a colored man and his wife to work for him,—he on the farm, and she in the house. They were very respectable people, and we thought a great deal of them. One Sunday the woman went to church, and was seated near the door, or somewhere back. This aroused father's indignation at once. He asked both of them to go the next Sunday; they followed the family in, and he seated them in his pew. The whole congregation were shocked; the minister looked angry; but I remember father's firm, determined look. The whole church were down on him then." She adds: "My brothers were so disgusted to see such a mockery of religion that they left the church, and have never belonged to another."

*　*　*　*　*

"The first recollection I have of father was being carried through a piece of woods on Sunday, to attend a meeting held at a neighbor's house. After we had been at the house a little while, father and mother stood up and held us, while the minister put water on our faces. After we sat down, father wiped my face with a brown silk handkerchief with yellow spots on it in diamond shape. It seemed beautiful to me, and I thought how good he was to wipe my face with that pretty handkerchief. He showed a great deal of tenderness in that and other ways. He sometimes seemed very stern and strict with me; yet his tenderness made me forget that he was stern. He told me, a few years before his death, to reason calmly with my children when they had done wrong, and in that way encourage them to be truthful; and never to punish them, whatever they had done, if they told the truth about it. Said he: 'If I had my life to live over again, I should do very differently with my children. I meant to do right, but I can see now where I failed.'

"Whenever he and I were alone, he never failed to give me the best of advice, just such as a true and anxious mother would give a daughter. He always seemed interested in my work, and would come around and look at it, when I was sewing or knitting; and when I was learning to spin he always praised me, if he saw that I was improving. He used to say: 'Try to do whatever you do in the very best possible manner.'"

The Reverend Edward Brown, a cousin of John Brown, relates the story of a meeting in November 1837, in Hudson, Ohio, in memory of Elijah P. Lovejoy, the anti-slavery editor who had been slain on November 7, 1837, in Alton, Illinois, by a pro-slavery mob. It was at this meeting, Mr. Brown notes, that John Brown publicly vowed to consecrate his life to the destruction of slavery. At the time of the meeting, Mr. Brown was a student at Western Reserve College in Hudson, Ohio, where John Brown was living with his family. Mr. Brown, who died in 1895, recorded the incident in a series of thirteen articles, primarily of a reminiscent nature, which appeared in *The Northwestern Congregationalist* of Minneapolis, Minnesota, in 1892. The description of the meeting and John Brown's vow apparently went unnoticed until J. Newton Brown, who had been editor of *The Northwestern Congregationalist*, referred to them in a letter to *The Nation*, which appeared in its issue of February 12, 1914, and from which the following is taken. He subsequently wrote an article on this theme for *The Magazine of History* (Vol. XXIII, pp. 97-102, September-October, 1916), entitled, "Lovejoy's Influence on John Brown."

Among the earliest of the pioneers at Hudson, O., was Owen Brown, my father's brother, in after years a trustee of Oberlin

College. His eldest son, John, a very bright and energetic young man, making a religious profession at sixteen years of age, was desirous of studying for the ministry, incited thereto chiefly by that ardent founder of the American Board, Samuel J. Mills, a kinsman. Unable to furnish him money, his father gave him two horses, which he took, riding one and leading the other, to Connecticut and sold. Then he went to Plainfield, Mass., where, at an academy and under the private instruction of one Moses Hallock,[5] he was fitted to enter the junior class of Yale College, which he was prevented from doing by a chronic disease of the eyes. . . .

With his father he was among the earliest of Abolitionists. He had been a surveyor in the mountains near Harper's Ferry,[6] Va., and had often remarked that, with a good leader, the slaves, escaping to those fastnesses and fortifying themselves, could compel emancipation.

Prof. Laurens P. Hickok (since president of Union College and a distinguished preacher and writer of philosophical works) became, in 1836, professor of theology in Western Reserve College. He was regarded as conservative on the question of emancipation. One afternoon in November, 1837, we heard a rapid tramping through the college, halls, and every room entered. Soon we saw it was Professor Hickok, who entered greatly excited. He said, "I want you all to come down to the old chapel-room immediately on the ringing of the four o'clock bell. I have some very important news to tell you." Promptly on time the room was filled with both faculty and students. Professor Hickok had brought an account of the murder of the Rev. Elijah P. Lovejoy and the destruction of his press at Alton, Ill. (where he was publishing a religious paper of decidedly anti-slavery views), by a Missouri mob from St. Louis. They had before destroyed his presses, both at St. Louis and at Alton. After reading it, he proposed to us to call a meeting at the Congregational church in the village two days later.

The next day he mounted his horse and rode all over the township, calling at every house and inviting the people to the meeting. At the meeting he made a most eloquent speech, burning with indignation, in which he said, "The crisis has come. The question now before the American citizens is no longer alone, 'Can the slaves be made free?' but, 'Are we free, or are we slaves under

---

[5] Actually, John Brown left the Hallock school to enter Morris Academy at Litchfield, Conn. His ultimate aim was Amherst College.
[6] John Brown never surveyed in the mountains near Harpers Ferry, and probably never saw the region until his arrival there in July, 1859, in preparation for his attack in October. In 1840, he did do some surveying in the Ohio Valley of West Virginia, a region far removed from the Allegheny Mountains.

Southern mob law?' I propose that we take measures to procure another press and another editor. If a like fate attends them, send another, till the whole country is aroused; and if you can find no fitter man for the first victim, send me." During the afternoon many speeches were made and strong resolutions passed.

Just before the close of the meeting, John Brown, who had sat silent in the back part of the room, rose, lifting up his right hand, saying, "Here, before God, in the presence of these witnesses, from this time, I consecrate my life to the destruction of slavery!" His aged father then rose, and, with stammering speech (for he was a great stammerer), said, "When John the Baptist was beheaded, the disciples took up his body and laid it in a tomb and went and told Jesus. Let us now go to Jesus and tell him." Then, in a very fervent prayer, weeping (but not stammering, for he scarcely ever stammered in prayer), he closed the meeting. . . .

John Brown, Jr., tells of his father's refusal to countenance racial segregation in church.

"About 1837 mother, Jason, Owen and I joined the Congregational Church at Franklin [now Kent, Ohio], the Rev. Mr. Burritt pastor. Shortly after the other societies, including Methodists and Episcopalians, joined ours in an undertaking to hold a protracted meeting under the special management of an Evangelist preacher from Cleveland, named Avery. The house of the Congregationalists being the largest, it was chosen as the place for this meeting. Invitations were sent out to Church folks in adjoining towns to 'come up to the help of the Lord against the mighty;' and soon the house was crowded, the assembly occupying by invitation the pews of the church generally. Preacher Avery gave us in succession four sermons from one text,—'Cast ye up, cast ye up! Prepare ye the way of the Lord; make his paths straight!' Soon lukewarm Christians were heated up to a melting condition, and there was a bright prospect of a good shower of grace. There were at that time in Franklin a number of free colored persons and some fugitive slaves. These became interested and came to the meetings, but were given seats by themselves, where the stove had stood, near the door,—not a good place for seeing ministers or singers. Father noticed this, and when the next meeting (which was at evening) had fairly opened, he

189

rose and called attention to the fact, that, in seating the colored portion of the audience, a discrimination had been made, and said that he did not believe God is 'a respecter of persons.' He then invited the colored people to occupy his slip. The blacks accepted, and all of our family took their vacated seats. This was a bomb-shell, and the Holy Spirit in the hearts of Pastor Burritt and Deacon Beach at once gave up his place to another tenant. Next day father received a call from the Deacons to admonish him and 'labor' with him; but they returned with new views of Christian duty. The blacks during the remainder of that protracted meeting continued to occupy our slip, and our family the seats around the stove. We soon after moved to Hudson, and though living three miles away, became regular attendants at the Congregational Church in the centre of the town. In about a year we received a letter from good Deacon Williams, informing us that our relations with the church in Franklin were ended in accordance with a rule made by the church since we left, that 'any member being absent a year without reporting him or herself to that church should be cut off.' This was the first intimation we had of the existence of the rule. Father, on reading the letter, became white with anger. This was my first taste of the proslavery diabolism that had intrenched itself in the Church, and I shed a few uncalled for tears over the matter, for instead I should have rejoiced in my emancipation. From that date my theological shackles were a good deal broken, and I have not worn them since (to speak of),—not even for ornament."

Reminiscences of his father by Salmon Brown. Salmon was not " the only survivor." Anne Brown Adams was then alive. Salmon died on May 10, 1919; Annie, on October 5, 1926.

MY FATHER, JOHN BROWN

BY SALMON BROWN,

THE ONLY SURVIVOR OF TWENTY CHILDREN

Salmon Brown, aged and infirm, lives at Montavilla, Oregon. A married daughter, Agnes Brown-Evans, cares for her father in addition to her other family duties. In reminiscent mood at times, Mr.

Brown gave the facts as set down here, and the daughter gathered them and compiled them for publication, with the assistance of Mr. A. H. Harris, of the Portland, Oregon "Labor Press."—The Editors.[7]

Perhaps the most striking characteristic of my father, as his children knew him, was his faith in God, his faith in his family, and his sense of equity. For whatever else may be said of John Brown, he was true to his God as he knew his duty, he was strongly devoted to the interests of his family, and he never wronged a man where the interests of justice—as he saw the situation—did not demand it of him. He was stern when need be, but sympathetic and just always.

My memory goes back to the days long before the war, when slavery was not considered such a National sin as it was about the time Lincoln came on the scene. My early recollections of my father have to do with his hatred of slavery, his hatred for everything that would take from one man a single right and give to his fellow even a petty advantage. He was just in his conception of the rights of men, and could never understand why others were determined to reap where they had not sown, to profit unjustly by the efforts of others.

My early recollections go back clearly to the old home at Hudson, Ohio, where I was born, October 2, 1836. Our home was an old-fashioned house, with a great rock nearly covering half an acre of land and nearly as high as the house. A spring bubbled out of the side of the rock, forming a basin and then running off in a " creek," as we called it. I have clear recollections of being chased by Aunt Martha and my sister Ruth all over the big rock in an effort to make me eat butter on my bread. Like my father, I have always disliked butter; why, I do not know.

In a large living-room was a fireplace ten feet long, with huge andirons and a crane and hooks to hang kettles upon. We boys would cut logs two and three feet through for the fireplace, and at night, in winter, two great back-logs were covered with ashes to hold fire. Father would sit in front of a lively fire and take up us children one, two, or three at a time, and sing until bedtime. We all loved to hear him sing as well as to talk of the conditions in the country, over which he seemed worried. A favorite song with father and us children was " Blow Ye the Trumpet, Blow."

We lived in an old whitewashed log house at Richfield, Ohio, with a mill-pond and creek dam, with mud-turtles, which we boys would fatten and eat. The turtles would jerk for twenty-four hours after being cooked, it seemed to us. At Richfield three children died—

7 This introductory note accompanied the article when it first appeared.

three in less than three weeks—a calamity from which father never fully recovered. Two years later another, a year old, was burned to death. Of the three that died at Richfield, Charles was very swift and strong, his legs and arms straight as broomsticks, of sandy complexion, quiet as a cat, but brave as a tiger. Peter was very stout, darker, the best-looking member of the family.

Father had fine Saxony sheep at Richfield. Later in his career, at Akron, while running sheep with Simon Perkins, he took first prize at the first World's Fair ever held (at London, England) in competition with all countries, exhibiting one hundred fleeces of Saxony lambs.

Father was a strict observer of the Sabbath. Sunday evenings he would gather the family and hired help together, and have the Ten Commandments and the Catechism repeated. Sometimes he would preach a regular sermon to us. Besides we had prayers morning and night of every day, with Bible reading, all standing during prayer, father himself leaning on a chair upreared on the forward legs, the old-fashioned Presbyterian way. He was greatly concerned over the spiritual welfare of us boys, whose beliefs were more or less reactionary. He constantly expostulated when with us, and in letters when away. His expressed hope was "that ye sin not, that you form no foolish attachments, that you be not a companion of fools."

Father had great confidence in us children. He never said "Don't tell," but simply trusted to our not telling. Before a child of seven or eight he would calmly discuss plans he would not have breathed before older persons.

Father was five feet ten inches in height, slightly stoop-shouldered after middle life, with eyes sky blue, hair dark brown till tinged with gray, nose hawked and thin, skin florid, spare but muscular in build. His form and features attracted the attention of strangers quickly. He always dressed in snuff-colored broadcloth for good clothes, and was always neat. He wore boots, as was the custom of those days, and wore white shirts with a plait on each side of the bosom. Usually he walked with his hands clasped behind him, often with his eyes on the ground, as if in deep thought. So far as I know he was never sick a day, and never missed a meal on account of his own illness. This was also true of his father.

Blood has always been thick in the Brown family. Family ties were firm, and the tendency has been strong to "stick together." I first noticed this family trait in my father's case when he would go to grandfather's bed—after he became old—and tuck the covers about him as a mother would do with her children.

Our old home was a model of orderliness, and quiet always prevailed when father was about. The meals were served leisurely, but with due order and silence. The long table where twelve children, the largest number ever living at any time (1843), sat down with keen appetites was a model of the time.

A favorite dish with us children was corn-meal mush cooked the whole afternoon long in a huge iron caldron, and served with rich milk or cream. It left a crust a half-inch thick in the caldron, and tasted, so I affirm to this day, like no other mush ever made. The table was always neatly set, never without a white tablecloth; the food was coarse, hearty farmers' food, always in abundance, and always well served. Frugality was observed from a moral standpoint; but, one and all, we were a well-fed, well-clad lot. Considerable hardship was entailed when father left to engage in the Kansas warfare; but real poverty never obtruded itself till his death.

There were no drones in the Brown hive. Little toddlers unable to help were at least not allowed to hinder; as soon as they had achieved a show of stable control of their uncertain little legs the world of work opened to them. There was no pampering, little petting. The boys could turn a steak or brown a loaf as well as their mother.

Despite his relentless sternness, and underlying it, cropping through in his later years, when paternalism of necessity gave way to comradeship, there ran in John Brown's nature a strain of intense tenderness. Suffering in himself he bore without a murmur; but every fiber of his being was wrung by the suffering of others. It brought out the woman in him, the John Brown little known to history, who sat around the great open fireplace at night with his children in his arms and sang them to sleep; who rose on the coldest night and paced the floor with a collicky child, while his wife, worn by child-bearing and child-rearing, lay in bed asleep; and who was ever the nurse in sickness, watchful, tireless, tender, allowing no one to lift the burden of the night watch from him. During a protracted illness of my mother he hovered over her night and day, sleeping for a fortnight only at intervals in his chair, unrelieved of his clothes, afraid to go to bed lest he oversleep.

His kindness toward dumb animals was proverbial. He was like the Israelite of old, sheltering the ninety-and-nine, but refusing shelter for himself till the straying hundredth was safely folded. A chilled and dying lamb was a spectacle upon which he would spend his energies till it either died or stood solidly upon its crooked legs. Even the Monday's wash, soaking in the tubs, was once put aside in order to thaw in the warm, soapy water the numbing death chill from a little straggler's bones.

Family worship was as inexorably a matter of habit as eating or sleeping. The burden of father's soul was the souls of his children, and he strove with them without ceasing. The day's work was ushered in and out with Scripture and prayer. Provided each with a Bible, we read in rotation, father leading with several verses from the large family Bible; mother following with several more from an old Bible bound in sheepskin which father himself had tanned; then on through the long line of children. During prayers all stood, father leaning against the back of a chair upreared on its forward legs, dead to the world and to the pranks of his unregenerate boys, who slyly prodded each other with pins and trampled upon each other's toes to relieve the tension. The week was opened by a Sunday service.

Our long trip from New York to Kansas brought many unusual experiences to the large family. Father outfitted well for the trip, which was beset with unforeseen hardships. But no one questioned the wisdom of the undertaking or feared the result.

At Brunswick, Missouri, we crossed the Missouri River. Near Independence was a slave pen, built like a chicken coop, only stronger and higher. Inside the pen was the auction block. This slave-selling stirred father to the depths of his soul. As he waited for the ferry he saw slaves handcuffed for the journey down the river to New Orleans. Cholera at that time was fearfully epidemic, people dying by hundreds on the boats. Jason's boy, four years old, contracted the disease and died there. The following spring father had the child's body removed to Kansas, thinking Jason would feel better to have the boy's body off Missouri soil.

On the first trip to Kansas father traded dogs with an old Quaker. The Quaker's dog was a ratter, which father wanted as a watch-dog. The trade was made on Sunday, but father would not exchange dogs till Monday.

One day an old Missourian came up to our wagon. "Whar you going?" he asked.

"To Osawatomie."

"Whar you from?"

"New York."

"You'll never live to get thar," informed the Missourian.

" We are prepared not to die alone," answered father quietly, and the man slouched off.

Father was a man of intense earnestness in all things that interested him. Events which changed the course of his life occurred unexpectedly and even strangely. While he was living in Pennsylvania it was the custom for every farmer to have a barrel of whisky in the house. It was also the custom to have " bees " and barn-raisings. A tavern-keeper was to have a barn-raising, and father was to be there. The tavern-keeper needed more liquor and sent to Meadville by father, then scarcely in middle life, for a three-gallon jug. The liquor cost twenty-five cents a gallon. On the road from Meadville father became thirsty and began taking "nips" from the jug. He was accustomed to drinking from his own barrel, and did not think the practice wrong. On the way to the barn-raising father realized that liquor was getting hold of him, and he became alarmed. He afterward spoke of the occurrence frequently. He reasoned that if liquor would lead him to drink from another man's jug it was surely gaining control over him—a thing he could not allow. Coming to a large rock by the roadway, he smashed the jug upon it, vowing that he would not be responsible for his neighbor's drinking at the barn-raising, where accidents might happen. He paid for the liquor, and when he reached home rolled his whisky barrel into the back yard and smashed it to pieces with an ax. No liquor was allowed about the house afterwards.

Father was strongly fixed in most of his habits. He worked with the same earnestness year after year; he ate regularly, and went to bed and arose at the same hours, whenever it was possible. It was always difficult for him to fit himself to circumstances; he wanted conditions to change for him—and he usually brought about the things he most desired. His persistence was as strongly developed as was his firmness. With it all the large family of boys usually held firmly to the idea that father was right; that his foresight was unusual.

Until the Harper's Ferry "trip" was planned father had never found reaction in the spirits of his boys. Where he had led we were glad to follow—and every one of us had the courage of his convictions. Whatever else may be said of the Brown family, I feel that no one will charge us with lacking in bravery at the time when the shadows lowered and there was that dreadful feeling that a great mistake had been made. When death—and the gallows—enters a family it is a time that tries men's souls.

It may have been fear that led me to revolt against the proposed trip to Virginia, which father urged us boys to join him in. I thought the matter over and concluded that I would not go, that for the first time I could not go side by side with father. He urged and reasoned, and regretted my determination to stay at home, perhaps as he had never regretted the act of any of his children. But I felt that the trip was a mistake, that it was not the wise thing to do, and stayed at home. The slaughter at Harper's Ferry showed me clearly that father had miscalculated somewhere; I had no fears of death as the result of the effort against slavery. We never learned just how father accounted for his being trapped as he was.

Father never did anything that he thought was not worth doing well. As a boy he learned the lessons of thoroughness from his father, a tanner who lived in Ohio. Before father was fifteen years of age he learned something of tanning skins and determined to learn the trade of a tanner. He had not told his father of his intentions, but one day a currying-knife would not take an edge until father put it on the stone. In trying the knife father began graining a skin, and it was discovered that he had mastered much of the detail of the trade. Soon afterwards he was charged with a large part of the management of the tannery.

At eighteen the religious nature of father had developed until he determined to go to a New England college and study for the ministry. After a period of hard study he gave up the effort on account of inflammation of the eyes which had fastened itself upon him. At twenty he married and removed to Pennsylvania, where he took up wild land and built a tannery near Meadville. The land was covered with a heavy growth of hemlock, maple, and beech, and the task of clearing it was heartbreaking. The tannery was built of stone, and remains to this day. A great tan-bark yard—several acres of refuse—was soon developed, and here the first children had their playground. Every influence of the surroundings was rugged at least.

While father operated the tannery successfully and engaged in the sheep business with profit, his spirit was constantly struggling with the problems of the National life. He established at Springfield, Massachusetts, the first wool commission house in the United States, and operated it at a profit to himself and to wool-growers. When the Fugitive Slave Law was passed, he quickly made his warehouse a "station" on the "underground railway," sacrificing business and profit to principle. His blooded sheep industry was also sacrificed on the altar of freedom for the black man. Father may have been a fanatic, but he had some intensely practical and homely ideas which were lost sight of when his acts tended to throw the Nation into sectional strife and warfare. The country saw him as a reckless adventurer; his family knew him as a just and generous man.

Following the dark days at Harper's Ferry, the suffering of mother and the family was intense. Despised bitterly by all who sympathized with slavery and considered as the victims of a righteous wrath by many of the North, our family was long buffeted from pillar to post. Efforts to forget were fruitless. The passing years did not heal the horrible wounds made by the country father had tried so hard to help to a plane of higher living.

With nearly all my brothers and sisters gone to their reward, many of them before the Nation realized the importance of father's work, with more than half a century intervening since the tragedy at Harper's Ferry, during which time public judgment has calmed and changed materially, I feel that no apology is needed on behalf of John Brown, husband and father kind and true, however much some may still doubt the saneness of his work for the abolition of that horrible National curse, slavery.

Salmon Brown writes of the events leading up to the Pottawatomie killings in Kansas, in May, 1856. The "foreword" and footnotes are in the original article, with the exception of those footnotes inserted by the present editor, which are indicated by the letter "a."

JOHN BROWN AND SONS IN KANSAS TERRITORY

BY SALMON BROWN

Foreword

Salmon Brown was the last of the many sons of John Brown of Osawatomie to die. He participated in the stirring events that occurred in Kansas Territory, but was opposed to the Harper's Ferry project of his father and had no part in it. After the opening of the Civil War, he raised a company of men at North Elba, New York, during the winter of 1861-1862. The recruits were afraid, however, to go to Virginia for service under a son of John Brown, so no commission was received and Salmon Brown remained a private citizen. Having married in 1859, the family migrated to California during the Civil War where they lived for almost a quarter of a century, when they moved to Portland, Oregon.

Dr. Linneus N. Hines, until recently President of the Indian State Teachers' College at Terre Haute, went to Portland in 1917 to attend the National Educational Association. Learning before his departure from Indiana that a son of John Brown was living in Portland, Dr. Hines hunted up the plain but comfortable home of Salmon Brown and became acquainted with the old gentleman and his wife. Finding that his mind was clear and that he thought about the violence of the Kansas conflict without passion or rancor, Dr. Hines urged this last reviving [sic] son of John Brown to prepare an account of the Kansas struggle. With the aid of a daughter, Mrs. Ethel Brown Chamberlain, the following narrative was written and sent to Dr. Hines, about a year before the death of the author, which occurred on May 10, 1919, in Portland, Oregon. Through the kindness of Dr. Hines, the interesting story, save for the omission of the first section, as it came from the lips of Salmon Brown and was written down by his daughter is presented to the readers of the *Indiana Magazine of History.—Editor.*

THE NARRATIVE[8]

. . . .

BORDER COURT OFFENSIVE

In the Spring of 1856 we were all very busy building houses and doing Spring work, also attending free state settlement meetings. The free state men had a free state legislature run by the bona fide settlers of the territory.[9] It was located at Topeka. If I remember rightly, Judge Cato, of Alabama, was located with his border court at Dutch Henry's Crossing of the Pottawatomie.[10] The free state settlers held a meeting to consider what was to be done in this clash in their territorial government. There were over 100 men present,

---

[8] Salmon Brown and four of his brothers went from Ohio to Kansas Territory in the spring of 1855. They settled near Osawatomie, where their father joined them in the fall of that year. The point covered in the omitted portion of the narrative is the conference held in the hotel at Lawrence at which Dr. Charles Robinson, Governor Wilson Shannon and Col. James H. Lane were present. John Brown with some of his sons, including Salmon Brown, were in the town, but all of them remained outside the hotel. Though Robinson and Lane were both free-state leaders, there was at times considerable friction between them, but both, along with Shannon, signed the agreement drawn up on Dec. 8, 1855, in the Free State Hotel. (See Daniel W. Wilder, *Annals of Kansas*, 72.)

[9] In an attempt to ignore the Territorial government, the free-state men had set up a government of their own at Topeka and were seeking statehood.

[10] Pottawatomie Creek flowed northeastward about thirty miles south of Lawrence. John Brown lived on the Osage River at Osawatomie, about thirty-five miles south and a little east of Lawrence, where Pottawatomie Creek flows into the Osage.

including my brother John's company of nearly 100 trained men. They passed resolutions to warn Cato not to try any one under the "border ruffian laws."[11] My father and my brother were selected to deliver a copy of these resolutions to Judge Cato. I went along to see how Cato would receive the warning. He paid no attention to it but went on organizing his court. He got out warrants for all of the Browns and the members of the free state legislature that were in his district. My brother John and H. H. Williams were two of them. At this time Colonel Buford's men were located somewhere within two or three miles a little southwest of the Pottawatomie crossing.[12] My father, to ascertain what their future purposes were, took his surveying instruments and flagmen and chainmen and ran a line right into their camp. I carried one end of the chain. At this time all of the Pierce Administration surveyors were Southern sympathizers. That made us all hail fellows well met.[13] The Buford men talked very freely, saying, among other things, that they had come to Kansas to help themselves first and the South next. And there was one thing they would do—they would annihilate every one of "those damned Browns" and would stand by Judge Cato "until every damned abolitionist was in hell."

LAWRENCE THREATENED AGAIN

We returned home well served up for future action. They did not know at that time that they were talking to Puritan stock. The warrants for the arrests were put into the hands of the Constable, who was old man Doyle, and two sons who were deputies, to serve upon the whole Brown crowd, and Henry Thompson, Brown's son-in-law. As soon as father heard this he sent Henry Thompson and me to Cato's courthouse unarmed, ten miles away, on foot, to see if they would arrest us. If we were arrested father promised to secure us next day. We remained around the courtroom nearly half a day but they were not quite ready to act. I never could approve of father's act in sending Thompson and myself on such a hazardous scheme just to bring about the issue between freedom and slavery. I thought he trusted a little too much to Providence.

11 Laws of the Territorial Legislature. Free-state men called the Legislature, whose members were elected in 1855, a "bogus Legislature," claiming that the pro-slavery men gained control of it through the votes of Missourians ("border ruffians") who invaded the Territory on election day.
12 Major Jefferson Buford organized and conducted to Kansas Territory a company of men from Alabama to hold the free-state men in check. See Walter L. Fleming, "The Buford Expedition to Kansas" in *America Historical Review*, VI, 38-48.
13 The Browns were pretending to be surveyors in the employ of the Pierce Administration.

While all this was going on in the Pottawatomie region, we had another call to make haste to the defense of Lawrence, as the border riders were marching in force in that direction. My brother John's company of Pottawatomie rifles, 100 strong, augumented with troops from the surrounding country, including Osawatomie, with father's squad, made a forced march in the night for the defense of Lawrence.

HOTEL IS DESTROYED

We traveled all night in the dark and at daybreak in the morning we were on the top of the hills south of Waukarusa, where we could see Lawrence very distinctly. There were about 200 men standing there, tired and hungry, gazing at the Free State hotel all in flames. Just at this time a messenger on horseback came up the hill from the Waukarusa in great haste. Our men made him a prisoner at once. He said, "Who are you?" We replied, "We are free state men, going to the defense of Lawrence." He said, "You are the very men I want to see and I have a hurry-up call for you." He then took a paper out of his boot leg and it was read to our men in the gray of the early morning. The import of the message was to hasten to save Lawrence. The messenger did not know until he got to the top of the hill that Lawrence was on fire.

This messenger told us that Senator Charles Sumner, of Massachusetts, had been knocked down on the floor of the United States Senate by Brooks, of South Carolina. I do not think there was a tired or hungry man in that crowd as they were too much excited to think of creature comforts. This messenger gave his name but I do not remember it. He was soon mixed up with the other men and lost to my view. Some of our men got weak in the knees and expressed the belief that the South had us whipped, and were ready to give up the fight. Others were more on the fight than ever before.

SOME ARE FRIGHTENED

We all turned back to our troubles on the Pottawatomie. My brother John and some of his men had freed some slaves of a man who had settled near our route back. Some of the weak-kneed ones commenced a howl against the act and soon had the company all torn into shreds. They did not want to mix up with "niggers" or abolitionists. In the meantime father's little company went back on the road toward Ottawa,[14] Jones' place. I think, as near as I can remember, it was about twelve miles from the Waukarusa hills to the Jones home place. Near there was a station where they served meals, I think, from a tent. Anyway they had a grindstone. There were a good many men there when we arrived, among them being H. H. Williams, of Pottawatomie, an old comrade of my brother John, and later a resident of Osawatomie, I understand. He was a very fine man but got badly cowed after he was taken to Lecompton a prisoner.

He knew everybody on the Pottawatomie. My father told him we were going back there to break up Cato's court and get away with some of his vile emissaries before they got away with us. "I mean to steal a march on the slave hounds, Williams," my father said. "That is just right," replied Williams, "and I will write down their names," which he did. I stood within two feet of him when he gave the names of all those that were later killed, and some others. We all had implicit confidence in Williams and knew that he was giving us the truth.

GUIDE IS WEAK-KNEED

We then ground all of our swords on the grindstone. When we had finished, old man Tousley[15] in high glee volunteered to haul all of our crowd back in his lumber wagon. We started off with the cheers of the crowd, with their hats in the air, they all knowing the purport of the mission. On the way, old man Tousley got weak in the knees and wanted to quit from sheer fear, but we couldn't let him go, fearing he might turn traitor and foil all of our plans.

We went down to near the crossing at Dutch Henry's and turned off to the right in a deep grass canyon next to the timber on the creek, far away from all travel. We stayed there all that night and all of the next day until late in the evening. The reason for taking the night for our work was because it was impossible to take the men in the daytime. And the broadswords were used because it could be done in a noiseless manner, while shooting would have aroused the whole neighborhood.

[14a] Comma in original doesn't belong there. The man was called Ottawa Jones.
[15a] James Townsley.

DOYLES ARE SLAIN

We went to Doyle's first and encountered a number of savage dogs. Old man Tousley went after the dogs with a broadsword and he and my brother Fred soon had them all laid out. Tousley then went in without being asked and worked with all his might, but not as a prisoner as he afterwards claimed. The three Doyles were taken out of the house to a point a half mile or so away and were slain with broadswords. Owen Brown cut down one of them and another of the Browns cut down the old man and the other. Old Man Doyle's wife gave the Doyles a terrible scoring as they were being taken from the house. She said, "I told you you would get into trouble for all your devilment; and now you see it has come."

Henry Sherman was killed by Henry Thompson, and also Wilkinson, at about the same time the Doyles were. Our party divided, Thompson and Winer[16] in one party and Owen Brown, Fred Brown, Salmon Brown,[17] Oliver Brown and old man Tousley in the other, father running back and forth between the two parties. Father never raised a hand in slaying the men. He shot a bullet into the head of old man Doyle about a half hour after he was dead, but what for I do not know. Perhaps it was to call Thompson and Winer so that they could locate us and we could all get together and return to our camp. We all soon got to camp and remained there all of the following day and until quite late at night. We left and Tousley was more than willing to go with us.

SLAYING IS REGRETTED

The night of the slaying I went alone to the house of Mr. Harris, who worked for Dutch Henry, and had the care of a fine gray stallion. I made Harris saddle the animal and hold the stirrup for me to mount. I said, "Thank you and goodbye." I never saw him again. He made a report of this just as here given before an investigating committee.

We moved back toward our place near Middle Creek and camped. My brother Owen felt terribly conscience-smitten because he had killed one of the Doyles, and he cried and took on at an agonizing

16a Theodore Wiener, an Austrian of the Jewish faith, owned a store in the vicinity of Dutch Henry's Crossing, with two other Jewish settlers as partners: August Bondi and Jacob Benjamin.
17 The writer of this account.

rate. My brother John made his way back to Osawatomie, where his family had gone, in a very dejected state of mind, bordering on a breakdown. He hid himself in the timber near Adair's old place, as the Missouri militia was taking prisoners and scouring the country in every direction.

Father sent Owen with a fine race-horse that we had got by trading the gray stallion to some parties up north that had taken the race-horse from some Missouri invaders and then brought the animal down to trade with us and get something of their own to take back. Owen was to see John and get him to come to our camp. Father told Owen that if John would not come to leave the race-horse with him. Owen went along the ridge towards Osawatomie until he came to the bluff about four miles west of that place to the right of the trail.

OWEN BROWN CHASED

Under the bluffs there was a settler's house and about 40 men with as many horses all saddled. The men were seemingly taking a little rest. Owen rode down the bluff and was seen by the crowd. They began to yell: "There goes one of them damned Browns." They at once mounted their horses and took after Owen, yelling like demons. Owen put spurs to his horse and made for Osawatomie, which place he easily made, distancing his would-be captors. He saw John in the woods, but he could do nothing with him as his head was still wild. He would not take the horse, and Owen came back, most of the way through the timber. When he got back he was so used up that he could not keep from going to sleep when he was talking of his trip.

The next day Howard Carpenter, who lived near Palmyra,[18] came to our camp on a branch of Middle Creek and wanted our company, which was somewhat increased in numbers, to go up to Palmyra, as Henry Clay Pate was camped at Black Jack Springs, and his men were robbing houses in all directions and taking free state prisoners. We had increased our stock of horses since leaving Pottawatomie Crossing by taking them from pro-slavery men, and were now pretty well mounted. We started that night for Palmyra, led by Carpenter. When we got to the line south of the creek at Ottawa Jones' place we found a company of soldiers, a part of Colonel Wood's com-

18 Palmyra was about half way between Osawatomie and Lawrence.

mand, rank pro-slavery men, camped at the end of the lane to intercept us in case we should try to get through.

SOLDIERS LIE IN WAIT

We came up to the lane in single file and were halted by their guards. It was a very dark night. The men were lying along both sides of the road with their feet to the road. There were still coals in the middle of the road where they had fires earlier in the night. My brother Frederick was in the lead and he commenced to talk to the guard, his horse champing the bit and prancing around. Suddenly and before the guard had time to think, Fred rushed his horse through the lane over the coals and we all followed like a flash of lightning. I was behind, riding a mule and carrying the blankets for the crowd, which were fastened to the mule with a circingle. I looked back after we had got through and the road was full of men, who had been startled out of their sleep, but their commander was not in sight.

We got to the Ottawa Jones' place where we found my brother Jason. He asked father if we killed those men. Father told him they had been killed and that he, John Brown, Sr., was responsible for it. Jason replied, "Then you have committed a very wicked crime." Father said, "God is my judge." Jason started for Osawatomie to give himself up and was arrested with his brother John and they were horribly treated and taken to Lecompton to be tried by the border laws.

JUDGE CATO'S COURT KNOCKED OUT

We left the Pottawatomie region with the Cato Court knocked to the pit and the pro-slavery people flying over to Missouri with their slaves and families as fast as their underpinning would take them. We went from Jones' place up to near Palmyra and camped. James Redpath[19] was a reporter for some newspaper and he came to our camp to get something in the way of news. He wanted to know what father wanted him to say to the Eastern newspapers. Father

[19] James Redpath was one of the famous anti-slavery newspaper correspondents, who served in Kansas Territory during the period of conflict. The Jones so often mentioned was Samuel J. Jones, sheriff of Douglas County.

told him to say that it was a "summary execution," which was all he had to say.

. . . .

The following account by James Townsley, a member of the group that committed the Pottawatomie killings, appeared in the Lawrence (Kansas) *Daily Journal* of December 10, 1879. It was preceded by the editor's explanation, which is herewith presented in its entirety. There are details in Townsley's account which conflict with those of Salmon Brown. For a fair and moderate account of an incident that has aroused more passion than any other in John Brown's life except Harpers Ferry itself, the reader would do well to read Chapter V, "Murder on the Pottawatomie," in Oswald Garrison Villard's *John Brown*.

THE POTAWATOMIE TRAGEDY

JOHN BROWN'S CONNECTION WITH IT

STATEMENT OF JAMES TOWNSLEY, AN EYE-WITNESS

[We are enabled to lay before our readers, this morning, the most important contribution ever made to Kansas history, viz: A full and circumstantial account of the Potawatomie tragedy, in May, 1856, from one who was an eye-witness and participated in that terrible affair.

The history of the paper which we publish below is as follows: In the course of the various articles which have been recently published in the Journal in regard to this affair, and the discussion which has ensued, it became important, if possible, to determine just where John Brown and his company went after they left camp on that historic afternoon when the old man called for volunteers and departed upon his secret expedition; whether John Brown remained with the company; if he did, what part he took, if any, in the killing; where the party went that night after the killing was done; and their subsequent movements until they returned to John Brown Jr.'s company at Ottawa Jones'.

It was evident that these facts could only be obtained from *some one who was a member of the party*. The only person supposed to be living in Kansas, and known to have been one of the party, was Mr. James Townsley, of Osawatomie. John Hutchings, Esq., of this city, who has taken the deepest interest in this history, volunteered to visit Mr. Townsley and if possible procure from him a full and circumstantial statement. On Thursday, December 4, Mr. Hutchings left Lawrence and reached Lane, Franklin county, in the afternoon, and put up with Judge Hanway. He called into requisition the services of Judge Hanway and Johnson Clark, Esq. Mr. Townsley, in response to an invitation from these gentlemen came to Judge Hanway's house, and after spending several hours in conversation respecting all the points and details of the tragedy dictated to Mr. Hutchings the following statement, which is so far the only full authentic and detailed history of the Potawatomie tragedy ever given to the public. It is needless to say that both the *Journal* and the public are under deep obligations to Mr. Hutchings for the efforts he has made to get at the bottom facts of this most tragical event in Kansas history. The following is the statement.—Ed.]

I am a native of Harford County, State of Maryland, and was born August 29th, 1815. In August, 1839, I enlisted in Company I, Capt. Benjamin L. Bell, Second United States Dragoons, and served five years in the Florida war waged against the Seminole and Creek Indians, a part of the time under the command of General Taylor, and was discharged in August, 1844, at Fort Washita, Indian Territory. I am a painter by trade, and followed that business in Fallston, in my native county, until Oct. 20, 1855, when I emigrated to Kansas with my family, and settled in Anderson county, on the Potawatomie Creek, about one mile west of Greeley. I joined the Potawatomie rifle company at its reorganization in May, 1856, at which time John Brown Jr. was elected captain. On the 21st of the same month information was received that the Georgians were marching on Lawrence, threatening its destruction. The company was immediately called together, and about four o'clock p.m. we started on a forced march to aid in its defense. About two miles south of Middle Creek we were joined by the Osawatomie company, under Captain Dayton, and proceeded to Mount Vernon, where we waited about two hours until the moon rose. We then marched all night, camping the next morning—the 22d, for breakfast, near Ottawa Jones'.

Before we arrived at this point news had been received that Lawrence had been destroyed, and a question was raised whether we should return or go on. During the forenoon, however, we proceeded up Ottawa creek to within about five miles of Palmyra; and went into camp near the residence of Captain Shore. Here we remained undecided over night. About noon the next day, the 23d, old John Brown came to me and said he had just received information that trouble was expected on the Potawatomie, and wanted to know if I would take my team and take him and his boys back so that they could keep watch of what was going on. I told him I would do so. The party, consisting of old John Brown, Frederick Brown, Owen Brown, Watson Brown, Oliver Brown, Henry Thompson, (John Brown's son-in-law,) and Mr. Winer, were soon ready for the trip, and we started as near as I can remember about two o'clock p.m. All of the party, except Mr. Winer, who rode a pony, rode with me in my wagon. When within two or three miles of the Potawatomie creek we turned off the main road to the right, drove down into the edge of the timber between two deep ravines and camped about one mile above Dutch Henry's crossing.

After my team was fed and the party had taken supper, John Brown told me for the first time what he proposed to do. He said he wanted me to pilot the company up to the forks of the creek some five or six-miles above, into the neighborhood in which I lived, and show them where all the pro-slavery men resided; that he proposed to sweep the creek as he came down of all the pro-slavery men living on it. I positively refused to do it. He insisted upon it, but when he found that I would not go he decided to postpone the expedition until the following night. I then wanted to take my team and go home, but he refused to let me do so and said I should remain with them. We remained in camp that night, and all day the next day. Sometime after dark we were ordered to march.

We started, the whole company, in a northerly direction, crossing Mosquito creek above the residence of the Doyles. Soon after crossing the creek some one of the party knocked at the door of a cabin but received no reply—I have forgotten whose cabin it was, if I knew at the time. The next place we came to was the residence of the Doyles. John Brown, three of his sons and son-in-law went to the door, leaving Frederick Brown, Winer and myself a short distance from the house. About this time a large dog attacked us. Frederick Brown struck the dog a blow with his short two-edged sword, after which I dealt him a blow on the head with my sabre and heard no more from him. The old man Doyle and two sons were called out and marched some distance from the house toward Dutch Henry's in the road, where a halt was made. Old John Brown drew his revolver and shot the old man Doyle in the forehead, and Brown's two youngest sons immediately fell upon the younger Doyles with their short two-edged swords.

One of the young Doyle's was stricken down in an instant, but the other attempted to escape, and was pursued a short distance by his assailant and cut down. The company then proceeded down Musquito creek to the house of Allen Wilkinson. Here the old man Brown, three of his sons and son-in-law, as at the Doyle residence, went to the door and ordered Wilkinson to come out, leaving Frederick Brown, Winer, and myself, standing in the road east of the house. Wilkinson was taken and marched some distance south of his house and slain in the road with a short sword by one of the younger Browns. After he was killed his body was dragged out to one side and left.

We then crossed the Potawatomie and came to the house of Henry Sherman, generally known as Dutch Henry. Here John Brown and the party, excepting Frederick Brown, Winer, and myself, who were left outside a short distance from the door, went into the house and brought out one or two persons, talked with them some, and then took them in again. They afterward brought out William Sherman, Dutch Henry's brother, marched him down into the Potawatomie Creek, where he was slain with swords by Brown's two youngest sons, and left lying in the creek.

It was the expressed intention of Brown to execute Dutch Henry also, but he was not found at home. He also hoped to find George Wilson, Probate Judge of Anderson county, there, and intended, if he did, to kill him too. Wilson had been notifying Free State men to leave the Territory. I had received such a notice from him myself.

I desire to say here that it is not true that there was any intentional mutilation of the bodies after they were killed. They were slain as quickly as possible and left, and whatever gashes they received were inflicted in the process of cutting them down with swords. I understand that the killing was done with these swords, so as to avoid alarming the neighborhood by the discharge of firearms.

I desire also to say that I did not then approve of the killing of those men, but Brown said it must be done for the protection of the Free State settlers; that the pro-slavery party must be terrified, and that it was better that a score of bad men should die than that one man who came here to make Kansas a free state should be driven out.

Brown wanted me to pilot the party into the neighborhood where I lived, and point out all the pro-slavery men in it, whom he proposed to put to death. I positively refused to do it, and on account of my refusal we remained in camp all of the night upon which the attack was first intended to be made, and the next day. I told him I was willing to go with him to Lecompton and attack the leaders, or fight the enemy in open field anywhere, but I did not want to engage in killing these men. That night and the acts then perpetrated, are vividly fixed in my memory, and I have thought of them many times since.

I then thought that the transaction was terrible, and have mentioned it to but few persons since. In after time, however, I became satisfied that it resulted in good to the Free State cause, and was especially beneficial to Free State settlers on Potawatomie Creek. The pro slavery men *were dreadfully* terrified, and large numbers of them soon left the Territory. It was afterwards said that one Free State man could scare a company of them. I always understood that Geo. W. Grant came to our camp on Ottawa Creek, near Captain Shore's, with a message from his father, John T. Grant, to John Brown, asking for protection from threatened assaults of the Shermans and other pro slavery ruffians. But I did not know Geo. W. Grant at the time and do not remember of seeing him. I frequently heard the circumstance mentioned as a fact.

After the killing of William Sherman, sometime after midnight, we all went back to camp, about one mile distant, where we had left my team and other things. We remained in camp until after noon of the following day, and then started to again join the Potawatomie company under Captain John Brown, Jr. When we reached Ottawa Jones' about midnight, we found them in camp at that place.

The next morning the company was called together just after breakfast, and John Brown, Jr., announced his resignation, and requested the company to elect another Captain in his place. The name of H. H. Williams, now of Osawatomie, and my own were presented and a vote taken which resulted in the election of Williams. The company then broke camp and started for home. After crossing Middle creek at Mount Vernon, John Brown, with the rest of the party who accompanied him on the Potawatomie expedition, fell back from the balance of the company and struck off to the left of the main Potawatomie road in the direction of the cabins of John Brown, Jr., and Jason Brown. That night we staid at the cabin of the former, keeping up a guard all night. The next night we went to Jason Brown's about one mile and a half away. Here we remained several days, all the time on the watch. While we remained here August Bundy,[20] and I think Benjamin L. Cochran, joined us.

After several days, as I now remember, a young man by the name of Carpenter came to us from Prairie City and gave the information that Capt. Pate was in the vicinity in search of Brown. That evening we all took horses and started for Prairie City, where we arrived the next morning about daylight and camped in the timber on Ottawa Creek near Captain Shore's. While John Brown was cooking breakfast for the company, James Redpath came into our camp and had some conversation with Captain Brown.

I saw Redpath again after the battle of Black Jack, near Blue Mound, and I desire to say, in this connection, that I never told Redpath at any time that John Brown was not present at the Potawatomie tragedy. His statement, which has been read to me, to the effect that "two squatters, who aided in the execution," gave him such information, is totally false, so far as I am concerned. As Winer and myself were the only settlers in the neighborhood, not members of Brown's family, who were present at the tragedy, I can only conclude he referred to us. In the afternoon after we camped in the timber near Captain Shore's, we moved up into Prairie City. We picketed out our horses and laid down not over a hundred yards from the store. About the middle of the afternoon six of Pate's men came riding into town, four of whom we captured and held as prisoners.

During the afternoon Captain Shore raised a company of about thirty men and in the evening we started in pursuit of Pate. The next morning before daylight we obtained information that he was camped at Black Jack Point, and we moved forward with about twenty-four men to attack him. When within a mile of Pate's forces we all dismounted, left seven men in charge of the horses, and with seventeen men made the attack. In about fifteen minutes we drove them into the ravine. The fight continued about three hours when Pate surrendered. About the time we got the captured arms loaded into the wagons ready to move, Maj. Abbott's company came up and we all marched back to Prairie City with the prisoners. Here we remained until Col. Sumner released them.

At this time I left John Brown, and in company with Charley

20 August Bondi.

Lenhart and some other Lawrence parties, camped in the timber near Ottawa Jones'. A day or two after we went to Blue Mound, a few miles south of Lawrence. Here I again met Winer, Bundy, and also saw Redpath as before stated. Wiener, from this point, went to Leavenworth, and thence to St. Louis, as I have been informed. I went on to Lawrence, and from there to Topeka, where I staid one night and then returned to Lawrence, which place I made a sort of headquarters for several weeks. I was acquainted with Martin F. Conway and his brother Jefferson, and saw them frequently while I was there. I knew the Conways in Maryland, and they were the first persons of my acquaintance that I met after I came to the Territory. I visited my cabin on the Potawatomie occasionally, but not to stay any length of time, and in July I went to Birmingham, Iowa, to get work. I was taken sick on the way with the ague, and was unable to do much of anything for weeks. In the later part of the season, Col. S. W. Eldridge passed through Iowa with a company for Lawrence. I joined them at Oskaloosa, Iowa, and accompanied them to Topeka. From Topeka I went home to the Potawatomie, passing through Lawrence again on my way. On my return from Iowa I met John Brown in Nebraska, on his way east. I talked with him, and he advised me not to return. This was the last time I ever saw him.

There is an error in the published statement of Mr. Johnson Clark, fixing the time of the killing of the Doyles, Wilkinson, and Sherman, on the night of the day we left the camp of John Brown, Jr., at Ottawa creek. Mr. Clark must have misunderstood me. I certainly did not understand his statement as it now reads. It was immediately, or soon after we camped that night that I refused to go any farther, because Brown required me to take them into the neighborhood where I lived, to commence operations, and hence nothing was done until the next night.

I make this statement at the urgent request of my friends and neighbors, Judge James Hanway, and Hon. Johnson Clarke, who have been present during all the time occupied in writing it out and in whose hearing it has been several times read before signing.

JAMES TOWNSLEY

Lane, Kansas, Dec. 6th, 1879.

This article from the Lawrence *Daily Journal* of December 5, 1879, throws valuable light on the conditions in Kansas which provoked the Pottawatomie killings.

THE POTAWATOMIE TRAGEDY

New and Important Testimony . . . What George and Henry Grant Say About It.

We are enabled to lay before our readers this morning one of the most important contributions that has yet been furnished to the history of the Potawatomie massacre. It will be remembered that in the article from the Kansas Biographical Dictionary by Johnson Clark, published by us some time since, he speaks of Mr. J. T. Grant as a Free State settler living on the Potawatomie at the time of the massacre, of the border ruffians going to his house and warning him off, and of his sending his son, George, to old John Brown's camp to tell the old man of the threat. We have been exceedingly anxious to meet some member of this Grant family ever since reading the above, for the purpose of inquiring more particularly into the alleged provocation given by the pro-slavery men. We have never been able to believe that the massacre occurred without *some* previous provocation on the part of the men who were killed. By a remarkable good fortune we happened to meet, Thursday morning, Mr. Geo. W. Grant, who had just arrived from California, where he has been living ever since 1869, and Mr. Henry C. Grant, his brother, who lives near Vinland, this county, and who had come to town to meet his brother and take him out to his house. The two gentlemen came to the Journal office, and we had a long and satisfactory interview with them, which we will proceed to give in the form of questions and answers, to and by Mr. George Grant. We may say they are very intelligent men, now in middle life, and well known to many of our citizens.

Q.—When did your father settle in Kansas?

A.—My father, John T. Grant, came from Oneida county, New York, and settled on Potawatomie Creek in 1854. He is now in California, having removed there last fall. We were near neighbors of the Shermans, of the Doyles, and of Wilkinson, who were afterwards killed.

Q.—What do you know about the Potawatomie affair?

A.—When the news came that the border ruffians were about to attack Lawrence, the Free State men of Potawatomie Creek raised a company to go to the rescue. It was under command of Captain John Brown, Jr. I was a member of the company. We started for Lawrence, but on the way there a messenger reached us saying it was too late, that the town was already sacked. While lying in camp the company was drawn up one day and old John Brown called for volunteers, saying, "How many men will volunteer to go with me and obey my orders?" When he called for volunteers John Brown, Jr., said, "Father, I object to any of the men leaving. We are getting up here near the enemy and may need them." After the number had volunteered John Brown, Jr., said, "Father, be careful and commit no rash act." The volunteers were Fred. Owen, Salmon and Oliver Brown, Thompson, John Brown's son-in-law, Mr. Winer, and Mr. Townsley with his team. After they had volunteered they went into camp by themselves and ground up their sabers. They were armed with short swords and sabers.

Q.—When did you first see the party on their return?

A.—When we were at Ottawa Jones', the Brown party came in during the night. The next morning I saw one of Dutch Henry's horses which they had brought in. It was a gray horse, with his mane and tail sheared. We had heard of the killing, on Potawatomie Creek, at Palmyra, and had returned.

Q.—What effect, if any, did the news of the massacre have upon John Brown Jr.?

A.—A very marked effect. He showed great agitation, and gave up the command of the company to H. H. Williams.

Q.—Mr. Grant, it has been asserted that there had been no provocation given by these pro-slavery men. What do you know about that?

A.—The assertion is not true. There was a company of Georgia border ruffians encamped on the Marias [Marais] des Cygnes, about four miles away from us, who had been committing outrages upon the Free State people, and these pro-slavery men were in constant communication with them. They had a courier who went backwards and forwards, carrying messages between them. When we heard on the Potawatomie creek that the border ruffians were threatening Lawrence, and that the Free State men wanted help, we immediately began to prepare to go to their assistance. Frederick Brown, one of the sons of old John Brown, went to a store at Dutch Henry's crossing,—it stood very near where Mr. Wassen's house now stands,—kept by a Mr. Morse, from Michigan, known as old 'Squire' Morse, a quiet, inoffensive old Free State man, living there with his two boys, and bought some bars of lead—some twenty or thirty pounds. He brought the lead to my father's house on Sunday morning, and my brother Henry C. Grant, and my sister Mary, spent the whole day in running Sharpe's and other rifle bullets for the company. As Frederick Brown was bringing this lead to our house, he passed by Henry Sherman's house, and several pro-slavery men, among them Doyle and his sons, Wm. Sherman, and others, were sitting on the fence, and inquired what he was going to do with it? He told them he was going to run it into bullets for Free State guns. They were apparently much incensed at his reply, as they knew that the Free State company was then preparing to go to Lawrence. The next morning, after the company had started to go to Lawrence, a number of these pro-slavery men—Wilkinson, Doyle, his two sons, and Wm. Sherman, known as " Dutch Bill," took a rope and went to old Squire Morse's house, and said they were going to hang him for selling the lead to the Free State men. They frightened the old man terribly, but finally told him he must leave the country before eleven o'clock, or they would hang him. They then left, and went to the Shermans', and went to drinking. About eleven o'clock a portion of them, half drunk, went back to Mr. Morse's, and were going to kill him with an axe. His little boys—one was only nine years old—set up a violent crying and begged for their father's life. They finally gave him till sundown to leave. He left everything and came at once to our house. He was nearly frightened to death. He came to our house carrying a blanket and leading his little boy by the hand. When night came he was so afraid that he would not stay in the house but went out doors and slept on the prairie in the grass. For a few days he laid about in the brush, most of the time getting his meals at our house. He was then taken violently ill and died in a very short time. Dr. Gilpatrick attended him during his brief illness, and said that his death was directly caused by the fright and excitement of that terrible day when he was driven from his store. The only thing they had against Mr. Morse was his selling the lead, and this he had previously bought of Henry Sherman, who had brought it from Kansas City. Mr. Morse was a quiet, inoffensive man, nearly sixty years old and in feeble health.

While the Free State company was gone to Lawrence, Henry Sherman came to my father's house and said, " We have ordered old Morse out of the country and he has got to go, and a good many others of the Free State families have got to go."

The general feeling among the Free State people was one of

terror while the company was gone, as we did not know at what moment the Georgia ruffians might come in and drive us all out.

Q.—Were you sent to Brown's camp as stated in some of the accounts?

A.—No; I was with John Brown, Jr.'s company.

Q.—Was there any other evidence of a premeditated assault upon the Free State men on the creek?

A.—My father, who was an old man, and Dr. Gilpatrick had been to Kansas City for provisions. They were on their way home the day before the massacre and failed to reach home with the teams, and had camped on the prairie about a mile from Potawatomie Creek. Dr. Gilpatrick stayed with the wagons and my father came over and slept at home. In the morning they brought the wagons in. The first place they struck was Wilkinson's. He kept the post office. They called at the house for their mail and found Mrs. Wilkinson crying. She said that a party of men had been to the house during the night and taken him out. She had heard that morning that Mr. Doyle had been killed during the night, and she was afraid that her husband had been killed also.

Among other reasons that she gave for fearing that he was killed, was that he had said to her the night before that there was going to be an attack made upon the Free State men, and that by the next Saturday night there would not be a Free State settler left on the creek. These, she said, were the last words he said to her, the night before.

Q.—What sort of a man was this Wilkinson?

A.—He was a dangerous man. Everybody feared him. He was the most evil-looking man I ever saw. He abused his wife shamefully. She was a very nice woman, and well liked by the neighbors.

Q.—What happened next?

A.—Mrs. Wilkinson desired my father and Dr. Gilpatrick to go and look for her husband. They did so, and found his body in the brush, near the house.

Q.—Was there anything said about the bodies of Wilkinson and the others being mutilated?

A.—They were apparently killed by a thrust with the short sword and by cuts over the head with the sabre, except Doyle, who was shot in the forehead and also stabbed. There was no idea at that time that the bodies had been purposely mutilated. The wounds in the hands had apparently been made either in attempting to ward off blows or in grasping the blades of the short swords.

Q.—Was it understood at that time, that John Brown was present and did any of the killing?

A.—Mrs. Wilkinson's description of the leader pointed out Brown. She mentioned his being an old man and his wearing a black stock about his neck, which Brown habitually wore. Nobody on the creek doubted that John Brown was the leader of the party. As to the killing, it was the current story that Brown shot Doyle, but personally did nothing more, and that the cutting and stabbing was done by other members of the party.

Q.—What was the effect of this massacre on the inhabitants of the creek?

A.—Both parties were greatly alarmed. The pro-slavery settlers almost entirely left at once, and the Free State people were constantly fearful of vengeance. As a matter of fact, there was no more killing on either side in that neighborhood. Dutch Henry—Henry Sherman, was killed in the spring of 1857, but politics had nothing to do with it.

We have read the above and it is correct.

Geo. W. Grant.
H. C. Grant.

William Addison Phillips (January 14, 1824—November 30, 1893), was born in Scotland and came to this country with his parents about 1838. After practicing law in Illinois, he went to Kansas in 1855 as special correspondent for the New York Tribune. In 1856 he wrote a volume called "The Conquest of Kansas by Missouri and Her Allies," which was widely read and did much to popularize the anti-slavery cause in Kansas. Thomas Wentworth Higginson later referred to it as " altogether the best and fairest book upon the confused history of that time and place."

He served as an officer in the Union Army during the Civil War, was actively engaged in politics and writing following the war, and was elected to Congress from Kansas in 1872, 1874, and 1876. The following article by Phillips appeared in the Atlantic Monthly for December, 1879, pp. 738-744.

THREE INTERVIEWS WITH OLD JOHN BROWN

W. A. PHILLIPS

Upon the 2d of July, 1856, Captain John Brown called on me at the Eastern House, In Lawrence, Kansas. He had left his company, twenty-two men, camped on the Wakerusa,[21] a few miles from town.

[21] Wakarusa.

The free-state legislature was to assemble at noon, at Topeka, on the 4th. Franklin Pierce was then president, and the federal officials of the Territory, who all sympathized with the pro-slavery party, had determined that the legislature should not meet. There had been a lull in the winter, but with the spring hostilities set in. Finding the Missourians unable longer to cope with the free-state men, Buford and his men came from the far Southern States to reinforce them. Lawrence had been sacked and the Free State hotel and printing-houses bombarded and burned in May. From that time forward there had been a skirmish or a fight almost every day. Bands of armed men, of both parties, roamed over the country. At first the pro-slavery men had the best of it; but Captain Brown captured Pate[22] at Black Jack, after a sharp struggle, and the enemy lost some of their artillery at Franklin, and as the tide was turning the other way the United States troops came on the scene, for the alleged purpose of keeping the peace. Altogether it was neither a place nor a time for conservative men. The free-state governor and other officials were under guard at Lecompton, charged with treason. The pro-slavery party determined that the legislature under the Topeka constitution should not assemble. Their original purpose was to lead a Border Ruffian army to Topeka, to break it up; but the events of June rendered that a precarious enterprise. Topeka was seventy-five miles from the border. It would be difficult to get a large force up there, and as matters stood might be more difficult to get it back. Provisions and ammunition were stored at Topeka, and it was expected that a thousand armed free-state men would be there, if necessary, to defend the legislature. In this situation of affairs the programme was changed. A proclamation was issued, denouncing the legislature as a treasonable body, and commanding that it disperse. United States troops were sent to enforce this order. Colonel E. V. Sumner, with several hundred of the first cavalry and a battery, moved from Fort Leavenworth, and on the 3d of July camped close to the capitol on the southeast, while Colonel Philip St. George Cooke, with a still larger force, moved simultaneously from Fort Riley, and camped on the northwest of the town. The federal territorial officers, with marshals and deputy-marshals, clustered in the federal camp. From all directions companies of armed men were going to Topeka.

It was a part of this general plan that John Brown and his company were on their way from Ossawatomie[23] to Topeka. He was not

---

[22] Henry Clay Pate, correspondent of the St. Louis *Missouri Republican*, captain in the Missouri militia and a deputy United States Marshal.
[23] The correct spelling is with one " s."

in the habit of subjecting himself to the orders of anybody. He intended to aid the general result, but to do it in his own way.

During the day he stayed with me in Lawrence I had my first good opportunity to judge the old man's character. I had seen him in his camp, had seen him in the field, and he was always an enigma, a strange compound of enthusiasm and cold, methodic stolidity,—a volcano beneath a mountain of snow. He told me of his experiences as a wool merchant and manufacturer in Ohio, and of his travels in Europe. I soon discovered that his tastes ran in a military rather than a commercial channel. He had visited many of the fortifications in Europe, and criticised them sharply, holding that the modern system of warfare did away with them, and that a well-armed, brave soldier was the best fortification. He criticised all the arms then in use, and showed me a fine specimen of repeating-rifle which had long-range sights, and, he said, would carry eight hundred yards; but, he added, the way to fight was to press to close quarters. He had a couple of small pamphlets or circulars; one he had had printed on the armies and military systems of Europe; the other was addressed to the soldiers of the armies of the United States,[24] and was an odd mixture of advice as to discipline and soldierly habits, and wound up by advising them to desert whenever there was an attempt made to use them against a free government and human liberty. He looked upon passing political movements as mere preliminaries or adjuncts to more important events in the future. With him men were nothing, principles everything.

I had intended to drive from Lawrence to Topeka with a friend that day, but he urged me to wait until evening and go with him, and I was so interested in him that I did so. We rode down Massachusetts Street, followed by one of his men, a sort of orderly, if I may so designate him. We ascended Mount Oread, and proceeded to the point where the state university now stands, and there reined our horses and looked at the scene, while we waited for the company, which was now slowly winding towards the base of the hill, where the old California road ascended it. It was a glorious landscape. Lawrence lay to the northeast, at our feet. Kaw River, like a sheet of silver, could be seen here and there through breaks in the forest. Away to our right was the Wakerusa, winding and twisting to meet it. A few miles distant rose the double-peaked Blue Mound.

[24] *Manual of the Patriotic Volunteer in Active Service in Regular and Irregular War. . .* by Hugh Forbes. (New York, 1857.) A pamphlet condensed from a two-volume work by the same author and printed at Brown's expense. The second pamphlet was *Tract No. 1. The Duty of the Soldier,* a four-page folder written by Forbes from ideas given by John Brown. Issued in 1857, place of printing unknown. I am indebted to Mr. Boyd B. Stutler for this information.

The streams and creeks were marked by feathery lines of trees, and away five or six miles before us, where the Kaw and Wakerusa met, there was an immense mass of timber veiling the meeting of the waters. The sun went down as we looked at it, and as I turned my eyes to his I saw he had drunk in the glorious beauty of the landscape.

"What a magnificent scene, captain!" I exclaimed.

"Yes," he said, in his slow, dry way; "a great country for a free State."

The company had climbed the hill, riding by twos, and we rode towards them. There was no recognition. We silently took our places at the head of the little column; he gave the command to march, and we rode up the California road. Darkness set in long before we reached "Coon Point." While on the march the captain was reticent, and apologized to me for being so on the ground of discipline. The road runs, or ran, some four miles to the south of Lecompton, the pro-slavery capital, and as we neared that region he carefully examined his men, and all appeared to be more vigilant. It was late when we reached Big Springs, and there we left the road, going in a southwesterly direction for a mile, when we halted on a hill, and the horses were stripped of their saddles and other articles, and picketed out to graze. The grass was wet with dew. The men ate of what provision they had with them, and I received a portion from the captain. I was not at all hungry, and if I had been I doubt if I could have eaten it. It was dry beef, which was not so bad; but the bread had been made from corn bruised between stones, and then rolled in balls and cooked in the coal and ashes of the camp fire. These ashes served for saleratus. Captain Brown observed that I nibbled it very gingerly, and said,—

"I am afraid you will be hardly able to eat a soldier's harsh fare."

"I must be frank enough to say that I have doubts on that subject myself," I responded.

We placed our two saddles together, so that our heads lay only a few feet apart. He spread his blanket on the wet grass, and, when we lay together upon it, mine was spread over us. Previous to doing this he had stationed a couple of guards. It was past eleven o'clock, and we lay there until two in the morning, scarcely time enough for sleep; indeed, we slept none. He seemed to be as little disposed to sleep as I was, and we talked; or rather he did, for I said little more than enough to keep him going. I soon found that he was a very thorough astronomer, and he enlightened me on a good many matters in the starry firmament above us. He pointed out the different constellations and their movements. "Now," he said, "it is midnight," and he pointed to the finger marks of his great clock in the sky.

In his ordinary moods the man seemed so rigid, stern, and unimpressible when I first knew him that I never thought a poetic and impulsive nature lay behind that cold exterior. The whispering of the wind on the prairie was full of voices to him, and the stars as they shone in the firmament of God seemed to inspire him. "How admirable is the symmetry of the heavens; how grand and beautiful. Everything moves in sublime harmony in the government of God. Not so with us poor creatures. If one star is more brilliant than others, it is continually shooting in some erratic way into space."

He discussed and criticised both parties in Kansas. Of the pro-slavery men he spoke in bitterness. He said that slavery besotted everything, and made men more brutal and coarse. Nor did the free-state men escape his sharp censure. He said that we had many noble and true men, but that we had too many broken-down politicians from the older States. These men, he said, would rather pass resolutions than act, and they criticised all who did real work. A professional politician, he went on, you never could trust; for even if he had convictions, he was always ready to sacrifice his principles for his advantage.

One of the most interesting things in his conversation that night, and one that marked him as a theorist (and perhaps to some extent he might be styled a visionary), was his treatment of our forms of social and political life. He thought society ought to be organized on a less selfish basis; for while material interests gained something by the deification of pure selfishness, men and women lost much by it. He said that all great reforms, like the Christian religion, were based on broad, generous, self-sacrificing principles. He condemned the sale of land as a chattel, and thought that there was an infinite number of wrongs to right before society would be what it should be, but that in our country slavery was the "sum of all villainies," and its abolition the first essential work. If the American people did not take courage and end it speedily, human freedom and republican liberty would soon be empty names in these United States.

He ran on during these midnight hours in a conversation I can never forget. The dew lay cold and heavy on the grass and on the blanket above us. The stars grew sharper and clearer, and seemed to be looking down like watchers on that sleeping camp. My companion paused for a short time, and I thought he was going to sleep, when he said,—

"It is nearly two o'clock, and as it must be nine or ten miles to Topeka it is time we were marching," and he again drew my attention to his index marks in the sky. He rose and called his men. They responded with more alacrity than I expected. In less than ten minutes the company had saddled, packed, and mounted, and was again on the march.

He declined following the road any farther, but insisted on taking a straight course over the country, guided by the stars. It was in vain that I expostulated with him, and told him that three or four creeks were in the way, and that the country was rough and broken, and that it would be difficult to find our way in the dark. He was determined not to go by Tecumseh. We had, it is needless to say, a rough time of it that night, and day broke while we were floundering in the thickets of a creek bottom some miles from Topeka. As soon as daylight came and we could see our way, we rode more rapidly; but the sun had risen above the horizon before we rode down the slopes to Thung-gahnung. Across the creek and nearly two miles to the right we saw the tents, and in the morning stillness could hear the bugles blow in Colonel Sumner's camp.

John Brown would not go into Topeka, but halted in the timber of the creek, sending one of his men with me, who was to be a messenger to bring him word when his company was needed. He had his horse picketed, and walked down by the side of my horse to the place where I crossed the creek. He sent messages to one or two of the gentlemen in town, and, as he wrung my hand at parting, urged that we should have the legislature meet, and resist all who should interfere with it, and fight, if necessary, even the United States troops.

The second interview occurred, I think, in February, 1857. It was a cold, snowy Sabbath morning, about eight o'clock, when a son of Mr. Whitman rode into Lawrence, and told me the "old man" was at his father's, and wanted to see me. He brought a led horse for me. It was a cold and disagreeable ride that morning, but as I had not heard of the whereabouts of Captain Brown for some time, I concluded to go.

When I reached Mr. Whitman's I found him, and with him Kagi and Whipple, or Stevens, and Cook; in fact, most of the men who were with him at Harper's Ferry. He took me to an apartment where we could be alone, and then he first inquired as to the condition of the free-state cause. He was very apprehensive that many of the free-state leaders would jeopardize the principles of the party in order to get power. He said whenever the free-state party gave itself over to selfish interests, its virtue and usefulness ended, and for good results it was far more desirable that it should be kept on the strain and suffer than make selfish compromises with the enemy. He asked earnestly many questions about the free-state leaders. One very good man he criticised for several things he had done, and in response to my assurances about him he used one of his striking comparisons. He took out a large pocket compass, and unscrewing its brass lid laid it down on the table before me, and pointing at the needle fixed his eyes on me, while he said : —

"You see that needle; it wabbles about and is mighty unsteady, but *it wants to point to the north*. Is he like that needle? "

He told me that some friends in the East had raised for him and placed in his hands a very large sum of money, in all nearly five thousand dollars. He had picked his company, and would like a few more, if he could get the right kind of men. He had spent some time in Iowa and some on the Kansas border. He was drilling and educating his company, and training them to hardship and to be perfectly faithful and reliable. He desired, he said, to get my advice as to the best way of using his force and resources, so as to advance the great interests of freedom and humanity.

Long before that time I had understood John Brown well enough to know that there was little probability about our agreeing on that subject, or of his being governed by the advice of anybody. He urged me so strenuously, however, that for a short time I actually permitted myself to suppose that he might really take advice. I had just previously discovered the site and location for a town, where the city of Salina now stands, and as it was then fifty miles beyond the settlement I told him I would give him any interest I then had in the place, and advised him to go there with his company. Each of them, I said, could take claims on the rich farming lands adjacent; they could be the pioneer builders of the town, could invest their funds in a stock of goods and a mill, and drill, if he thought it best, an hour each morning, and maintain in everything perfect descipline, and be ready for any emergency.

Before I had concluded my rather practical and conservative advice, I could perceive that it did not at all harmonize with the views and purposes of Captain Brown, and I suspected that a location one hundred and eighty miles from the Missouri border was in his opinion rather remote from the scene of operations. He suggested that it was only fair, as Missouri had undertaken to make a slave State of Kansas and failed, that Kansas should make a free State of Missouri, and proceeded at length to show, in the most logical manner, that it was not for the interests of Kansas to have a powerful slave State so close to it, and that the process of putting an end to slavery there was exceedingly simple. He said that he intended to spend some time near Tabor, Iowa, where he expected to be joined by others, who would need discipline and organization; and that he expected also to visit Canada, with the view of studying personally its suitability for receiving and protecting negro emigration. And so we parted on that occasion.

I heard of the old man occasionally, sometimes in one place, sometimes in another. It was during the ensuing winter that he made one or two raids into the State of Missouri, generally, if not always, visiting those who had taken an active part in the Kansas outrages. He was on hand on the southeast border very soon after the Mer du Cygne [Marais des Cygnes] massacre, no doubt to punish the perpetrators. Many persons will remember when he took from Missouri a large number of negroes, and led them through Kansas, Iowa, and other States and Territories to Canada. During that march several parties tried to catch old John Brown, but they invariably caught a Tartar. He passed through Kansas some miles to the south of Lawrence, and the night they camped at the nearest point Kagi and Stevens came up to town and gave me all the particulars of that adventure, which were in the New York Tribune at the time. They also brought from the old man the text of his celebrated "parallels" to show me.

The most important interview, the one that has peculiar historical significance, was the last I ever had with him. It occurred during the same year of the Harper's Ferry affair, although several months before. He had been absent from Kansas for some time. Now we could hear of him in New England, now in Canada, now in Ohio or Pennsylvania. I had lost track of him, when one day Kagi came to my house in Lawrence, and told me that the old man had arrived and was at the Whitney House, and wished to see me. At first I refused to go, and sent him word by Kagi that as he never took my advice I did not see any use in giving him any. Kagi soon returned, and said that the old man must see me; he was going away, and might never see me again.

I found him in a small room at the Whitney House, then one of

223

the Lawrence hotels, down towards the river. He had changed a little. There was in the expression of his face something even more dignified than usual; his eye was brighter, and the absorbing and consuming thoughts that were within him seemed to be growing out all over him. He evinced his customary caution by telling Kagi to go out and close the door, and watch on the outside, for fear that some one should come to listen. Then he began.

He sketched the history of American slavery from its beginnings in the colonies, and referred to the States that were able to shake it off. He recalled many circumstances that I had forgotten, or had never heard of. He said the founders of the republic were all opposed to slavery, and that the whole spirit and genius of the American constitution antagonized it, and contemplated its early overthrow. He said this remained the dominant sentiment for the first quarter of a century of the republic. Afterwards slavery became more profitable, and as it did the desire grew to extend and increase it. The condition of the enslaved negroes steadily became worse, and the despotic necessities of a more cruel system constantly pressed on the degraded slaves. Rights they at first possessed were taken from them. The little of domestic happiness and independence that had been left them was taken away. The slave-trade being ended, it was profitable to breed negroes for sale. Gradually the pecuniary interests that rested on slavery seized the power of the government. Public opinion opposed to slavery was placed under ban. The politicians of the South became slavery propagandists, and the politicians of the North trimmers. When the religious and moral sentiment of the country indicated a desire to check this alarming growth, a threat of secession was uttered, and appeals were made not to risk the perpetuation of this glorious republic by fanatical antislavery-ism. Then began an era of political compromises, and men full of professions of love of country were willing, for peace, to sacrifice everything for which the republic was founded.

"And now," he went on, "we have reached a point where nothing but war can settle the question. Had they succeeded in Kansas, they would have gained a power that would have given them permanently the upper hand, and it would have been the death-knell of republicanism in America. They are checked, but not beaten. They never intend to relinquish the machinery of this government into the hands of the opponents of slavery. It has taken them more than half a century to get it, and they know its significance too well to give it up. If the republican party elects its president next year, there will be war. The moment they are unable to control they will go out, and as a rival nation along-side they will get the countenance and aid of the European nations, until American republicanism and freedom are overthrown."

I have endeavoured to quote him, but it is quite impossible to quote such a conversation accurately. I well remember all its vital essentials and its outlines. He had been more observant than he had credit for being. The whole powers of his mind (and they were great) had been given to one subject. He told me that a war was at that very moment contemplated in the cabinet of President Buchanan; that for years the army had been carefully arranged, as far as it could be, on a basis of Southern power; that arms and the best of the troops were being concentrated, so as to be under control of its interests if there was danger of having to surrender the government; that the secretary of the navy was then sending our vessels away on long cruises, so that they would not be available, and that the treasury would be beggared before it got into Northern hands.

All this has a strangely prophetic look to me now; then it simply appeared incredible, or the dream and vagary of a man who had allowed one idea to carry him away. I told him he surely was mistaken, and had confounded everyday occurrences with treacherous designs.

" No," he said, and I remember this part distinctly,—" no, the war is not over. It is a treacherous lull before the storm. We are on the eve of one of the greatest wars in history, and I fear slavery will triumph, and there will be an end of all aspirations for human freedom. For my part, I drew my sword in Kansas when they attacked us, and I will never sheathe it until this war is over. Our best people do not understand the danger. They are besotted. They have compromised so long that they think principles of right and wrong have no more any power on this earth."

My impression then was that it was his purpose to carry on incursions on the borders of the free and slave States, and I said to him :

" Let us suppose that all you say is true. If we keep companies on the one side, they will keep them on the other. Trouble will multiply; there will be collision, which will produce the very state of affairs you deprecate. That would lead to war, and to some extent we should be responsible for it. Better trust events. If there is virtue enough in this people to deserve a free government, they will maintain it."

"You forget the fearful wrongs that are carried on in the name of government and law."

"I do not forget them,—I regret them."

"I regret and will remedy them with all the power that God has given me."

He then went on to tell me of Spartacus and his servile war, and was evidently familiar with every step in the career of the great gladiator. I reminded him that Spartacus and Roman slaves were warlike people in the country from which they were taken, and were trained to arms in the arena, in which they slew or were slain, and that the movement was crushed when the Roman legions were concentrated against it. The negroes were a peaceful, domestic, inoffensive race. In all their sufferings they seemed to be incapable of resentment or reprisal.

"You have not studied them right," he said, "and you have not studied them long enough. Human nature is the same everywhere." He then went on in a very elaborate way to explain the mistakes of Spartacus, and tried to show me how he could easily have over-thrown the Roman empire. The pith of it was that the leader of that servile insurrection, instead of wasting his time in Italy until his enemies could swoop on him, should have struck at Rome; or, if not strong enough for that, he should have escaped to the wild northern provinces, and there have organized an army to overthrow Rome.

I told him that I feared he would lead the young men with him into some desperate enterprise, where they would be imprisoned and disgraced.

He rose. "Well," he said, "I thought I could get you to under-stand this. I do not wonder at it. The world is very pleasant to you; but when your household gods are broken, as mine have been, you will see all this more clearly."

I rose, somewhat offended, and said, "Captain, if you thought this, why did you send for me?" and walked to the door.

He followed me, and laid his hand on my shoulder, and when I turned to him he took both my hands in his. I could see that tears stood on his hard, bronzed cheeks. "No," he said, "we must not part thus. I wanted to see you and tell you how it appeared to me. With the help of God, I will do what I believe to be best," He held my hands firmly in his stern, hard hands, leaned forward and kissed me on the cheek, and I never saw him again.

Thomas Wentworth Higginson (1823-1911), of Worcester, Massachusetts, Unitarian minister, writer and anti-slavery leader, first met John Brown in Boston in March, 1858. He was so deeply impressed that he became one of Brown's most ardent supporters. The following essay first appeared in James Redpath's *Life of Captain John Brown* (1859) and was reprinted, with slight changes, in Higginson's volume, *Contemporaries*, pp. 219-243.

A VISIT TO JOHN BROWN'S HOUSEHOLD IN 1859

The traveler into the enchanted land of the Adirondacks has his choice of two routes from Keeseville to the Lower Saranac Lake, where his outdoor life is to begin. The one least frequented and most difficult should be selected, for it has the grandest mountain pass that the Northern States can show. After driving twenty-two miles of mountain road from Keeseville, past wild summits bristling with stumps, and through villages where every other man is black from the iron foundry, and every alternate one black from the charcoal pit, your pathway makes a turn at the little hamlet of Wilmington, and you soon find yourself facing a wall of mountain, with only glimpses of one wild gap, through which you must penetrate. In two miles more you have passed the last house this side the Notch, and you then drive on over a rugged way, constantly ascending, with no companion but the stream which ripples and roars below. Soon the last charcoal clearing is past, and thick woods of cedar and birch close around you : the high mountain on your right comes nearer and nearer, and close beside, upon your left, are glimpses of a wall, black and bare as iron, rising sheer for four hundred feet above your head. Coming from the soft marble country of Vermont, and from the pale granite of Massachusetts, there seems something weird and forbidding in this utter blackness. On your left the giant wall now appears nearer—now retreats again; on your right foams the merry stream, breaking into graceful cascades—and across it the great mountain Whiteface, seamed with slides. Now the woods upon your left are displaced by the wall, almost touching the roadside; against its steep abruptness scarcely a shrub can cling, scarcely a fern flutter—it takes your breath away; but five miles of perilous driving conduct you through it; and beyond this stern passway, this cave of iron, lie the lovely lakes and mountains of the Adirondacks, and the homestead of John Brown.

The Notch seems beyond the world, North Elba and its half-dozen houses are beyond the Notch, and there is a wilder little mountain road which rises beyond North Elba. But the house we seek is not even on that road, but behind it and beyond it; you ride a mile or two, then take down a pair of bars; beyond the bars, faith takes you across a half-cleared field, through the most difficult of wood paths, and after half a mile of forest you come out upon a clearing. There is a little frame house, unpainted, set in a girdle of black stumps, and with all heaven about it for a wider girdle; on a high hill-side, forests on north and west,—the glorious line of the Adirondacks on the east, and on the south one slender road leading off to Westport,—a road so straight that you could sight a United States marshal for five miles.

There stands the little house with no ornament or relief about it —it needs none with the setting of mountain horizon. Yes, there is one decoration which at once takes the eye, and which, stern and misplaced as it would seem elsewhere, seems appropriate here. It is a strange thing to see any thing so old, where all the works of man are new! but it is an old, mossy, time-worn tombstone—not marking any grave, not set in the ground, but resting against the house as if its time were either past or not yet come. Both are true—it has a past duty and a future one. It bears the name of Captain John Brown, who died during the Revolution, eighty-three years ago; it was brought hither by his grandson bearing the same name and title; the latter caused to be inscribed upon it, also, the name of his son Frederick, "murdered at Osawatomie for his adherence to the cause of freedom" (so reads the inscription); and he himself has said, for years, that no other tombstone should mark his own grave.

For two years now, that stone has stood there. No oath has been taken upon it, no curses been invoked upon it. It marks the abode of a race who do not curse. But morning and noon, as the sons have gone out to their work on that upland farm, they have passed by it; the early light over the Adirondacks has gilded it, the red reflection of sunset has glowed back upon it; its silent appeal has perpetually strengthened and sanctified that home—and as the two lately wedded sons went forth joyfully on their father's call to keep their last pledge at Harper's Ferry, they issued from that doorway between their weeping wives on the one side and that ancestral stone upon the other.

The farm is a wild place, cold and bleak. It is too cold to raise corn there; they can scarcely, in the most favorable seasons, obtain a few ears for roasting. Stock must be wintered there nearly six months in every year. I was there on the first of November; the ground was snowy, and winter had apparently begun, and it would last till the middle of May. They never raise anything to sell off that farm, except sometimes a few fleeces. It was well, they said, if they raised their own provisions, and could spin their own wool for clothing.

Do you ask why they live in such a bleak spot? With John Brown and his family there is a reason for everything, and it is always the same reason. Strike into their lives anywhere, and you find the same firm purpose at bottom, and to the widest questioning the same prompt answer comes ringing back,—the very motto of the tombstone,—"For adherence to the cause of freedom." The same purpose, nay, the selfsame project that sent John Brown to Harper's Ferry sent him to the Adirondacks.

Twenty years ago John Brown made up his mind that there was an irrepressible conflict between freedom and slavery, and that in that conflict he must take his share. He saw at a glance, moreover, what the rest of us are only beginning to see, even now—that slavery must be met, first or last, on its own ground. The time has come to tell the whole truth now—that John Brown's whole Kansas life was the result of this self-imposed mission, not the cause of it. Let us do this man justice; he was not a vindictive guerrilla, nor a maddened Indian; nor was he of so shallow a nature that it took the death of a son to convince him that right was right, and wrong was wrong. He had long before made up his mind to sacrifice every son he ever had, if necessary, in fighting slavery. If it was John Brown against the world, no matter; for, as his friend Frederick Douglass had truly said, "In the right *one* is a majority." On this conviction, therefore, he deliberately determined, twenty years ago this summer, that at some future period he would organize an armed party, go into a slave State, and liberate a large number of slaves. Soon after, surveying professionally in the mountains of Virginia, he chose the very ground for his purpose. Visiting Europe afterwards, he studied military strategy for this purpose, even making designs (which I have seen) for a new style of forest fortification, simple and ingenious, to be used by parties of fugitive slaves when brought to bay. He knew the ground, he knew his plans, he knew himself; but where should he find his men? He came to the Adirondacks to look for them.

Ten years ago Gerrit Smith gave to a number of colored men tracts of ground in the Adirondack Mountains. The emigrants were grossly defrauded by a cheating surveyor, who, being in advance of his age, practically anticipated Judge Taney's opinion, that black men have no rights which white men are bound to respect. By his villainy the colony was almost ruined in advance; nor did it ever recover itself; though some of the best farms which I have seen in that region are still in the hands of colored men. John Brown heard of this; he himself was a surveyor, and he would have gone to the Adirondacks, or anywhere else, merely to right this wrong. But he had another object—he thought that among these men he should find coadjutors in his cherished plan. He was not wholly wrong, and yet he afterwards learned something more. Such men as he needed are not to be found ordinarily; they must be reared. John Brown did not merely look for men, therefore; he reared them in his sons. During long years of waiting and postponement, he found others; but his sons and their friends (the Thompsons) formed the nucleus of his force in all his enterprises. What services the women of his family may have rendered it is not yet time to tell; but it is a satisfaction to think that he was repaid for his early friendship to these New York colored men by some valuable aid from freed slaves and fugitive slaves at Harper's Ferry; especially from Danger-field Newby, who, poor fellow! had a slave wife and nine slave children to fight for, all within thirty miles of that town.

To appreciate the character of the family, it is necessary to know these things; to understand that they have all been trained from childhood on this one principle, and for this one special project; taught to believe in it as they believed in their God or their father. It has given them a wider perspective than the Adirondacks. Five years before, when they first went to Kansas, the father and sons had a plan of going to Louisiana, trying the same project, and then retreating into Texas with the liberated slaves. Nurtured on it so long, for years sacrificing to it all the other objects of life, the thought of its failure never crossed their minds; and it is an extra-ordinary fact that when the disastrous news first came to North Elba, the family utterly refused to believe it and were saved from suffering by that incredulity till the arrival of the next weekly mail.

I had left the world outside, to raise the latch of this humble door amid the mountains; and now my pen falters on the threshold, as my steps did then. This house is a home of sacred sorrow. How shall we enter it? Its inmates are bereft and ruined men and women, as the world reckons; what can we say to them? Do not shrink;

you are not near the world, you are near John Brown's household. "In the world ye shall have tribulation; but be of good cheer: they have overcome the world."

It had been my privilege to live in the best society all my life— namely, that of abolitionists and fugitive slaves. I had seen the most eminent persons of the age: several men on whose heads tens of thousands of dollars had been set; a black woman, who, after escaping from slavery herself, had gone back secretly eight times into the jaws of death to bring out persons whom she had never seen; and a white man, who, after assisting away fugitives by the thousand, had twice been stripped of every dollar of his property in fines, and, when taunted by the court, had mildly said, "Friend, if thee knows any poor fugitive in need of a breakfast, send him to Thomas Garrett's door." I had known these, and such as these; but I had not known the Browns. Nothing short of knowing them can be called a liberal education. Lord Byron could not help clinging to Shelley, because he said he was the only person in whom he saw anything like disinterested benevolence. He really believed that Shelley would give his life for another. Poor Byron! he might well have exchanged his wealth, his peerage, and his genius for a brief training at North Elba.

Let me pause a moment, and enumerate the members of the family. John Brown was born in 1800 and his wife in 1816, though both might have been supposed older than the ages thus indicated. He has had in all twenty children—seven being the offspring of his first wife, thirteen of his second. Four of each race are living—eight in all. The elder division of the surviving family comprises John and Jason, both married, and living in Ohio; Owen, unmarried, who escaped from Harper's Ferry, and Ruth, the wife of Henry Thompson, who lives on an adjoining farm at North Elba, an intelligent and noble woman. The younger division consists of Salmon, aged twenty-three, who resides with his young wife in his mother's house, and three unmarried daughters, Anne (sixteen), Sarah (thirteen), and Ellen (five). In the same house dwell also the widows of the two slain sons—young girls, aged but sixteen and twenty. The latter is the sister of Henry Thompson and of the two Thompsons who were killed at Harper's Ferry; they also lived in the same vicinity, and one of them also has left a widow. Thus complicated and intertangled is this genealogy of sorrow.

All these young men went deliberately from North Elba for no other purpose than to join in this enterprise. "They could not," they told their mother and their wives, "live for themselves alone;" and so they went. One young wife, less submissive than the others, prevailed on her husband to remain; and this is the only reason why Salmon Brown survives. Oliver Brown, the youngest son, only twenty, wrote back to his wife from Harper's Ferry in a sort of premonition of what was coming, "If I can do a single good action, my life will not have been all a failure."

Having had the honor of Captain Brown's acquaintance for some years, I was admitted into the confidence of the family, though I could see them observing me somewhat suspiciously as I approached the door. Everything that was said of the absent father and husband bore testimony to the same simple, upright character. Though they had been much separated from him for the last few years, they all felt it to be a necessary absence, and had not only no complaint to make, but cordially approved it. Mrs. Brown had been always the sharer of his plans. "Her husband always believed," she said, "that he was to be an instrument in the hands of Providence," and she believed it too. "This plan had occupied his thoughts and prayers for twenty years." "Many a night he had lain awake and prayed concerning it." "Even now," she did not doubt, "he felt satisfied because he thought it would be overruled by Providence for the best." "For herself," she said, "she had always prayed that her husband might be killed in fight rather than fall alive into the hands of slaveholders; but she could not regret it now, in view of the noble words of freedom which it had been his privilege to utter." When, the next day, on the railway, I was compelled to put into her hands the newspaper containing the death warrant of her husband, I felt no fears of her exposing herself to observation by any undue excitement. She read it, and then the tall, strong woman bent her head for a few minutes on the back of the seat before us; then she raised it, and spoke calmly as before.

I thought that I had learned the lesson once for all in Kansas, which no one ever learns from books of history alone, of the readiness with which danger and death fit into the ordinary grooves of daily life, so that on the day of a battle, for instance, all may go on as usual,—breakfast and dinner are provided, children cared for, and all external existence has the same smoothness that one observes at Niagara, just above the American Fall; but it impressed me anew on visiting this household at this time. Here was a family out of which four young men had within a fortnight been killed. I say nothing of a father under sentence of death, and a brother fleeing

232

for his life, but only speak of those killed. Now that word "killed" is a word which one hardly cares to mention in a mourning household circle, even under all mitigating circumstances, when sad unavailing kisses and tender funeral rites have softened the last memories; how much less here, then, where it suggested not merely wounds and terror, and agony, but also coffinless graves in a hostile land, and the last ignominy of the dissecting-room.

Yet there was not one of that family who could not pronounce that awful word with perfect quietness; never, of course, lightly, but always quietly. For instance, as I sat that evening, with the women busily sewing around me, preparing the mother for her sudden departure with me on the morrow, some daguerreotypes were brought out to show me and some one said, "This is Oliver, one of those who were killed at Harper's Ferry." I glanced up sidelong at the young, fair-haired girl, who sat near me by the little table—a wife at fifteen, a widow at sixteen; and this was her husband, and he was killed. As the words were spoken in her hearing, not a muscle quivered, and her finger did not tremble as she drew the thread. Her life had become too real to leave room for wincing at mere words. She had lived through, beyond the word, to the sterner fact, and having confronted that, language was an empty shell. To the Browns, killing means simply dying—nothing more; one gate into heaven, and that one a good deal frequented by their family; that is all.

There was no hardness about all this, no mere stoicism of will; only God had inured them to the realities of things. They were not supported by any notions of worldly honor or applause, nor by that chilly reflection of it, the hope of future fame. In conversing with the different members of this family, I cannot recall a single instance of any heroics of that description. There, in that secluded home among the mountains, what have they to do with the world's opinion, even now, still less next century? You remember Carlyle and his Frenchman, to whom he was endeavoring to expound the Scottish Covenanters. "These poor, persecuted people," said Carlyle,—"they made their appeal." "Yes," interrupted the Frenchman, "they appealed to posterity, no doubt." "Not a bit of it," quoth Carlyle,—"they appealed to the Eternal God!" So with these whom I visited. I was the first person who had penetrated their solitude from the outer world since the thunderbolt had fallen. Do not imagine that they asked, What is the world saying of us? Will justice be done to the memory of our martyrs? Will men build the tombs of the prophets? Will the great thinkers of the age affirm that our father "makes the gallows glorious like the cross?" Not at all; they asked but one question after I had told them how little hope there was of acquittal or rescue. "Does it seem as if freedom were to gain or lose by this?" That was all. Their mother spoke the spirit of them all to me, next day, when she said, "I have had thirteen children, and only four are left; but if I am to see the ruin of my house, I cannot but hope that Providence may bring out of it some benefit to the poor slaves."

No; this family works for a higher price than fame. You know it is said that in all Wellington's dispatches you never meet with the word Glory; it is always Duty. In Napoleon's you never meet with the word Duty; it is always Glory. The race of John Brown is of the Wellington type. Principle is the word I brought away with me as most familiar in their vocabulary. That is their standard of classification. A man may be brave, ardent, generous; no matter—if he is not all this from principle, it is nothing. The daughters, who knew all the Harper's Ferry men, had no confidence in Cook because "he was not a man of principle." They would trust Stevens round the world, because "he was a man of principle." "He tries the hardest to be good," said Annie Brown, in her simple way, "of any man I ever saw."

It is pleasant to add that this same brave-hearted girl, who had known most of her father's associates, recognized them all but Cook as being men of principle. "People are surprised," she said, "at father's daring to invade Virginia with only twenty-three men; but I think if they knew what sort of men they were, there would be less surprise. I never saw such men."

And it pleases me to remember that since this visit, on the day of execution, while our Worcester bells were tolling their melancholy refrain, I took from the post-office a letter from this same young girl, expressing pity and sorrow for the recreant Cook, and uttering the hope that allowances might be made for his conduct, "though she could not justify it." And on the same day I read that infuriated letter of Mrs. Mahala Doyle—a letter which common charity bids us suppose a forgery, uttering fiendish revenge in regard to a man against whom, by her own showing, there is not one particle of evidence to identify him with her wrongs.[25] Nothing impressed me more in my visit to the Brown family, and in subsequent correspon-

[25] Mrs. Doyle's husband and two sons were among the five slain in the Pottawatomie killings. Although John Brown did not commit any of the killings himself, he did lead and direct the men who did them.

dence with them, than the utter absence of the slightest vindictive spirit, even in words.

The children spoke of their father as a person of absolute rectitude, thoughtful kindness, unfailing foresight, and inexhaustible activity. On his flying visits to the farm, every moment was used; he was "up at three A.M., seeing to everything himself," providing for everything, and giving heed to the minutest points. It was evident that some of the older ones had stood a little in awe of him in their childish years. "We boys felt a little pleased sometimes, after all," said the son, "when father left the farm for a few days." "We girls never did," said the married daughter, reproachfully, the tears gushing to her eyes. "Well," said the brother, repenting, "we were always glad to see the old man come back again; for if we did get more holidays in his absence, we always missed him."

Those dramatic points of character in him, which will of course make him the favorite hero of all American romance hereafter, are nowhere appreciated more fully than in his own family. In the midst of all their sorrow, their strong and healthy hearts could enjoy the record of his conversations with the Virginians, and applaud the keen, wise, simple answers which I read to them, selecting here and there from the ample file of newspapers I carried with me. When, for instance, I read the inquiry, "Did you go out under the auspices of the Emigrant Aid Society?" and the answer, "No, sir; I went out under the auspices of John Brown," three voices eagerly burst in with, "That's true," and "That's so." And when it was related that the young Virginia volunteer taxed him with want of military foresight in bringing so small a party to conquer Virginia, and the veteran imperturbably informed the young man that probably their views on military matters would materially differ, there was a general delighted chorus of, "That sounds just like father." And his sublimer expressions of faith and self-devotion produced no excitement or surprise among them,—since they knew in advance all which we now know of him—and these things only elicited, at times, a half-stifled sigh as they reflected that they might never hear that beloved voice again.

References to their father were constant. This book he brought them; the one sitting-room had been plastered with the last money he sent; that desk, that gun, were his; this was his daguerrotype; and at last the rosy little Ellen brought me, with reverent hands, her prize treasure. It was a morocco case, inclosing a small Bible; and in the beginning, written in the plain, legible hand I knew so well, the following inscription, which would alone (in its touching simplicity) have been worthy the pilgrimage to North Elba to see.

This Bible, presented to my dearly beloved daughter Ellen Brown, is not intended for common use, but to be carefully preserved *for her* and *by her*, in remembrance of her father (of whose care and attentions she was deprived in her infancy), he being absent in the territory of Kansas from the summer of 1855.

May the Holy Spirit of God incline your heart, *in earliest childhood*, "to receive the truth in the love of it," and to form your thoughts, words, and actions by its wise and holy precepts, is *my best wish* and *most earnest* prayer to Him in whose care I leave you. Amen.

From your affectionate father,
John Brown.

April 2, 1857.

This is dated two years ago; but the principles which dictated it were permanent. Almost on the eve of his last battle, October 1, 1859, he wrote home to his daughter Anne, in a letter which I saw, "Anne, I want you first of all to become a sincere, humble, and consistent Christian, and then [this is characteristic], to acquire good and efficient business habits. Save this to remember your father by, Anne. God Almighty bless and save you all."

John Brown is almost the only radical abolitionist I have ever known who was not more or less radical in religious matters also. His theology was Puritan, like his practice; and accustomed as we now are to see Puritan doctrines and Puritan virtues separately exhibited, it seems quite strange to behold them combined in one person again. He and his wife were regular communicants of the Presbyterian church; but it tried his soul to see the juvenile clerical gentlemen who came into the pulpits up that way, and dared to call themselves Presbyterians[26]—preachers of the gospel with all the hard applications left out. Since they had lived in North Elba, his wife said, but twice had the slave been mentioned in the Sunday services, and she had great doubts about the propriety of taking part in such worship as that. But when the head of the family made his visits home from Kansas, he commonly held a Sunday meeting in the little church, "under the auspices of John Brown," and the Lord heard the slave mentioned pretty freely then.

26 John Brown was received into the Congregational Church at Hudson, Ohio, in 1816, and remained, at least nominally, a member of that denomination until his death.

In speaking of religious opinions, Mrs. Brown mentioned two preachers whose sermons her sons liked to read, and "whose anti-slavery principles she enjoyed, though she could not agree with all their doctrines." She seemed to regard their positions as essentially the same. I need not say who the two are—the thunders of Brooklyn and Boston[27] acquire much the same sound as they roll up among the echoes of the Adirondacks.

In respect to politics, Mrs. Brown told me that her husband had taken little interest in them since the election of Jackson, because he thought that politics merely followed the condition of public senti-ment on the slavery question, and that this public sentiment was mainly created by actual collisions between slavery and freedom. Such, at least, was the view which I was led to attribute to him, by combining this fact which she mentioned with my own personal knowledge of his opinions. He had an almost exaggerated aversion to words and speeches, and a profound conviction of the importance of bringing all questions to a direct issue, and subjecting every theory to the test of practical application.

I did not, of course, insult Mrs. Brown by any reference to that most shallow charge of insanity against her husband, which some even of his friends have, with what seems most cruel kindness, encouraged,—thereby doing their best to degrade one of the age's prime heroes into a mere monomaniac,—but it may be well to record that she spoke of it with surprise, and said that if her husband were insane, he had been consistent in his insanity from the very first moment she knew him.

Now that all is over, and we appear to have decided, for the present, not to employ any carnal weapons, such as steel or iron, for the rescue of John Brown, but only to use the safer metals of gold and silver for the aid of his family, it may be natural for those who read this narrative to ask, What is the pecuniary condition of this household? It is hard to answer, because the whole standard is different, as to such matters, in North Elba and Massachusetts. The ordinary condition of the Brown family may be stated as follows: They own the farm, such as it is, without incumbrance, except so far as unfelled forest constitutes one. They have ordinarily enough to eat of what the farm yields, namely, bread and potatoes, pork and mutton—not any great abundance of these, but ordinarily enough. They have ordinarily enough to wear, at least of woolen clothing, spun by themselves. And they have absolutely no money.

27 Henry Ward Beecher and Theodore Parker.

When I say this I do not merely mean that they have no superfluous cash to go shopping with, but I mean almost literally that they have none. For nearly a whole winter, Mrs. Brown said, they had no money with which to pay postage, except a tiny treasury which the younger girls had earned for that express object, during the previous summer, by picking berries for a neighbor three miles off.

The reason of these privations simply was, that it cost money to live in Kansas in "adherence to the cause of freedom" (see the tombstone inscription), but not so much to live at North Elba; and therefore the women must stint themselves that the men might continue their Kansas work. When the father came upon his visits he never came empty-handed, but brought a little money, some plain household stores, flour, sugar, rice, salt fish; tea and coffee they do not use. But what their standard of expense is may be seen from the fact that Mrs. Brown seemed to speak as if her youngest widowed daughter were not totally and absolutely destitute, because her husband had left a property of five sheep, which would belong to her. These sheep, I found on inquiry, were worth, at that place and season, two dollars apiece: a child of sixteen, left a widow in the world, with an estate amounting to ten dollars! The immediate financial anxieties of Mrs. Brown herself seemed chiefly to relate to a certain formidable tax bill, due at New Year's time; if they could only weather that, all was clear for the immediate future. How much was it, I asked, rather surprised that that wild country should produce a high rate of taxation. It was from eight to ten dollars, she gravely said; and she had put by ten dollars for the purpose, but had had occasion to lend most of it to a poor black woman, with no great hope of repayment. And one of the first things done by her husband, on recovering his money in Virginia, was to send her, through me, fifteen dollars, to make sure of that tax bill.

I see, on looking back, how bare and inexpressive this hasty narrative is; but I could not bear to suffer such a privilege as this visit to pass away unrecorded. I spent but one night at the house, and drove away with Mrs. Brown, in the early frosty morning, from that breezy mountain home, which her husband loved (as one of them told me) "because he seemed to think there was something romantic in that kind of scenery." There was, indeed, always a sort of thrill in John Brown's voice when he spoke of mountains. I shall never forget the quiet way in which he once told me that "God had established the Alleghany Mountains from the foundation of the world that they might one day be a refuge for fugitive slaves." I did not then know that his own home was among the Adirondacks.

Just before we went, I remember, I said something or other to Salmon Brown about the sacrifices of their family; and he looked up in a quiet, manly way, which I shall never forget, and said briefly, "I sometimes think that is what we came into the world for—to make sacrifices." And I know that the murmuring echo of those words went with me all that day, as we came down from the mountains, and out through the iron gorge; and it seemed to me that any one must be very unworthy the society I had been permitted to enter who did not come forth from it a wiser and a better man.

This letter was written by George B. Gill to Richard J. Hinton, John Brown's biographer. In May, 1858, at John Brown's constitutional convention, in Chatham, Canada, Gill had been appointed Secretary of the Treasury for the provisional government. In the winter of 1858-59, he was one of the band that accompanied Brown on the foray into Missouri, in which eleven slaves were liberated and brought to Canada. Gill refused, however, in August, 1859, to join Brown at Harpers Ferry.

Milan, Sumner Co., Kan.
July 7 1893

My dear friend;

It seems that all great men have their foibles or what we in our differance from them call their weaknesses. In our intimacy we find the vulnerable points, hence "A man is never a hero to his valet." And I am about to give you an expression of truthfulness which I have never given to any one yet.

The great father of his country was not personally a loveable man, but an aristocrat in all that the title can claim where it implies selfishness and intolerance. Men to make their marks in the world must have some leading characteristic, prominent either in its great strength or its great weakness. I admit that I am sadly deficient as a god or hero worshiper. I cannot avoid the feeling that men have their merits or demerits without any volition of their own. We may love one for his pretty attractiveness, and abhor another for his repulsiveness, yet neither the one or the other is responsible for these divergent ways. Egotism, love of approbation, love of adventure, love of command and many personal characteristics coupled with firmness, combativeness, destructiveness and sometimes vindictiveness may prompt us to act. These promptings whatever they may be come from a source which we did not originate and are as natural to our being as the flow of blood in our veins, hence we merit neither praise or blame for our acts, and the man who may do his fellows or the world the most good may be far from the goody goody kind but may be personaly absolutely offensive.

My intimate acquaintance with Brown demonstrated to me that he was very human. The angel wings were so dim and shadowy as to be almost unseen, very superstitious, very selfish and very intolerant with great self esteem. His immense egotism coupled with love of approbation and his god idea begot in him a feeling that he was the Moses that was to lead the Exodus of the colored people from their southern taskmasters. Brooding on this, in time he believed that he was Gods chosen instrument, and the *only one*, and that whatever methods he used, God would be his guard and shield, rendering the most illogical movements into a grand success. Other ways than his own, other men than himself were not awarded one iota of credit from him. When the colored people would designate him as the second Moses, which they frequently did, it would elate him through and through. He could not brook a rival. At first he was very fond of Montgomery,[28] but when he found that Montgomery had thoughts of his own and could not be dictated to, why he loved him no longer. Montgomery Lane[29] and all other leaders went down before his imperial self. He was intolerant in little things, and in little ways, for instance his drink was tea, others wanted coffee. He would wrangle and compel them to drink tea or nothing as he was cook and would not make coffee for them. I had it from Owen in a quiet way, and from other sources in quite a loud way, that in his family his methods were of the most arbitrary kind. The row that he raised in the Masonic fraternity was most probably a resultant of his imperial egotism. I have known Stevens to sometimes raise merry hell when the old man would get too dictatorial. He was iron and had neither sympathy or feeling for the timid and weak of will. Notwithstanding claims to the contrary, he was essentualy vindictive in his nature. Just before we left Kansas during a trip that Brown and myself were some days away from the rest, the boys arrested a man (I think by the name of Jackson). Montgomery gave him a trial and he was released by general consent as not meriting punishment. When we returned Brown was furious because the man had not been shot. His Calvinism and general organism would have

28 James Montgomery, a Free-State guerrilla leader in Kansas.
29 James H. Lane, a Free-State politician and guerrilla leader in Kansas.

treated Servetus as Calvin did. I cannot now recall an instance in which he gave to another the unstinted and unqualified praise that you and I would give.

And yet this very concentration in self commanded the grand advance on American slavery. It bearded the lion in his den, the monster in his home and in the end vindicated an apparent absurd assault by accelerating the forces which in the end gave success. I still feel that Brown "builded wiser than he knew." The dream which peopled the mountains with dusky freemen and created an army all his own, led as only a Moses could lead, sustained as only a God could sustain, ended only in a dreamless sleep yet the wave moved on upon whose bloody crest the slave rode to freedom.

It seems harsh and cruel in me to tell you of Browns individuality as I have told you, yet it seemed to me that you, perhaps the last writer on the theme, should know all, whether it be of any use to you or not.

The men in the ranks are too often forgotten in the adulation we give the leaders. Browns memory will never be as sacred a thing to me as the memory of some who fell with him, for there were some of these whose aspirations were only for others, whose dreams and hopes and loves never centered in self, and whose devotion to friends or cause led them to the deaths that only martyrs and heroes find.

You are the only one that I have ever mentioned these things to, and will be the last.

You and I, almost the last links in the chain, and knowing human nature as we do, can never expect to clothe our heroes with the beauty and goodness of mythical angels. Yet henceforth as in the past I'll remember only his or their goodness. Your men will record their virtues. May the lines live when Thermopylaes myth or Tells romance will be covered by the dust of centuries, and the fable of the Moses of the Nile will have been forgotten. In all the years to come men will read the story of how these heroes gave their lives for the freedom of a people not their own, when they themselves were free.

Some two weeks ago I sent you a package by express. I have not heard from you since. We are expecting "The Strip"[30] to open the 15th of Sep. and hope to get claims for self and boys. We will probably not have to go more than from twenty to fifty miles from here. Please keep your eye open for some one who will give me some

---

[30] Cherokee Strip in Oklahoma where in 1893 the famous of the "runs" for homesteads was made when that section was opened for homesteading.

money in exchange for that knife or for my commission. It seems like a sacrilege but our crop is very short and we will need money so badly. If we should succeed in getting good claims three hundred dollars would make me rich. I have so far done no work this season.

Yours as ever

Geo[rge] B. Gill

This account of an interview with the wife of Judge Thomas Russell (one of the most highly respected and influential citizens of Boston during the years preceding and following the Civil War), was written by Katherine Mayo, and appeared in the New York *Evening Post* on October 23, 1909. Miss Mayo was then a reporter for the *Evening Post* and was also serving as secretary and research assistant to Oswald Garrison Villard, helping him to gather material for his biography of John Brown. She later became a well-known author in her own right.

BROWN IN HIDING AND IN JAIL

Katherine Mayo

When Capt. John Brown came out of Kansas in the late fall of 1856, his name walked before him. As a free-lance leader in the wars between the anti-slavery and pro-slavery factions then wrangling over the new Territory as debatable ground, his deeds of arms had become almost famous. And when, early in the new year, he appeared in Boston in search of friends and means to sustain him in further aggressions of the old stripe, he found his welcome ready. Men of conservative mind and practical habits somewhat inclined, it is true, to look askance at his mysterious, lawless, and violent methods, while attracted by his rugged honesty and his picturesque career. But to a little group of extreme radical Abolitionists his appeal was sovereign. Naming him the "Old Covenanter," the "border chieftain," their "Roundhead hero," they united to his support with word and purse. Gerrit Smith, Dr. S. G. Howe, Theodore Parker, George Luther Stearns, F. B. Sanborn, and T. W. Higginson found a centre of sympathy and effort in their common admiration; and if this was not made known to all their world, it was because Brown's past record and future plans alike demanded cover for prosperity. If the old man's views were warlike, and his acts matched to his views, he met scant check at the hands of his friends. When, in April, 1857, he was compelled to go into eclipse for a space, to escape the assiduities of a United States marshal from Kansas, it was Theodore Parker who wrote to Brown's immediate protector a fiery message of thinly veiled advice : " If I were in his [Brown's] position, I should shoot dead any man who attempted to arrest me." And such, it may fairly be said, was the general spirit of the group.

This period of hiding, " to let the track get cold," Brown spent in Boston, in the house of the late Hon. Thomas Russell, then judge of the Superior Court of Massachusetts and later United States minister to Caracas. In his whole-hearted shielding of the hunted man, Judge Russell had the skilful co-operation of his beautiful, witty, and charming young wife. And when, in the working out of his tragic fate, John Brown lay, wounded and imprisoned in a hostile land, under sentence of death, these two alone of all the Boston friends dared to visit him.

The following is Mrs. Russell's narrative, as recently given, in her home near Boston to a representative of the *Evening Post* :

" One day my husband said to me, ' John Brown is coming to stay with us for a week.' ' Very well,' said I, and was ready to receive him when he presently arrived alone.

" ' You would like to see your room at once, would you not ? ' I asked, as soon as we had exchanged greetings. I had never met John Brown before, but I felt that he must be anxious, hunted as he was, to learn ' the lay of the land ' in his new quarters, and what safety they offered from the sheriff's pursuit. So I led him, myself, up the two flights to his room.

" ' There,' said I, ' you can barricade the door with all of the furniture if you like, and if there is not enough of it here, we will bring in as much more as you want.'

A WEEK'S REFUGE

" Our house was chosen as a refuge because no one would have dreamed of looking for Brown therein. It was in Hudson Street, an inconspicuous locality, and my husband never figured before the public as prominent in the Abolitionist ranks. His policy was to remain as far as possible unknown in his work for the cause, in order to enjoy greater freedom for action. They had nicknamed him ' The Stormy Petrel,' because, they said, whenever he did appear trouble was surely brewing.

" John Brown stayed with us a week, keeping his room almost always, except at meal time, and never coming down unless one of us went up to fetch him. He proved a most amiable guest, and when he left I missed him greatly. During his whole visit I waited on the front door myself, lest by chance some enemy should find the trail and should elicit from a servant an identifying word. That the servants themselves should suspect nothing was, of course, as desirable as it was difficult to maintain. In this respect my persistent waiting on the door had its dangerous side; yet I was shielded by the fact that their rooms were on the floor below and they not over alacritous to hasten upstairs in answer to the bell.

"The first time that I went up to call John Brown, I thought he would never open his door. Nothing ensued but an interminable sound of the dragging of furniture.

"'I have been finding the best way to barricade,' he remarked, when he appeared at last. 'I shall never be taken alive, you know. And I should hate to spoil your carpet.'

"'You may burn the house down, if you want to,' I exclaimed. He laughed his silent laugh. 'No, my dear, I shall not do that.'

KEEN SENSE OF HUMOR

"He had the keenest possible sense of humor, and never missed the point of a joke or of a situation. Negroes' long words, exaggeration, and grandiloquence afforded him endless amusement, as did pretentiousness of any sort; and he was very quick to see the ridiculous in people's assumption of greater grandeur than that to which they were born.

"He was acute in observing the quality of spoken English, and would often show himself highly diverted by the blunders of uneducated tongues. He himself spoke somewhat rustically, but his phrases were well formed, his words well chosen, and his construction always forcible and direct. When he laughed he made not the slightest sound, not even a whisper or an intake of breath; but he shook all over and laughed violently. It was the most curious thing imaginable to see him, in utter silence, rock and quake with mirth.

"One evening he and I alone were sitting together in our parlor. Suddenly he drew from one boot a long, evil-looking knife. Then, from the other boot, he extracted two smaller knives. Then he produced a big pistol, and a smaller one. He looked at me doubtfully; I think he had a third somewhere concealed about him, but felt it unadvisable to resort, in my presence, to the measures necessary to get at it. Then he drew all the charges from the barrels and solemnly deposited them in the palms of my hands, filling both with cartridges. I was paralyzed with fear of the things.

"'Now, don't be awk'ard,' said he, 'don't tremble, or they will all fire off!'

"I sat stiff with fright, while he solemnly blew down the barrels, looked at the locks, examined the blades of his knives, and finally reloaded the firearms. I think he really, seriously, wished to make sure that his defences were in good condition; also, it amused him to see the effect upon me.

"'You haven't had this in your parlor before, have you?' he remarked at last.

"One night at supper, when there was syrup on the table, he preferred it to butter or sugar for their several uses. On my observing it, he remarked that I would not be much struck with that small matter did I know of some of the things that life in the wilds led men to eat. And thereafter he persisted in gravely mentioning, from time to time, unspeakable articles upon which he said he had dined —joints and toes of creatures that surely no human being ever tasted.

"When the time came for his leave-taking, his safe departure was managed in this way: There was to be a dance on a certain night. Those of my husband's friends in the secret of John Brown's whereabouts would take pains to ask, at conspicuous moments and in general hearing, for some days before, 'Will you do this, or that,' on the night in question. 'No,' my husband would reply, 'I have promised to take my wife to Mrs. ——'s dance'; and so on, again and again, to establish the impression. When the night came I went to the dance alone, telling every one there that my husband had been delayed, but would appear directly. Meantime, he spirited John Brown to the station, watched his train depart, and so came on to the dance, not late enough to attract notice.

"It was in the spring of 1859 that I next saw Capt. Brown, and in our house once more. On this visit it was that he brought a present of maple sugar to our little daughter Minnie, and held her, standing, on his outstretched palm. 'Now,' said he, 'when you are a young lady and I am hanged, you can say that you stood on the hand of Old Brown.'

245

"A few months later, when our third and last meeting occurred, this laughing, tragic prophecy had drawn close upon fulfilment. The Harper's Ferry raid had come to its bloody end; the trial of the survivors was in progress; and my husband determined to go to Virginia to offer Capt. Brown his professional advice and his sympathy as a friend. I would not let him go alone.

"Arriving in Charlestown, we went at once to the hotel, where my husband left me, and himself proceeded straight to the court. He arrived just in time to hear sentence pronounced. . . . After an interval we were allowed to go to the jail. It proved to be simply a good, old-fashioned dwelling-house, and the cell one of its large rooms. Within, on a cot, lay Capt. Brown, looking as calm, rugged, and comfortable as ever. He rose to receive us. His lips trembled a little as he looked at me, and he said, very softly : ' Oh, my dear, this is no place for you! ' He asked our pardon for lying down again.

"Now, before we left home, my husband had said to me : ' Take your scissors and needle and thimble, and some black thread. He will need mending, and you know how he loves neatness.' Excellent advice, as the event proved; for Capt. Brown's coat, that in which he had been taken, was all torn and cut and stained with mud and blood.

" ' Wouldn't you like to have this put right? ' I asked him.

" ' Oh, my dear, do you think you could sew these buttons on? ' The buttons were hanging. ' And wouldn't you like it cleaned? ' I went on.

"His face brightened. ' But that isn't possible, is it? ' ' I can do it,' I replied; and he laughed.

"Loitering around an opening that had once been a door, but which had been partly closed up and was now neither door nor window, stood a poor white, who had idled there, very obnoxiously, from the first. I walked over to this aperture with the coat. ' Take that,' I told the man, ' and clean it, and bring it back in ten minutes.'

" ' Yes, ma'am '; and he hurried away. When he returned with it, an hour later, it was marvelously clean, wonderfully clean, and he must have worked hard to accomplish it so quickly.

"Mr. Avis (the jailer) behaved like a gentleman. As soon as we entered he left the cell, retiring quite out of earshot, although we should have had to pass him in leaving the jail; and so he remained, beyond hearing, during all our visit. But when we had been there perhaps two hours Capt. Brown himself spoke to the jailer, saying, in that measured, deliberate way so entirely his own:

"'Have you any objection to my writing to my wife to tell her that I am to be hanged on the 2d of December at noon?'

"'Certainly not, Mr. Brown,' answered the jailer.

That query, so cool and slow, was Brown himself. I walked over and spoke to Stevens (Brown's young lieutenant, shot in the raid), who lay on the other cot. I can see yet the beautiful, sweet smile with which he said, when I asked if I could do anything for him: 'It is too late now.' He was so terribly wounded that it seemed scarcely possible that he could live another day.

IT HAD GONE WRONG

"I did not talk about the raid with Capt. Brown. I had never sympathized with his ideas on such subjects, and had always avoided them in our conversations. But I loved *John Brown*. To my husband he said but little of the raid, yet in that little it was evident that something had gone very wrong—that something had been done that he had expressly forbidden, or which was against his will. He had no fondness for Fred Douglass. Once I heard him say to my husband, of some defeated plan, some great opportunity lost, '*That* we owe to the famous Mr. Frederick Douglass!' and he shut his mouth in a way he had when he thought no good.

"In all our talk he had been the farthest possible removed from showing any approach to self-commiseration, or to any quarrel with fate. He was calm and at peace, and earnestly desired to maintain that mind, with unshaken self-control, to the end. Of his sons who fell in the raid he said one thing only: 'I have seen my two boys killed, and,' he added, in his very measured, quiet fashion, 'not gently killed.'

"At last we had to take our leave. I kissed him, weeping. His mouth trembled, ever so little, but he merely said: 'Now, go.' I went out and down the street in tears to the hotel, and we took the next train homeward.

"At the station Col. Lewis Washington (one of the principal gentlemen of the region, who had been Brown's prisoner during the raid) came and spoke to me. We walked up and down the platform together while awaiting the train—and a dear old gentleman he was.

247

He questioned me very closely. 'Why,' asked he, 'do you like such a miserable man?'

" 'I think you are a very bad Southerner, sir, to speak so to a lady of her friends.'

"He considered, and thought the point perhaps just. 'But why,' he persisted, 'did he come to your house, as you say?'

" 'To bring maple sugar to my children.'

" 'I believe you are only a spoiled child, after all. You would better come home with me. My wife will be delighted to see you.' Moreover, he meant it.

"I had assured him that I had no knowledge, part, or sympathy as to slave-takings, insurrections, or raids, and that I had merely come to see my friend in prison. He accepted my assurance, yet, despite himself, some little doubt remained in his mind, for as our train left, he said: 'I am not certain that I do right in letting you go.' Before we had been two hours away, the mail brought a letter from a Mrs. Russell, containing $50 for Brown. The inference was that she was a former as well as a present supporter, and that she and I were one. Great excitement arose over it, and I felt very badly on account of my dear old colonel. I could not bear to have him think I would have deceived him, and wrote to him at once to explain the facts.

"My husband, until this day, had never appeared publicly in connection with John Brown, but he had known of Brown's career and had always entertained the most absolute confidence in his integrity, high purpose, courage and singleness of heart. John Brown was without vanity or personal ambition. He could never have done a weak or mean or underhanded deed; nor could he ever have done a cruel one unless he felt that some great ultimate good required the sacrifice. John Brown was an idealist. He could form beautiful dreams of things, as they should occur, and forthwith go into action on the basis of those dreams, making no sufficient allowance for some things occurring as they should not. John Brown's dreams were not always practical. But we loved and trusted *John Brown*."

Osborn Perry Anderson (1830-1872) met John Brown in 1858, accompanied him on his raid to Harpers Ferry, and succeeding in escaping. He later fought in the Civil War. In *A Voice from Harper's Ferry*, Boston, 1861, Anderson offers an interesting evaluation of Brown and describes the events immediately preceding and following the attack on Harpers Ferry. The following selections are from pp. 23-24, 24-25, and 28-29 of his book.

A VOICE FROM HARPER'S FERRY

CHAPTER V

More Correspondence—My Journey to the Ferry— A Glance at the Family

. . . .

I found all the men concerned in the undertaking on hand when I arrived,[31] except Copeland, Leary and Merriam; and when all had collected, a more earnest, fearless, determined company of men it would be difficult to get together. There, as at Chatham, I saw the same evidence of strong and commanding intellect, high-toned morality, and inflexibility of purpose in the men, and a profound and holy reverence for God, united to the most comprehensive, practical, systematic philanthropy, and undoubted bravery in the patriarch leader, brought out to view in lofty grandeur by the associations and surroundings of the place and the occasion. There was no milk and water sentimentality—no offensive contempt for the negro, while working in his cause; the pulsations of each and every heart beat in harmony for the suffering and pleading slave. I thank God that I have been permitted to realize to its furthest, fullest extent, the moral, mental, physical, social harmony of an Anti-Slavery family, carrying out to the letter the principles of its antetype, the Anti-Slavery cause. In John Brown's house, and in John Brown's presence, men from widely different parts of the continent met and united into one company, wherein no hateful prejudice dared intrude its ugly self—no ghost of a distinction found space to enter.

31 At the Kennedy Farm.

CHAPTER VI

Life At Kennedy Farm

To a passer-by, the house and its surroundings presented but indifferent attractions. Any log tenement of equal dimensions would be as likely to arrest a stray glance. Rough, unsightly, and aged, it was only those privileged to enter and tarry for a long time, and to penetrate the mysteries of the two rooms it contained—kitchen, parlor, dining-room below, and the spacious chamber, attic, store-room, prison, drilling room, comprised in the loft above—who could tell how we lived at Kennedy Farm.

Every morning, when the noble old man was at home, he called the family around, read from his Bible, and offered to God most fervent and touching supplications for all flesh; and especially pathetic were his petitions in behalf of the oppressed. I never heard John Brown pray, that he did not make strong appeals to God for the deliverance of the slave. This duty over, the men went to the loft, there to remain all the day long; few only could be seen about, as the neighbors were watchful and suspicious. It was also important to talk but little among ourselves, as visitors to the house might be curious. Besides the daughter and daughter-in-law, who superin-tended the work, some one or other of the men was regularly detailed to assist in the cooking, washing, and other domestic work. After the ladies left, we did all the work, no one being exempt, because of age or official grade in the organization.

The principal employment of the prisoners, as we severally were when compelled to stay in the loft, was to study Forbes' Manual, and to go through a quiet, though rigid drill, under the training of Capt. Stevens, at some times. At others, we applied a preparation for bronzing our gun barrels—discussed subjects of reform—related our personal history; but when our resources became pretty well exhausted, the *ennui* from confinement, imposed silence, etc., would make the men almost desperate. At such times, neither slavery nor slaveholders were discussed mincingly. We were, while the ladies remained, often relieved of much of the dullness growing out of restraint by their kindness. As we could not circulate freely, they would bring in wild fruit and flowers from the woods and fields. We were well supplied with grapes, paw-paws, chestnuts, and other small fruit, besides bouquets of fall flowers, through their thoughtful consideration.

During the several weeks I remained at the encampment, we were under the restraint I write of through the day; but at night, we sallied out for a ramble, or to breathe the fresh air and enjoy the beautiful solitude of the mountain scenery around, by moonlight.

Captain Brown loved the fullest expression of opinion from his men, and not seldom, when a subject was being severely scrutinized by Kagi, Oliver, or others of the party, the old gentleman would be one of the most interested and earnest hearers. Frequently his views were severely criticized, when no one would be in better spirits than himself. He often remarked that it was gratifying to see young men grapple with moral and other important questions, and express themselves independently; it was evidence of self-sustaining power.

· · · · · · · · · · · · · · · ·

CHAPTER VIII

Council Meetings—Orders Given—The Charge—Etc.

On Sunday morning, October 16th, Captain Brown arose earlier than usual, and called his men down to worship. He read a chapter from the Bible, applicable to the condition of the slaves, and our duty as their brethren, and then offered up a fervent prayer to God to assist in the liberation of the bondmen in that slaveholding land. The services were impressive beyond expression. Every man there assembled seemed to respond from the depths of his soul, and throughout the entire day, a deep solemnity pervaded the place. The old man's usually weighty words were invested with more than ordinary importance, and the countenance of every man reflected the momentous thought that absorbed his attention within.

After breakfast had been despatched, and the roll called by the Captain, a sentinel was posted outside the door, to warn by signal if any one should approach, and we listened to preparatory remarks to a council meeting to be held that day. At 10 o'clock, the council was assembled. I was appointed to the Chair, when matters of importance were considered at length. After the council adjourned, the Constitution was read for the benefit of the few who had not before heard it, and the necessary oaths taken. Men who were to hold military positions in the organization, and who had not received commissions before then, had their commissions filled out by J. H. Kagi, and gave the required obligations.

In the afternoon, the eleven orders presented in the next chapter were given by the Captain, and were afterwards carried out in every particular by the officers and men.

In the evening, before setting out to the Ferry, he gave his final charge, in which he said, among other things:—" *And now, gentlemen, let me impress this one thing upon your minds. You all know how dear life is to you, and how dear your life is to your friends. And in remembering that, consider that the lives of others are as dear to them as yours are to you. Do not, therefore, take the life of any one, if you can possibly avoid it; but if it is necessary to take life in order to save your own, then make sure work of it.*"

John G. Rosengarten, a Northerner, was a director of the Pennsylvania Railroad who wandered into Harpers Ferry at the time of the raid, was arrested on suspicion of complicity and released in time to witness the aftermath of the raid. The essay in which he described his experience, from which the following selection is taken, appeared in the *Atlantic Monthly*, June, 1865, pp. 711-717.

JOHN BROWN'S RAID: HOW I GOT INTO IT, AND HOW I GOT OUT OF IT

John G. Rosengarten

.   .   .   .

I paid my respects to Governor Wise, and thanked him for my release; was introduced to Colonel Lee, (now the Rebel general,) and to the officers of the little squad of marines who had carried the stronghold of the "invaders," as the Governor persistently called them. In company with "Porte Crayon," Mr. Strothers, a native of that part of Virginia, and well known by his sketches of Southern life in "Harper's Magazine," I went to the engine-house, and there saw the marks of the desperate defence and of the desperate bravery of John Brown and his men. I saw, too, John Brown himself. Wounded, bleeding, haggard, and defeated, and expecting death with more or less agony as it was more or less near, John Brown was the finest specimen of a man that I ever saw. His great, gaunt form, his noble head and face, his iron-gray hair and patriarchal beard, with the patient endurance of his own suffering, and his painful anxiety for the fate of his sons and the welfare of his men, his reticence when jeered at, his readiness to turn away wrath with a kind answer, his whole appearance and manner, what he looked, what he said,— all impressed me with the deepest sense of reverence. If his being likened to anything in history could have made the scene more solemn, I should say he was likest to the pictured or the ideal representation of a Roundhead Puritan dying for his faith, and silently glorying in the sacrifice not only of life, but of all that made life dearest to him. His wounded men showed in their patient endurance the influence of his example; while the vulgar herd of lookers-on, fair representatives of the cowardly militia-men who had waited for the little force of regulars to achieve the capture of the engine-house and its garrison, were ready to prove their further cowardice by maltreating the prisoners. The marines, who alone had sacrificed life in the attack, were sturdily bent on guarding them from any harsh handling. I turned away sadly from the old man's side, sought and got the information he wanted concerning "his people," as he called them, and was rewarded with his thanks in a few simple words, and in a voice that was as gentle as a woman's. The Governor, as soon as he was told of the condition of the prisoners, had them cared for, and, in all his bitterness at their doings, never spoke of them in terms other than honorable to himself and to them. He persistently praised John Brown for his bravery and his endurance; and he was just as firm in declaring him the victim of shrewd and designing men, whose schemes he would yet fathom.

.   .   .   .

In spite of many scenes of noble heroism and devoted bravery in legitimate warfare, and in the glorious campaigns of our own successful armies, I have never seen any life in death so grand as that of John Brown, and to me there is more than an idle refrain in the solemn chorus of our advancing hosts,—

> " John Brown's body lies mouldering in the ground,
>   As we go marching on! "

John Brown first met Theodore Parker in Boston through an introduction by Franklin B. Sanborn in January, 1857. Thereafter, Parker became one of Brown's loyal supporters and defended him vigorously after the attack on Harpers Ferry. The following letter was written to Francis Jackson, a lawyer and leading abolitionist, from Rome, Italy, where Parker was seeking to recover from the illness to which he ultimately succumbed. It constitutes the best thought-out defense of Brown on logical-philosophical grounds. Parker's basic assumption is that slavery is a social system based ultimately on the use of force and terror against the individual slave, whose friends are therefore justified in using force to achieve his freedom and to maintain it.

JOHN BROWN'S EXPEDITION REVIEWED IN A LETTER FROM ROME TO FRANCIS JACKSON, BOSTON

Rome, Nov. 24, 1859.

MY DEAR FRIEND,—I see by a recent telegraph, which the steamer of Nov. 2nd brought from Boston, that the court found Capt. Brown guilty, and passed sentence upon him. It is said Friday, Dec. 2nd, is fixed as the day for hanging him. So long before this reaches you my friend will have passed on to the reward of his magnanimous public services, and his pure, upright, private life. I am not well enough to be the minister to any congregation, least of all to one like that which, for so many years, helped my soul while it listened to my words. Surely the 28th Congregational Society in Boston needs a minister, not half dead, but alive all over; and yet, while reading the accounts of the affair at Harper's Ferry, and of the sayings of certain men at Boston, whom you and I know only too well, I could not help wishing I was at home again *to use what poor remnant of power is left to me in defence of the True and the Right.*

America is rich in able men, in skilful writers, in ready and accomplished speakers. But few men dare treat public affairs with reference to the great principles of justice, and the American Democracy: nay, few with reference to any remote future, or even with a comprehensive survey of the present. Our public writers ask what effect will this opinion have on the Democratic party, or the Republican party; how will it affect the next Presidential election; what will the great State of Pennsylvania or Ohio, or New York say to it? This is very unfortunate for us all, especially when the people have to deal practically, and that speedily, with a question concerning the very existence of Democratic institutions in America;

254

for it is not to be denied that we must give up DEMOCRACY if we keep SLAVERY, or give up SLAVERY if we keep DEMOCRACY.

I greatly deplore this state of things. Our able men fail to perform their natural function, to give valuable instruction and advice to the people; and at the same time they debase and degrade themselves. The hurrahs and the offices they get are poor compensation for falseness to their own consciences.

In my best estate, I do not pretend to much political wisdom, and still less now while sick; but I wish yet to set down a few thoughts for your private eye, and, it may be, for the ear of the fraternity. They are, at least, the result of long meditation on the subject; besides, they are not at all new nor peculiar to me, but are a part of the public knowledge of all enlightened men.

1. A MAN HELD AGAINST HIS WILL AS A SLAVE HAS A NATURAL RIGHT TO KILL EVERY ONE WHO SEEKS TO PREVENT HIS ENJOYMENT OF LIBERTY. This has long been recognized as a self-evident proposition, coming so directly from the primitive instincts of human nature, that it neither required proofs nor admitted them.

2. IT MAY BE A NATURAL DUTY OF THE SLAVE TO DEVELOPE THIS NATURAL RIGHT IN A PRACTICAL MANNER, AND ACTUALLY KILL ALL THOSE WHO SEEK TO PREVENT HIS ENJOYMENT OF LIBERTY. For if he continue patiently in bondage : First, he entails the foulest of curses on his children; and, second, he encourages other men to commit the crime against nature which he allows his own master to commit. It is my duty to preserve my own body from starvation. If I fail thereof through sloth, I not only die, but incur the contempt and loathing of my acquaintances while I live. It is not less my duty to do all that is in my power to preserve my body and soul from slavery; and if I submit to that through cowardice, I not only become a bondman, and suffer what thraldrom inflicts, but I incur also the contempt and loathing of my acquaintance. Why do freemen scorn and despise a slave? Because they think his condition is a sign of his cowardice, and believe that he ought to prefer death to bondage. The Southerners hold the Africans in great contempt, though mothers of their children. Why? Simply because the Africans are slaves; that is, because the Africans fail to perform the natural duty of securing freedom by killing their oppressors.

3. THE FREEMAN HAS A NATURAL RIGHT TO HELP THE SLAVES RECOVER THEIR LIBERTY, AND IN THAT ENTERPRISE TO DO FOR THEM ALL WHICH THEY HAVE A RIGHT TO DO FOR THEMSELVES.

This statement, I think, requires no argument or illustration.

4. IT MAY BE A NATURAL DUTY FOR THE FREEMAN TO HELP THE SLAVES TO THE ENJOYMENT OF THEIR LIBERTY, AND AS MEANS TO THAT END, TO AID THEM IN KILLING ALL SUCH AS OPPOSE THEIR NATURAL FREEDOM.

If you were attacked by a wolf, I should not only have a *right* to aid you in getting rid of that enemy, but it would be my DUTY to help you in proportion to my power. If it were a MURDERER, and not a wolf, who attacked you, the duty would be still the same. Suppose it is not a murderer who would kill you, but a KIDNAPPER who would enslave, does that make it less my duty to help you out of the hands of your enemy? Suppose it is not a kidnapper who would make you a bondman, but a SLAVEHOLDER who would keep you one, does that remove my obligation to help you?

5. THE PERFORMANCE OF THIS DUTY IS TO BE CONTROLLED BY THE FREEMAN'S POWER AND OPPORTUNITY TO HELP THE SLAVES. (The impossible is never the obligatory.) I cannot help the slaves in Dahomey or Bornou, and am not bound to try. I can help those who escape to my own neighbourhood, and I ought to do so. My duty is commensurate with my power; and as my power increases, my duty enlarges along with it. If I *could* help the bondmen in Virginia to their freedom as easily and effectually as I can aid the runaway at my own door, then I OUGHT to do so.

These five maxims have a direct application to America at this day, and the people of the Free States have a certain dim perception thereof, which, fortunately, is becoming clearer every year.

Thus, the people of Massachusetts *feel* that they ought to protect the fugitive slaves who come into our State. Hence come first the irregular attempts to secure their liberty, and the declarations of noble men, like Timothy Gilbert, George W. Carnes, and others, that they will do so even at great personal risk; and, secondly, the statute laws made by the legislature to accomplish that end.

Now, if Massachusetts had the power to do as much for the slaves in Virginia as for the runaways in her own territory, we should soon see those two sets of measures at work in *that* direction also.

I find it is said in the Democratic newspapers that " Capt. Brown had many friends at the North, who sympathized with him in general, and in special approved of this particular scheme of his; they furnished him with some twelve or twenty thousand dollars, it would seem." I think much more than that is true of us. If he *had* succeeded in running off one or two thousand slaves to Canada, even at the expense of a little violence and bloodshed, *the majority of men in New-England would have rejoiced, not only in the end, but also in the means.* The first successful attempt of a considerable number of slaves to secure their freedom by violence will clearly show how deep is the sympathy of the people for them, and how strongly they embrace the five principles I mentioned above. A little success of that sort will serve as *priming* for the popular cannon; it is already *loaded*.

Of course I was not astonished to hear that an attempt had been made to free the slaves in a certain part of Virginia, nor should I be astonished if another "insurrection" or "rebellion" took place in the State of ——, or a third in ——, or a fourth in ——. Such things are to be expected; for they do not depend merely on the private will of men like Capt. Brown and his associates, but on the great general causes which move all human kind to hate wrong and love right. Such "insurrections" will continue as long as slavery lasts, and will increase, both in frequency and in power, just as the people become intelligent and moral. Virginia may hang John Brown and all that family, but she cannot hang the HUMAN RACE; and until that is done, noble men will rejoice in the motto of that once magnanimous State—" *Sic semper Tyrannis!*" "Let such be the end of every oppressor."

It is a good anti-slavery picture on the Virginia shield:—a man standing on a tyrant and chopping his head off with a sword; only I would paint the sword-holder *black* and the tyrant *white*, to show the *immediate application* of the principle. The American people will have to march to rather severe music, I think, and it is better for them to face it in season. A few years ago it did not seem difficult first to check slavery, and then to end it without any bloodshed. I think this cannot be done now, nor ever in the future. All the great charters of HUMANITY have been writ in blood. I once hoped that of American Democracy would be engrossed in less costly ink; but it is plain, now, that our pilgrimage must lead through a Red Sea, wherein many a Pharaoh will go under and perish. Alas! that we are not wise enough to be just, or just enough to be wise, and so gain much at small cost!

Look, now, at a few notorious facts:

I. There are four million slaves in the United States violently withheld from their natural right to life, liberty, and the pursuit of happiness. Now, they are our fellow-countrymen—yours and mine, just as much as any four million *white* men. Of course, you and I owe them the duty which one man owes another of his own nation—the duty of instruction, advice, and protection of natural rights. If they are starving, we ought to help feed them. The colour of their skins, their degraded social condition, their ignorance, abates nothing from their natural claim on us, or from our natural duty toward them.

There are men in all the Northern States who feel the obligation which citizenship imposes on them—the duty to help those slaves. Hence arose the ANTI-SLAVERY SOCIETY, which seeks simply to excite the white people to perform their natural duty to their dark fellow-countrymen. Hence comes CAPT. BROWN'S EXPEDITION —an attempt to help his countrymen enjoy their natural right to life, liberty, and the pursuit of happiness.

He sought by violence what the Anti-Slavery Society works for with other weapons. The two agree in the end, and differ only in the means. Men like Capt. Brown will be continually rising up among the white people of the Free States, attempting to do their *natural duty* to their black countrymen—that is, help them to freedom. Some of these efforts will be successful. Thus, last winter Capt. Brown himself escorted eleven of his countrymen from bondage in Missouri to freedom in Canada. He did not snap a gun, I think, although then, as more recently, he had his fighting tools at hand, and would have used them, if necessary. Even now the under-ground railroad is in constant and beneficent operation. By-and-by it will be an over-ground railroad from Mason and Dixon's line clear to Canada : the only *tunnelling* will be in the slave States. Northern men applaud the brave conductors of that locomotive of liberty.

When Thomas Garrett was introduced to a meeting of political free-soilers in Boston, as "the man who had helped 1800 slaves to their natural liberty," even that meeting gave the righteous quaker *three times three*. All honest Northern hearts beat with admiration of such men; nay, with love for them. Young lads say, "I wish that heaven would make me such a man." The wish will now and then be father to the fact. You and I have had opportunity enough, in twenty years, to see that this philanthropic patriotism is on the increase at the North, and the special direction it takes is toward the liberation of their countrymen in bondage.

Not many years ago Boston sent money to help the Greeks in their struggle for *political freedom* (they never quite lost their *personal liberty*), but with the money she sent what was more valuable and far more precious, one of her most valiant and heroic sons, who staid in Greece to fight the great battle of humanity. Did your friend, Dr Samuel G. Howe, lose the esteem of New-England men by that act? He won the admiration of Europe, and holds it still.

Nay, still later, the same dear old Boston—Hunkers have never been more than rats and mice in her house, which she suffers for a time, and then drives out twelve hundred of them at once on a certain day of March, 1776,—that same dear old Boston sent the same Dr Howe to carry aid and comfort to the Poles, then in deadly struggle for their political existence. Was he disgraced because he lay seven and-forty days in a Prussian jail in Berlin? Not even in the eyes of the Prussian King, who afterwards sent him a gold medal, whose metal was worth as many dollars as that philanthropist lay days in the despot's jail. It is said, "Charity should begin at home." The American began a good way off, but has been working homeward ever since. The Dr Howe of to-day would and ought to be more ready to help an American to *personal liberty*, than a Pole or a Greek to mere political freedom, and would find more men to furnish aid and comfort to our own countrymen, even if they were black. It would not surprise me if there were other and well-planned attempts in other States to do what Captain Brown heroically, if not successfully, tried in Virginia. Nine out of ten may fail—the tenth will succeed. The victory over Gen. Burgoyne more than made up for all the losses in many a previous defeat; it was the beginning of the end. Slavery will not die a dry death, it may have as many lives as a cat; at last, it will die like a mad dog in a village, with only the enemies of the human kind to lament its fate, and they too cowardly to appear as mourners.

II. But it is not merely white men who will fight for the liberty of Americans; the negroes will take their defence into their own hands, especially if they can find white men to lead them. No doubt the African race is greatly inferior to the Caucasian in general intellectual power, and also in that instinct for liberty which is so strong in the Teutonic family, and just now obvious in the Anglo-Saxons of Britain and America; besides, the African race have but little desire for vengeance—the lowest form of the love of justice. Here is one example out of many: In Santa Cruz the old slave laws were the most horrible, I think, I ever read of in modern times, unless those of the Carolinas be an exception. If a slave excited others to run away, for the first offence his right leg was to be cut off; for the second offence, his other leg. This mutilation was not to be done by a surgeon's hand; the poor wretch was laid down on a log, and his legs chopped off with a plantation axe, and the stumps plunged into boiling pitch to stanch the blood, and so save the *property* from entire destruction; for the live *torso* of a slave might serve as a warning. No action of a court was requisite to inflict this punishment; any master could thus mutilate his bondman. Even from 1830 to 1846, it was common for owners to beat their offending victims with "tamarind rods" six feet long and an inch in thickness at the bigger end—rods thick set with ugly thorns. When that process was over, the lacerated back was washed with a decoction of the Manchineel, a poison tree, which made the wounds fester, and long remain open.

In 1846, the negroes were in "rebellion," and took possession of the island; they were 25,000, the whites 3000. But the blacks did not hurt the hair of a white man's head; they got their freedom, but they took no revenge! Suppose 25,000 Americans, held in bondage by 3000 Algerines on a little island, should get their masters into their hands, how many of the 3000 would see the next sun go down?

No doubt it is through the absence of this desire of natural vengeance that the Africans have been reduced to bondage, and kept in it.

But *there is a limit even to the negro's forbearance.* San Domingo is not a great way off. The revolution which changed its black inhabitants from tame slaves into wild men, took place after you had ceased to call yourself a boy.

It shows what may be in America, with no white man to help. In the slave States there is many a possible San Domingo, which may become actual any day; and, if not in 1860, then in some other "year of our Lord." Besides, America offers more than any other country to excite the slave to love of liberty, and the effort for it. We are always talking about "liberty," boasting that we are "the freest people in the world," declaring that "a man would die rather than be a slave." We continually praise our fathers "who fought the Revolution." We build monuments to commemorate even the humblest beginning of that great national work. Once a year we stop all ordinary work, and give up a whole day to the noisiest kind of rejoicing for the War of Independence. How we praise the "champions of liberty!" How we point out the "infamy of the British oppressors!" "They would make our fathers slaves," say we, "and we slew the oppressor—SIC SEMPER TYRANNIS!"

Do you suppose this will fail to produce its effect on the black man, one day? The South must either give up keeping "Independence Day," or else keep it in a little more thorough fashion. Nor is this all: the Southerners are continually taunting the negroes with their miserable nature. "You are only half human," say they, "not capable of freedom." "Hay is good for horses, not for hogs," said the *philosophic* American, who now "represents the great Democracy" at the court of Turin. *So, liberty is good for white men, not for negroes.* Have they souls? I don't know that—*non mi ricordo.* "Contempt," says the proverb, "will cut through the shell of the tortoise." And, one day, even the sluggish African will wake up under the three-fold stimulus of the fourth of July cannon, the whip of the slaveholder, and the sting of his heartless mockery. Then, if "oppression maketh wise men mad," what do you think it will do to African slaves, who are familiar with scenes of violence, and all manner of cruelty? Still more: if the negroes have not general power of mind, or instinctive love of liberty, equal to the whites, they are much our superiors in *power of cunning*, and in *contempt for death*—rather formidable qualities in a servile war. There already have been several risings of slaves in this century; they spread fear and consternation. The future will be more terrible. Now, in case of insurrection, not only is there, as Jefferson said, "no attribute of the Almighty" which can take sides with the master, but *there will be many white men who will take part with the slave.* Men, like the Lafayettes of the last century, and the Dr. Howes of this, may give the insurgent negro as effectual aid as that once rendered to America and Greece; and the public opinion of an enlightened world will rank them among its heroes of noblest mark.

If I remember rightly, some of your fathers were in the battle of Lexington, and that at Bunker Hill. I believe, in the course of the war which followed, every able-bodied man in your town (Newton) was in actual service. Now-a-days their descendants are proud of the fact. One day it will be thought not less heroic for a negro to fight for his personal liberty, than for a white man to fight for political independence, and against a tax of three pence a pound on tea. Wait a little, and things will come round.

III. The existence of slavery endangers all our Democratic institutions. It does this if only tolerated as an exceptional measure—a matter of present convenience, and still more when proclaimed as an instantial principle, a rule of political conduct for all time and every place. Look at this: In 1790 there were (say) 300,000 slaves;

soon they make their first doubling, and are 600,000; then their second, 1,200,000; then their third, 2,400,000. They are now in the process of doubling the fourth time, and will soon be 4,800,000; then comes the fifth double, 9,600,000; then the sixth, 19,200,000. Before the year of our Lord nineteen hundred there will be twenty million slaves!

An Anglo-Saxon with common sense does not like this Africanization of America; he wishes the superior race to multiply rather than the inferior. Besides, it is plain to a one-eyed man that slavery is an irreconcilable enemy of the progressive development of Democracy; that, if allowed to exist, it must be allowed to spread, to gain political, social, and ecclesiastical power; and all that it gains for the slaveholders is just so much taken from the freemen.

Look at this—there are twenty Southern representatives who represent nothing but property in man, and yet their vote counts as much in Congress as the twenty Northerners who stand for the will of 1,800,000 freemen. Slavery gives the South the same advantage in the choice of President; consequently the slaveholding South has long controlled the Federal power of the nation.

Look at the recent acts of the slave power! The Fugitive Slave bill, the Kansas-Nebraska bill, the Dred Scott decision, the fillibustering against Cuba (till found too strong), and now against Mexico and other feeble neighbours, and, to crown all, the actual re-opening of the African slave-trade!

The South has kidnapped men in Boston, and made the Judges of Massachusetts go under her symbolic chain to enter the courts of justice (!) She has burned houses and butchered innocent men in Kansas, and the perpetrators of that wickedness were rewarded by the Federal government with high office and great pay! Those things are notorious; they have stirred up some little indignation at the North, and freemen begin to think of defending their liberty. Hence came the Free-Soil party, and hence the Republican party—it contemplates no direct benefit to the slave, only the defence of the white man in his national rights, or his conventional privileges. It will grow stronger every year, and also bolder. It must lay down principles as a platform to work its measure on; the principles will be found to require much more than what was at first proposed, and even from this platform Republicans will promptly see that *they cannot defend the natural rights of freemen without destroying that slavery which takes away the natural rights of a negro.* So, first, the wise and just men of the party will sympathize with such as seek

262

to liberate the slaves, either peacefully or by violence; next, they will declare their opinions in public; and finally, the whole body of the party will come to the same sympathy and the same opinion. Then, of course, they will encourage men like Capt. Brown, give him money and all manner of help, and also encourage the slaves whenever they shall rise to take their liberty, at all hazards. When called to help put down an insurrection of the slaves, they will go readily enough and do the work by removing the cause of insurrection—that is—*by destroying slavery itself.*

An Anti-slavery party, under one name or another, will before long control the Federal Government, and will exercise its constitutional rights, and perform its constitutional duty, and "guarantee a Republican form of government to every State in the Union." That is a work of time and peaceful legislation. But the short work of violence will be often tried, and each attempt will gain something for the cause of humanity, even by its dreadful process of blood.

IV. But there is yet another agency that will act against slavery. There are many mischievous persons who are ready for any wicked work of violence. They abound in the city of New York (a sort of sink where the villany of both hemispheres settles down, and genders that moral pestilence which steams up along the columns of the *New York Herald* and the *New York Observer*, the great escape-pipes of secular and ecclesiastical wickedness), they commit the great crimes of violence and robbery at home, plunder emigrants, and engage in the slave-trade, or venture on fillibustering expeditions. This class of persons is common in all the South. One of the legitimate products of her "peculiar institution," they are familiar with violence, ready and able for murder. Public opinion sustains such men. Bully Brooks was but one of their representatives in Congress. Now-a-days they are fond of slavery, defend it, and seek to spread it. But the time must come one day—it may come any time—when the lovers of mischief will do a little fillibustering at home, and rouse up the slaves to rob, burn, and kill. Prudent carpenters sweep up all the shavings in their shops at night, and remove this food of conflagration to a safe place, lest the spark of a candle, the end of a cigar, or a friction-match should swiftly end their wealth, slowly gathered together. The South takes pains to strew her carpenter's shop with shavings, and fill it full thereof. She encourages men to walk abroad with naked candles in their hands and lighted cigars in their mouths; then they scatter friction-matches on the floor, and dance a fillibustering jig thereon. She cries, " Well done! Hurrah for Walker! " " Hurrah for Brooks! " " Hurrah for the bark Wanderer and its cargo of slaves! Up with the bowie-knife! Down with justice and humanity! " The South must reap as she sows; where she scatters the wind, the whirlwind will come up. It will be a pretty crop for her to reap. Within a few years the South has BURNED ALIVE eight or ten negroes. Other black men looked on, and learned how to fasten the chain, how to pile the green wood, how to set this hell-fire of slavery agoing. The apprentice may be slow to learn, but he has had teaching enough by this time to know the art and mystery of torture; and, depend upon it, the negro will one day apply it to his old tormentors. The fire of vengeance may be waked up even in an African's heart, especially when it is fanned by the wickedness of a white man : then it runs from man to man, from town to town. What shall put it out? *The white man's blood!*

Now, slavery is a wickedness so vast and so old, so rich and so respectable, supported by the State, the press, the market, and the Church, that all those agencies are needed to oppose it with—those, and many more which I cannot speak of now. You and I prefer the peaceful method; but I, at least, shall welcome the violent, if no other accomplish the end. So will the great mass of thoughtful and good men at the North; else why do we honour the heroes of the Revolution, and build them monuments all over our blessed New-England? I think you gave money for that of Bunker Hill : I once thought it a folly; now I recognize it as a great sermon in stone, which is worth not only all the money it cost to build it, but all the blood it took to lay its corner-stones. Trust me, its lesson will not be in vain—at the North, I mean, for the LOGIC OF SLAVERY will keep the South on its lower course, and drive it on more swiftly than before. " Capt. Brown's expedition was a failure," I hear it said. I am not quite sure of that. True, it kills fifteen men by sword and shot, and four or five men by the gallows. But it shows the weakness of the greatest slave State in America, the worthlessness of her soldiery, and the utter fear which slavery genders in the bosoms of the masters. Think of the condition of the city of Washington while Brown was at work!

Brown will die, I think, like a martyr, and also like a saint. His noble demeanour, his unflinching bravery, his gentleness, his calm, religious trust in God, and his words of truth and soberness, cannot fail to make a profound impression on the hearts of Northern men;

yes, and on Southern men. For "every human heart is human," &c. I do not think the money wasted, nor the lives thrown away. Many acorns must be sown to have one come up; even then, the plant grows slow; but it is an oak at last. None of the Christian martyrs died in vain; and from Stephen, who was stoned at Jerusalem, to Mary Dyer, whom our fathers hanged on a bough of "the great tree" on Boston Common, I think there have been few spirits more pure and devoted than John Brown's, and none that gave up their breath in a nobler cause. Let the American State hang his body, and the American Church damn his soul; still, the blessing of such as are ready to perish will fall on him, and the universal justice of the Infinitely perfect God will take him welcome home. The road to heaven is as short from the gallows as from a throne; perhaps, also, as easy.

I suppose you would like to know something about myself. Rome has treated me to bad weather, which tells its story in my health, and certainly does not mend me. But I look for brighter days and happier nights. The sad tidings from America—my friends in peril, in exile, in jail, killed, or to be hung—have filled me with grief, and so I fall back a little, but hope to get forward again. God bless you and yours, and comfort you!

Ever affectionately yours,
THEODORE PARKER.

TO HARRIET BEECHER STOWE

Oliver Wendell Holmes
1809-1894

. . . .

All through the conflict, up and down
Marched Uncle Tom and Old John Brown,
   One ghost, one form ideal;
And which was false and which was true,
And which was mightier of the two,
The wisest sibyl never knew,
   For both alike were real.

Wendell Phillips, (1811-1884), was one of the foremost anti-slavery leaders of his day, a friend and co-worker of William Lloyd Garrison, and a great orator. This eulogy was delivered at the grave of John Brown, at North Elba, on December 8, 1859.

BURIAL OF JOHN BROWN

Wendell Phillips

How feeble words seem here! How can I hope to utter what your hearts are full of? I fear to disturb the harmony which his life breathes round this home. One and another of you, his neighbors, say, "I have known him five years," "I have known him ten years." It seems to me as if we had none of us known him. How our admiring, loving wonder has grown, day by day, as he has unfolded trait after trait of earnest, brave, tender, Christian life! We see him walking with radiant, serene face to the scaffold, and think what an iron heart, what devoted faith! We take up his letters, beginning "My dear wife and children, every one,"—see him stoop on his way to the scaffold and kiss that negro child,—and this iron heart seems all tenderness. Marvellous old man! We have hardly said it when the loved forms of his sons, in the bloom of young devotion, encircle him, and we remember he is not alone, only the majestic centre of a group. Your neighbor farmer went, surrounded by his household, to tell the slaves there were still hearts and right arms ready and nerved for their service. From this roof four, from a neighboring roof two, to make up that score of heroes. How resolute each looked into the face of Virginia, how loyally each stood at his forlorn post, meeting death cheerfully, till that master-voice said, "It is enough." And these weeping children and widow seem so lifted up and consecrated by long, single-hearted devotion to his great purpose, that we dare, even at this moment, to remind them how blessed they are in the privilege of thinking that in the last throbs of those brave young hearts, which lie buried on the banks of the Shenandoah, thoughts of them mingled with love to God and hope for the slave.

He has abolished slavery in Virginia. You may say this is too much. Our neighbors are the last men we know. The hours that pass us are the ones we appreciate the least. Men walked Boston streets, when night fell on Bunker's Hill, and pitied Warren, saying, "Foolish man! Thrown away his life! Why didn't he measure his means better?" Now we see him standing colossal on that blood-stained sod, and severing that day the tie which bound Boston to Great Britain. That night George III. ceased to rule in New England. History will date Virginia Emancipation from Harper's Ferry. True, the slave is still there. So, when the tempest uproots a pine on your hills, it looks green for months,—a year or two. Still, it is timber, not a tree. John Brown has loosened the roots of the slave system; it only breathes,—it does not live,—hereafter.

Men say, "How coolly brave!" But matchless courage seems the least of his merits. How gentleness graced it! When the frightened town wished to bear off the body of the Mayor, a man said, "I will go, Miss Fowke,[1] under their rifles, if you will stand between them and me." He knew he could trust their gentle respect for woman. He was right. He went in the thick of the fight and bore off the body in safety. That same girl flung herself between Virginia rifles and your brave young Thompson. They had no pity. The pitiless bullet reached him, spite of woman's prayers, though the fight had long been over. How God has blessed him! How truly he may say, "I have fought a good fight, I have *finished* my course." Truly he has *finished*,—done his work. God granted him the privilege to look on his work accomplished. He said, "I will show the South that twenty men can take possession of a town, hold it twenty-four hours, and carry away all the slaves who wish to escape." Did he not do it? On Monday night he stood master of Harper's Ferry,—could have left unchecked with a score or a hundred slaves. The wide sympathy and secret approval are shown by the eager, quivering lips of lovers of slavery, asking, "O, why did he not take his victory and go away?" Who checked him at last? Not startled Virginia. Her he had conquered. The Union crushed,—seemed to crush him. In reality God said, "That work is done; you have proved that a Slave State is only fear in the mask of despotism; come up higher, and baptize by your martyrdom a million hearts into holier life." Surely such a life is no failure. How vast the change in men's hearts! Insurrection was a harsh, horrid word to millions a month ago. John Brown went a whole generation beyond it, claiming the right for white men to help the slave to freedom by arms. And now men run up and down, not disputing his principle, but trying to frame excuses for Virginia's hanging of so pure, honest, high-hearted, and heroic a man. Virginia stands at the bar of the civilized world on trial. Round her victim crowd the apostles and martyrs, all the brave, high souls who have said, "God is God," and trodden wicked

[1] Fouke.

laws under their feet. As I stood looking at his grandfather's grave-
stone, brought here from Connecticut, telling, as it does, of his death
in the Revolution, I thought I could hear our hero-saint saying, "My
fathers gave their swords to the oppressor,—the slave still sinks
before the pledged force of this nation. I give my sword to the slave
my fathers forgot." If any swords ever reflected the smile of Heaven,
surely it was those drawn at Harper's Ferry. If our God is ever the
Lord of Hosts, making one man chase a thousand, surely that little
band might claim him for their captain. Harper's Ferry was no single
hour, standing alone,—taken out from a common life,—it was the
flowering out of fifty years of single-hearted devotion. He must have
lived wholly for one great idea, when these who owe their being to
him, and these whom love has joined to the circle, group so har-
moniously around him, each accepting serenely his and her part.

I feel honored to stand under such a roof. Hereafter you will tell
children standing at your knees, "I saw John Brown buried,—I sat
under his roof." Thank God for such a master. Could we have asked
a nobler representative of the Christian North putting her foot on
the accursed system of slavery? As time passes, and these hours float
back into history, men will see against the clear December sky that
gallows, and round it thousands of armed men guarding Virginia
from her slaves. On the other side, the serene brow of that calm old
man, as he stoops to kiss the child of a forlorn race.[2] Thank God for
our emblem. May he soon bring Virginia to blot out hers in repent-
ant shame, and cover that hateful gallows and soldiery with thousands of broken fetters.

What lesson shall those lips teach us? Before that still, calm brow
let us take a new baptism. How can we stand here without a fresh
and utter consecration? These tears! how shall we dare even to
offer consolation? Only lips fresh from such a vow have the right to
mingle their words with your tears. We envy you your nearer place
to these martyred children of God. I do not believe slavery will go
down in blood. Ours is the age of thought. Hearts are stronger than
swords. That last fortnight! How sublime its lesson! the Christian
one of conscience,—of truth. Virginia is weak, because each man's
heart said amen to John Brown. His words,—they are stronger even
than his rifles. These crushed a State. Those have changed the
thoughts of millions, and will yet crush slavery. Men said, "Would
he had died in arms!" God ordered better, and granted to him and

2 The story that John Brown, on the way to the gallows, stooped to kiss a Negro child, originated
in the mind of an over-imaginative reporter. Although widely referred to and accepted as fact at
the time and for years afterward, it never actually occurred.

the slave those noble prison hours,—that single hour of death; granted him a higher than the soldier's place, that of teacher; the echoes of his rifles have died away in the hills,—a million hearts guard his words. God bless this roof,—make it bless us. We dare not say bless you, children of this home! you stand nearer to one whose lips God touched, and we rather bend for your blessing. God make us all worthier of him whose dust we lay among these hills he loved. Here he girded himself and went forth to battle. Fuller success than his heart ever dreamed God granted him. He sleeps in the blessings of the crushed and the poor, and men believe more firmly in virtue, now that such a man has lived. Standing here, let us thank God for a firmer faith and fuller hope.

Ralph Waldo Emerson met Brown in March, 1857, at Henry Thoreau's home. After Harpers Ferry, Emerson delivered several speeches in Brown's defense. His most famous remark concerning Brown was on November 8, 1859, in Boston, in a lecture on " Courage," in which he predicted that Brown's martyrdom " will make the gallows as glorious as the cross." On November 18th, he spoke at a meeting for the relief of Brown's family, in Boston's Tremont Temple. The following address was delivered at Salem, on January 6, 1860.

JOHN BROWN

Ralph Waldo Emerson

Mr. Chairman :

I have been struck with one fact, that the best orators who have added their praise to his fame,—and I need not go out of this house to find the purest eloquence in the country,—have one rival who comes off a little better, and that is *JOHN BROWN*. Every thing that is said of him leaves people a little dissatisfied; but as soon as they read his own speeches and letters they are heartily contented,—such is the singleness of purpose which justifies him to the head and the heart of all. Taught by this experience, I mean, in the few remarks I have to make, to cling to his history, or let him speak for himself.

John Brown, the founder of liberty in Kansas, was born in Torrington, Litchfield County, Conn., in 1800. When he was five years old his father emigrated to Ohio, and the boy was there set to keep sheep and to look after cattle and dress skins; he went bareheaded and barefooted, and clothed in buckskin. He said that he loved rough play, could never have rough play enough; could not see a seedy hat without wishing to pull it off. But for this it needed that the playmates should be equal; not one in fine clothes and the other in buckskin; not one his own master, hale and hearty, and the other watched and whipped. But it chanced that in Pennsylvania, where he was sent by his father to collect cattle, he fell in with a boy whom he heartily liked and whom he looked upon as his superior. This boy was a slave; he saw him beaten with an iron shovel, and otherwise maltreated; he saw that this boy had nothing better to look forward to in life, whilst he himself was petted and made much of; for he was much considered in the family where he then stayed, from the circumstance that this boy of twelve years had conducted alone a drove of cattle a hundred miles. But the colored boy had no friend, and no future. This worked such indignation in him that he swore an oath of resistance to Slavery as long as he lived. And thus his enterprise to go into Virginia and run off five hundred or a thousand slaves was not a piece of spite or revenge, a plot of two years or of twenty years, but the keeping of an oath made to Heaven and earth forty-seven years before. Forty-seven years at least, though I incline to accept his own account of the matter at Charlestown, which makes the date a little older, when he said, "This was all settled millions of years before the world was made."

He grew up a religious and manly person, in severe poverty; a fair specimen of the best stock of New England; having that force of thought and that sense of right which are the warp and woof of greatness. Our farmers were Orthodox Calvinists, mighty in the Scriptures; had learned that life was a preparation, a "probation," to use their word, for a higher world, and was to be spent in loving and serving mankind.

Thus was formed a romantic character absolutely without any vulgar traits; living to ideal ends, without any mixture of self-indulgence or compromise, such as lowers the value of benevolent and thoughtful men we know; abstemious, refusing luxuries, not sourly and reproachfully but simply as unfit for his habit; quiet and gentle as a child in the house. And, as happens usually to men of romantic character, his fortunes were romantic. Walter Scott would have delighted to draw his picture and trace his adventurous career. A shepherd and herdsman, he learned the manners of animals and knew the secret signals by which animals communicate. He made his hard bed on the mountains with them; he learned to drive his flock through thickets all but impassable; he had all the skill of a shepherd by choice of breed and by wise husbandry to obtain the best wool, and that for a course of years. And the anecdotes preserved show a far-seeing skill and conduct which, in spite of adverse accidents, should secure, one year with another, an honest reward, first to the farmer, and afterwards to the dealer. If he kept sheep, it was with a royal mind; and if he traded in wool, he was a merchant prince, not in the amount of wealth, but in the protection of the interests confided to him.

I am not a little surprised at the easy effrontery with which political gentlemen, in and out of Congress, take it upon them to say that there are not a thousand men in the North who sympathize with John Brown. It would be far safer and nearer the truth to say that all people, in proportion to their sensibility and self-respect, sympathize with him. For it is impossible to see courage, and disinterestedness, and the love that casts out fear, without sympathy. All women are drawn to him by their predominance of sentiment. All gentlemen, of course, are on his side. I do not mean by "gentlemen," people of scented hair and perfumed handkerchiefs, but men of gentle blood and generosity, "fulfilled with all nobleness," who, like the Cid, give the outcast leper a share of their bed; like the dying Sidney, pass the cup of cold water to the wounded soldier who needs it more. For what is the oath of gentle blood and knighthood? What but to protect the weak and lowly against the strong oppressor?

Nothing is more absurd than to complain of this sympathy, or to complain of a party of men united in opposition to Slavery. As well complain of gravity, or the ebb of the tide. Who makes the Abolitionist? The Slaveholder. The sentiment of mercy is the natural recoil which the laws of the universe provide to protect mankind from destruction by savage passions. And our blind statesmen go up and down, with committees of vigilance and safety, hunting for the origin of this new heresy. They will need a very vigilant committee indeed to find its birthplace, and a very strong force to root it out. For the arch-Abolitionist, older than Brown, and older than the Shenandoah Mountains, is Love, whose other name is Justice, which was before Alfred, before Lycurgus, before Slavery, and will be after it.

Thoreau delivered three addresses on John Brown. The first, on October 30, 1859, was read by Thoreau in the Concord Town Hall, at a meeting which he himself called, and which gave him the distinction of being, in the words of Henry Seidel Canby and Raymond William Adams, " the first American to make public utterance in defense of Brown." As the editor of Thoreau's collected *Writings* remarks, " When Captain Brown lay in prison, Thoreau did not wait for a public meeting, but went about among his neighbors, summoning them to come together to hear what he had to say." The second address, " After the Death of John Brown," was given at Concord on the day of Brown's execution; the third, " The Last Days of John Brown," which is reprinted here, was read at North Elba on July 4, 1860.

THE LAST DAYS OF JOHN BROWN

Henry David Thoreau

John Brown's career for the last six weeks of his life was meteor-like, flashing through the darkness in which we live. I know of nothing so miraculous in our history.

If any person, in a lecture or conversation at that time, cited any ancient example of heroism, such as Cato or Tell or Winkelried, passing over the recent deeds and words of Brown, it was felt by any intelligent audience of Northern men to be tame and inexcusably far-fetched.

For my own part, I commonly attend more to nature than to man, but any affecting human event may blind our eyes to natural objects. I was so absorbed in him as to be surprised whenever I detected the routine of the natural world surviving still, or met persons going about their affairs indifferent. It appeared strange to me that the " little dipper" should be still diving quietly in the river, as of yore; and it suggested that this bird might continue to dive here when Concord should be no more.

I felt that he, a prisoner in the midst of his enemies and under sentence of death, if consulted as to his next step or resource, could answer more wisely than all his countrymen beside. He best understood his position; he contemplated it most calmly. Comparatively, all other men, North and South, were beside themselves. Our thoughts could not revert to any greater or wiser or better man with whom to contrast him, for he, then and there, was above them all. The man this country was about to hang appeared the greatest and best in it.

Years were not required for a revolution of public opinion; days, nay hours, produced marked changes in this case. Fifty who were ready to say, on going into our meeting in honor of him in Concord, that he ought to be hung, would not say it when they came out. They heard his words read; they saw the earnest faces of the congregation; and perhaps they joined at last in singing the hymn in his praise.

The order of instructors was reversed. I heard that one preacher, who at first was shocked and stood aloof, felt obliged at last, after he was hung, to make him the subject of a sermon, in which, to some extent, he eulogized the man, but said that his act was a failure. An influential class-teacher thought it necessary, after the services, to tell his grown-up pupils that at first he thought as the preacher did then, but now he thought that John Brown was right. But it was understood that his pupils were as much ahead of the teacher as he was ahead of the priest; and I know for a certainty that very little boys at home had already asked their parents, in a tone of surprise, why God did not interfere to save him. In each case, the constituted teachers were only half conscious that they were not *leading*, but being *dragged*, with some loss of time and power.

The more conscientious preachers, the Bible men, they who talk about principle, and doing to others as you would that they should do unto you,—how could they fail to recognize him, by far the greatest preacher of them all, with the Bible in his life and in his acts, the embodiment of principle, who actually carried out the golden rule? All whose moral sense had been aroused, who had a calling from on high to preach, sided with him. What confessions he extracted from the cold and conservative! It is remarkable, but on the whole it is well, that it did not prove the occasion for a new sect of *Brownites* being formed in our midst.

They, whether within the Church or out of it, who adhere to the spirit and let go the letter, and are accordingly called infidel, were as usual foremost to recognize him. Men have been hung in the South before for attempting to rescue slaves, and the North was not much stirred by it. Whence, then, this wonderful difference? We were not so sure of *their* devotion to principle. We made a subtle distinction, forgot human laws, and did homage to an idea. The North, I mean the *living* North, was suddenly all transcendental. It went behind the human law, it went behind the apparent failure, and recognized eternal justice and glory. Commonly, men live according to a formula, and are satisfied if the order of law is observed, but in this instance they, to some extent, returned to

273

original perceptions, and there was a slight revival of old religion. They saw that what was called order was confusion, what was called justice, injustice, and that the best was deemed the worst. This attitude suggested a more intelligent and generous spirit than that which actuated our forefathers, and the possibility, in the course of ages, of a revolution in behalf of another and an oppressed people.

Most Northern men, and a few Southern ones, were wonderfully stirred by Brown's behavior and words. They saw and felt that they were heroic and noble, and that there had been nothing quite equal to them in their kind in this country, or in the recent history of the world. But the minority were unmoved by them. They were only surprised and provoked by the attitude of their neighbors. They saw that Brown was brave, and that he believed that he had done right, but they did not detect any further peculiarity in him. Not being accustomed to make fine distinctions, or to appreciate magnanimity, they read his letters and speeches as if they read them not. They were not aware when they *burned*. They did not feel that he spoke with authority, and hence they only remembered that the *law* must be executed. They remembered the old formula, but did not hear the new revelation. The man who does not recognize in Brown's words a wisdom and nobleness, and therefore an authority, superior to our laws, is a modern Democrat. This is the test by which to discover him. He is not willfully but constitutionally blind on this side, and he is consistent with himself. Such has been his past life; no doubt about it. In like manner he has read history and his Bible, and he accepts, or seems to accept, the last only as an established formula, and not because he has been convicted by it. You will not find kindred sentiments in his commonplace book, if he has one.

When a noble deed is done, who is likely to appreciate it? They who are noble themselves. I was not surprised that certain of my neighbors spoke of John Brown as an ordinary felon, for who are they? They have either much flesh, or much office, or much coarseness of some kind. They are not ethereal natures in any sense. The dark qualities predominate in them. Several of them are decidedly pachydermatous. I say it in sorrow, not in anger. How can a man behold the light who has no answering inward light? They are true to their *right*, but when they look this way they *see* nothing, they are blind. For the children of the light to contend with them is as if there should be a contest between eagles and owls. Show me a man who feels bitterly toward John Brown, and let me hear what noble verse he can repeat. He'll be as dumb as if his lips were stone.

It is not every man who can be a Christian, even in a very moderate sense, whatever education you give him. It is a matter of constitution and temperament, after all. He may have to be born again many times. I have known many a man who pretended to be a Christian, in whom it was ridiculous, for he had no genius for it. It is not every man who can be a freeman, even.

Editors persevered for a good while in saying that Brown was crazy; but at last they said only that it was "a crazy scheme," and the only evidence brought to prove it was that it cost him his life. I have no doubt that if he had gone with five thousand men, liberated a thousand slaves, killed a hundred or two slave-holders, and had as many more killed on his own side, but not lost his own life, these same editors would have called it by a more respectable name. Yet he has been far more successful than that. He has liberated many thousands of slaves, both North and South. They seem to have known nothing about living or dying for a principle. They all called him crazy then; who calls him crazy now?

All through the excitement occasioned by his remarkable attempt and subsequent behavior the Massachusetts Legislature, not taking any steps for the defense of her citizens who were likely to be carried to Virginia as witnesses and exposed to the violence of a slaveholding mob, was wholly absorbed in a liquor-agency question, and indulging in poor jokes on the word "extension." Bad spirits occupied their thoughts. I am sure that no statesman up to the occasion could have attended to that question at all at that time,—a very vulgar question to attend to at any time!

When I looked into a liturgy of the Church of England, printed near the end of the last century, in order to find a service applicable to the case of Brown, I found that the only martyr recognized and provided for by it was King Charles the First, an eminent scamp. Of all the inhabitants of England and of the world, he was the only one, according to this authority, whom that church had made a martyr and saint of; and for more than a century it had celebrated his martyrdom, so called, by an annual service. What a satire on the Church is that!

Look not to legislatures and churches for your guidance, nor to any soulless *incorporated* bodies, but to *inspirited* or inspired ones.

What avail all your scholarly accomplishments and learning, compared with wisdom and manhood? To omit his other behavior, see what a work this comparatively unread and unlettered man wrote within six weeks. Where is our professor of *belles-lettres*, or of logic and rhetoric, who can write so well? He wrote in prison, not a History of the World, like Raleigh, but an American book which I think will live longer than that. I do not know of such words, uttered under such circumstances, and so copiously withal, in Roman or English or any history. What a variety of themes he touched on in that short space! There are words in that letter to his wife, respecting the education of his daughters, which deserve to be framed and hung over every mantelpiece in the land. Compare this earnest wisdom with that of Poor Richard.

The death of Irving, which at any other time would have attracted universal attention, having occurred while these things were transpiring, went almost unobserved. I shall have to read of it in the biography of authors.

Literary gentlemen, editors, and critics think that they know how to write, because they have studied grammar and rhetoric; but they are egregiously mistaken. The *art* of composition is as simple as the discharge of a bullet from a rifle, and its masterpieces imply an infinitely greater force behind them. This unlettered man's speaking and writing are standard English. Some words and phrases deemed vulgarisms and Americanisms before, he has made standard American; such as "*It will pay.*" It suggests that the one great rule of composition—and if I were a professor of rhetoric I should insist on this—is, to *speak the truth*. This first, this second, this third; pebbles in your mouth or not. This demands earnestness and manhood chiefly.

We seem to have forgotten that the expression, a *liberal* education, originally meant among the Romans one worthy of *free* men; while the learning of trades and professions by which to get your livelihood merely was considered worthy of *slaves* only. But taking a hint from the word, I would go a step further, and say that it is not the man of wealth and leisure simply, though devoted to art, or science, or literature, who, in a true sense, is *liberally* educated, but only the earnest and *free* man. In a slaveholding country like this, there can be no such thing as a *liberal* education tolerated by the State; and those scholars of Austria and France who, however learned they may be, are contented under their tyrannies have received only a *servile* education.

Nothing could his enemies do but it redounded to his infinite advantage,—that is, to the advantage of his cause. They did not hang him at once, but reserved him to preach to them. And then there was another great blunder. They did not hang his four followers with him; that scene was still postponed; and so his victory was prolonged and completed. No theatrical manager could have arranged things so wisely to give effect to his behavior and words. And who, think you, *was* the manager? *Who* placed the slavewoman and her child, whom he stooped to kiss for a symbol, between his prison and the gallows?

We soon saw, as he saw, that he was not to be pardoned or rescued by men. That would have been to disarm him, to restore to him a material weapon, a Sharps rifle, when he had taken up the sword of the spirit—the sword with which he has really won his greater and most memorable victories. Now he has not laid aside the sword of the spirit, for he is pure spirit himself, and his sword is pure spirit also.

> " He nothing common did or mean
> Upon that memorable scene,
> Nor called the gods with vulgar spite,
> To vindicate his helpless right;
> But bowed his comely head
> Down as upon a bed."

What a transit was that of his horizontal body alone, but just cut down from the gallows-tree! We read that at such a time it passed through Philadelphia, and by Saturday night had reached New York. Thus like a meteor it shot through the Union from the Southern regions toward the North! No such freight had the cars borne since they carried him Southward alive.

On the day of his translation, I heard, to be sure, that he was *hung*, but I did not know what that meant; I felt no sorrow on that account; but not for a day or two did I even *hear* that he was *dead*, and not after any number of days shall I believe it. Of all the men who were said to be my contemporaries, it seemed to me that John Brown was the only one who *had not died*. I never hear of a man named Brown now,—and I hear of them pretty often,—I never hear of any particularly brave and earnest man, but my first thought is of John Brown, and what relation he may be to him. I meet him at every turn. He is more alive than ever he was. He has earned immortality. He is not confined to North Elba nor to Kansas. He is no longer working in secret. He works in public, and in the clearest light that shines on this land.

277

Frederick Douglass (1817-1895), an escaped slave, was a prominent Negro orator, journalist and anti-slavery leader. He met Brown in 1847 and became a close friend. This address, after being delivered on a number of previous occasions, was delivered at Harpers Ferry, on May 30, 1881, at the celebration of the fourteenth anniversary of the founding of Storer College, at Harpers Ferry, West Virginia—an institution for the education of Negro young people. The publication of the address in pamphlet form in 1881 was intended to provide funds for the endowment of a John Brown Professorship at Storer College.

The introduction to the pamphlet states that "Hon. Andrew Hunter, of Charlestown—the District Attorney who prosecuted John Brown and secured his execution—sat on the platform directly behind Mr. Douglass during the delivery of the entire address and at the close of it shook hands with him, and congratulated him, and invited him to Charlestown (where John Brown was hanged), adding that if Robert E. Lee were living, he would give him his hand also."

JOHN BROWN

Frederick Douglass

Not to fan the flame of sectional animosity now happily in the process of rapid and I hope permanent extinction; not to revive and keep alive a sense of shame and remorse for a great national crime, which has brought its own punishment, in loss of treasure, tears and blood; not to recount the long list of wrongs, inflicted on my race during more than two hundred years of merciless bondage; nor yet to draw, from the labyrinths of far-off centuries, incidents and achievements wherewith to rouse your passions, and enkindle your enthusiasm, but to pay a just debt long due, to vindicate in some degree a great historical character, of our own time and country, one with whom I was myself well acquainted, and whose friendship and confidence it was my good fortune to share, and to give you such recollections, impressions and facts, as I can, of a grand, brave and good old man, and especially to promote a better understanding of the raid upon Harper's Ferry of which he was the chief, is the object of this address.

In all the thirty years' conflict with slavery, if we except the late tremendous war, there is no subject which in its interest and importance will be remembered longer, or will form a more thrilling chapter in American history than this strange, wild, bloody and mournful drama. The story of it is still fresh in the minds of many who now hear me, but for the sake of those who may have forgotten its details, and in order to have our subject in its entire range more fully and clearly before us at the outset, I will briefly state the facts in that extraordinary transaction.

On the night of the 16th of October, 1859, there appeared near the confluence of the Potomac and Shenandoah rivers, a party of nineteen men—fourteen white and five colored. They were not only armed themselves, but had brought with them a large supply of arms for such persons as might join them. These men invaded Harper's Ferry, disarmed the watchman, took possession of the arsenal, rifle factory, armory and other government property at that place, arrested and made prisoners nearly all the prominent citizens of the neighborhood, collected about fifty slaves, put bayonets into the hands of such as were able and willing to fight for their liberty, killed three men, proclaimed a general emancipation, held the ground more than thirty hours, were subsequently overpowered and nearly all killed, wounded or captured, by a body of United States troops, under command of Colonel Robert E. Lee, since famous as the rebel Gen. Lee. Three out of the nineteen invaders were captured whilst fighting, and one of these was Captain John Brown, the man who originated, planned and commanded the expedition. At the time of his capture Capt. Brown was supposed to be mortally wounded, as he had several ugly gashes and bayonet wounds on his head and body; and apprehending that he might speedily die, or that he might be rescued by his friends, and thus the opportunity of making him a signal example of slave-holding vengeance would be lost, his captors hurried him to Charlestown two miles further within the border of Virginia, placed him in prison strongly guarded by troops, and before his wounds were healed he was brought into court, subjected to a nominal trial, convicted of high treason and inciting slaves to insurrection, and was executed. His corpse was given to his woe-stricken widow, and she, assisted by Anti-slavery friends, caused it to be borne to North Elba, Essex County, N. Y., and there his dust now reposes, amid the silent, solemn and snowy grandeur of the Adirondacks.

Such is the story; with no line softened or hardened to my inclining. It certainly is not a story to please, but to pain. It is not a story to increase our sense of social safety and security, but to fill the imagination with wild and troubled fancies of doubt and danger. It was a sudden and startling surprise to the people of Harper's Ferry, and it is not easy to conceive of a situation more abundant in all the elements of horror and consternation. They had retired as usual to rest, with no suspicion that an enemy lurked in the surrounding darkness. They had quietly and trustingly given themselves up to "tired Nature's sweet restorer, balmy sleep," and while thus all unconscious of danger, they were roused from their peaceful slumbers by the sharp crack of the invader's rifle, and felt the keen-edged sword of war at their throats, three of their number being already slain.

Every feeling of the human heart was naturally outraged at this occurrence, and hence at the moment the air was full of denunciation and execration. So intense was this feeling, that few ventured to whisper a word of apology. But happily reason has her voice as well as feeling, and though slower in deciding, her judgments are broader, deeper, clearer and more enduring. It is not easy to reconcile human feeling to the shedding of blood for any purpose, unless indeed in the excitement which the shedding of blood itself occasions. The knife is to feeling always an offence. Even when in the hands of a skillful surgeon, it refuses consent to the operation long after reason has demonstrated its necessity. It even pleads the cause of the known murderer on the day of his execution, and calls society half criminal when, in cold blood, it takes life as a protection of itself from crime. Let no word be said against this holy feeling; more than to law and government are we indebted to this tender sentiment of regard for human life for the safety with which we walk the streets by day and sleep secure in our beds at night. It is nature's grand police, vigilant and faithful, sentineled in the soul, guarding against violence to peace and life. But whilst so much is freely accorded to feeling in the economy of human welfare, something more than feeling is necessary to grapple with a fact so grim and significant as was this raid. Viewed apart and alone, as a transaction separate and distinct from its antecedents and bearings, it takes rank with the most cold-blooded and atrocious wrongs ever perpetrated; but just here is the trouble—this raid on Harper's Ferry, no more than Sherman's march to the sea can consent to be thus viewed alone.

There is, in the world's government, a force which has in all ages been recognized, sometimes as Nemesis, sometimes as the judgment of God and sometimes as retributive justice; but under whatever name, all history attests the wisdom and beneficence of its chastisements, and men become reconciled to the agents through whom it operates, and have extolled them as heroes, benefactors and demi-gods.

To the broad vision of a true philosophy, nothing in this world stands alone. Everything is a necessary part of everything else. The margin of chance is narrowed by every extension of reason and knowledge, and nothing comes unbidden to the feast of human experience. The universe, of which we are a part, is continually proving itself a stupendous whole, a system of law and order, eternal and perfect. Every seed bears fruit after its kind, and nothing is reaped which was not sowed. The distance between seed time and harvest, in the moral world, may not be quite so well defined or as clearly intelligible as in the physical, but there is a seed time, and there is a harvest time, and though ages may intervene, and neither he who ploughed nor he who sowed may reap in person, yet the harvest nevertheless will surely come; and as in the physical world there are century plants, so it may be in the moral world, and their fruitage is as certain in the one as in the other. The bloody harvest of Harper's Ferry was ripened by the heat and moisture of merciless bondage of more than two hundred years. That startling cry of alarm on the banks of the Potomac was but the answering back of the avenging angel to the midnight invasions of Christian slave-traders on the sleeping hamlets of Africa. The history of the African slave-trade furnishes many illustrations far more cruel and bloody.

Viewed thus broadly our subject is worthy of thoughtful and dispassionate consideration. It invites the study of the poet, scholar, philosopher and statesman. What the masters in natural science have done for man in the physical world, the masters of social science may yet do for him in the moral world. Science now tells us when storms are in the sky, and when and where their violence will be most felt. Why may we not yet know with equal certainty when storms are in the moral sky, and how to avoid their desolating force? But I can invite you to no such profound discussions. I am not the man, nor is this the occasion for such philosophical enquiry. Mine is the word of grateful memory to an old friend; to tell you what I knew of him—what I knew of his inner life—of what he did and what he attempted, and thus if possible to make the mainspring of his actions manifest and thereby give you a clearer view of his character and services.

It is said that next in value to the performance of great deeds ourselves, is the capacity to appreciate such when performed by others; to more than this I do not presume. Allow me one other personal word before I proceed. In the minds of some of the American people I was myself credited with an important agency in the John Brown raid. Governor Henry A. Wise was manifestly of that opinion. He was at the pains of having Mr. Buchanan send his Marshals to Rochester to invite me to acccompany them to Virginia. Fortunately I left town several hours previous to their arrival.

What ground there was for this distinguished consideration shall duly appear in the natural course of this lecture. I wish however to say just here that there was no foundation whatever for the charge that I in any wise urged or instigated John Brown to his dangerous work. I rejoice that it is my good fortune to have seen, not only the end of slavery, but to see the day when the whole truth can be told about this matter without prejudice to either the living or the dead. I shall however allow myself little prominence in these disclosures. Your interests, like mine, are in the all-commanding figure of the story, and to him I consecrate the hour. His zeal in the cause of my race was far greater than mine—it was the burning sun to my taper light—mine was bounded by time, his stretched away to the boundless shores of eternity. I could live for the slave, but he could die for him. The crown of martyrdom is high, far beyond the reach of ordinary mortals, and yet happily no special greatness or superior moral excellence is necessary to discern and in some measure appreciate a truly great soul. Cold, calculating and unspiritual as most of us are, we are not wholly insensible to real greatness; and when we are brought in contact with a man of commanding mold, towering high and alone above the millions, free from all conventional fetters, true to his own moral convictions, a "law unto himself," ready to suffer misconstruction, ignoring torture and death for what he believes to be right, we are compelled to do him homage.

In the stately shadow, in the sublime presence of such a soul I find myself standing to-night; and how to do it reverence, how to do it justice, how to honor the dead with due regard to the living, has been a matter of most anxious solicitude.

Much has been said of John Brown, much that is wise and beautiful, but in looking over what may be called the John Brown literature, I have been little assisted with material, and even less encouraged with any hope of success in treating the subject. Scholarship, genius and devotion have hastened with poetry and eloquence, story and song to this simple altar of human virtue, and have retired dissatisfied and distressed with the thinness and poverty of their offerings, as I shall with mine.

The difficulty in doing justice to the life and character of such a man is not altogether due to the quality of the zeal, or of the ability brought to the work, nor yet to any imperfections in the qualities of the man himself; the state of the moral atmosphere about us has much to do with it. The fault is not in our eyes, nor yet in the object, if under a murky sky we fail to discover the object. Wonderfully tenacious is the taint of a great wrong. The evil, as well as " the good that men do, lives after them." Slavery is indeed gone; but its long, black shadow yet falls broad and large over the face of the whole country. It is the old truth oft repeated, and never more fitly than now, "a prophet is without honor in his own country and among his own people." Though more than twenty years have rolled between us and the Harper's Ferry raid, though since then the armies of the nation have found it necessary to do on a large scale what John Brown attempted to do on a small one, and the great captain who fought his way through slavery has filled with honor the Presidential chair, we yet stand too near the days of slavery, and the life and times of John Brown, to see clearly the true martyr and hero that he was and rightly to estimate the value of the man and his works. Like the great and good of all ages—the men born in advance of their times, the men whose bleeding footprints attest the immense cost of reform, and show us the long and dreary spaces, between the luminous points in the progress of mankind,—this our noblest American hero must wait the polishing wheels of after-coming centuries to make his glory more manifest, and his worth more generally acknowledged. Such instances are abundant and familiar. If we go back four and twenty centuries, to the stately city of Athens, and search among her architectural splendor and her miracles of art for the Socrates of today, and as he stands in history, we shall find ourselves perplexed and disappointed. In Jerusalem Jesus himself was only the "carpenter's son"—a young man wonderfully destitute of worldly prudence—a pestilent fellow, "inexcusably and perpetually interfering in the world's business,"—"upsetting the tables of the money-changers"—preaching sedition, opposing the good old religion—"making himself greater than Abraham," and at the same time "keeping company" with very low people; but behold the change! He was a great miracle-worker, in his day, but time has worked for him a greater miracle than all his miracles, for now his name stands for all that is desirable in government, noble in life, orderly and beautiful in society. That which time has done for other great men of his class, that will time certainly do for John Brown. The brightest gems shine at first with subdued light, and the strongest characters are subject to the same limitations. Under the influence of adverse education and hereditary bias, few things are more difficult than to render impartial justice. Men hold up their hands to Heaven, and swear they will do justice, but what are oaths against prejudice and against inclination! In the face of high-sounding professions and affirmations we know well how hard it is for a Turk to do justice to a Christian, or for a Christian to do justice to a Jew. How hard for an Englishman to do justice to an Irishman, for an Irishman to do justice to an Englishman, harder still for an American tainted by slavery to do justice to the Negro or the Negro's friends. " John Brown," said the late Wm. H. Seward, " was justly hanged." " John Brown," said the late John A. Andrew, " was right." It is easy to perceive the sources of these two opposite judgments : the one was the verdict of slave-holding and panic-stricken Virginia, the other was the verdict of the best heart and brain of free old Massachusetts. One was the heated judgment of the passing and passionate hour, and the other was the calm, clear, unimpeachable judgment of the broad, illimitable future.

There is, however, one aspect of the present subject quite worthy of notice, for it makes the hero of Harper's Ferry in some degree an exception to the general rules to which I have just now adverted. Despite the hold which slavery had at that time on the country, despite the popular prejudice against the Negro, despite the shock which the first alarm occasioned, almost from the first John Brown received a large measure of sympathy and appreciation. New England recognized in him the spirit which brought the pilgrims to Plymouth rock and hailed him as a martyr and saint. True he had broken the law, true he had struck for a despised people, true he had crept upon his foe stealthily, like a wolf upon the fold, and had dealt his blow in the dark whilst his enemy slept, but with all this and more to disturb the moral sense, men discerned in him the greatest and best qualities known to human nature, and pronounced him "good." Many consented to his death, and then went home and taught their children to sing his praise as one whose " soul is marching on" through the realms of endless bliss. One element in explanation of this somewhat anomalous circumstance will probably be found in the troubled times which immediately succeeded, for " when judgments are abroad in the world, men learn righteousness."

The country had before this learned the value of Brown's heroic character. He had shown boundless courage and skill in dealing with the enemies of liberty in Kansas. With men so few, and means so small, and odds against him so great, no captain ever surpassed him in achievements, some of which seem almost beyond belief. With only eight men in that bitter war, he met, fought and captured Henry Clay Pate, with twenty-five well armed and mounted men. In this memorable encounter, he selected his ground so wisely, handled his men so skillfully, and attacked the enemy so vigorously, that they could neither run nor fight, and were therefore compelled to surrender to a force less than one-third of their own. With just thirty men on another important occasion during the same border war, he met and vanquished four hundred Missourians under the command of General Read. These men had come into the territory under an oath never to return to their homes till they had stamped out the last vestige of free State spirit in Kansas; but a brush with old Brown took this high conceit out of them, and they were glad to get off upon any terms, without stopping to stipulate. With less than one hundred men to defend the town of Lawrence, he offered to lead them and give battle to fourteen hundred men on the banks of the Waukerusia [Wakarusa] river, and was much vexed when his offer was refused by Gen. Jim Lane and others to whom the defense of the town was confided. Before leaving Kansas, he went into the border of Missouri, and liberated a dozen slaves in a single night, and, in spite of slave laws and marshals, he brought these people through a half dozen States, and landed them safely in Canada. With eighteen men this man shook the whole social fabric of Virginia. With eighteen men he overpowered a town of nearly three thousand souls. With these eighteen men he held that large community firmly in his grasp for thirty long hours. With these eighteen men he rallied in a single night fifty slaves to his standard, and made prisoners of an equal number of the slave-holding class. With these eighteen men he defied the power and bravery of a dozen of the best militia companies that Virginia could send against him. Now, when slavery struck, as it certainly did strike, at the life of the country, it was not the fault of John Brown that our rulers did not at first know how to deal with it. He had already shown us the weak side of the rebellion, had shown us where to strike and how. It was not from lack of native courage that Virginia submitted for thirty long hours and at last was relieved only by Federal troops; but because the attack was made on the side of her conscience and thus armed her against herself. She beheld at her side the sullen brow of a black Ireland. When John Brown proclaimed emancipation to the slaves of Maryland and Virginia he added to his war power the force of a moral earthquake. Virginia felt all her strong-ribbed mountains to shake under the heavy tread of armed insurgents. Of his army of nineteen her conscience made an army of nineteen hundred.

Another feature of the times, worthy of notice, was the effect of this blow upon the country at large. At the first moment we were stunned and bewildered. Slavery had so benumbed the moral sense of the nation, that it never suspected the possibility of an explosion like this, and it was difficult for Captain Brown to get himself taken for what he really was. Few could seem to comprehend that freedom to the slaves was his only object. If you will go back with me to that time you will find that the most curious and contradictory versions of the affair were industriously circulated, and those which were the least rational and true seemed to command the readiest belief. In the view of some, it assumed tremendous proportions. To such it was nothing less than a wide-sweeping rebellion to overthrow the existing government, and construct another upon its ruins, with Brown for its President and Commander-in-chief; the proof of this was found in the old man's carpet-bag in the shape of a constitution for a new Republic, an instrument which in reality had been executed to govern the conduct of his men in the mountains. Smaller and meaner natures saw in it nothing higher than a purpose to plunder. To them John Brown and his men were a gang of desperate robbers, who had learned by some means that government had sent a large sum of money to Harper's Ferry to pay off the workmen in its employ there, and they had gone thence to fill their pockets from this money. The fact is, that outside of a few friends, scattered in different parts of the country, and the slave-holders of Virginia, few persons understood the significance of the hour. That a man might do something very audacious and desperate for money, power or fame, was to the general apprehension quite possible; but, in face of plainly-written law, in face of constitutional guarantees protecting each State against domestic violence, in face of a nation of forty million of people, that nineteen men could invade a great State to liberate a despised and hated race, was to the average intellect and conscience, too monstrous for belief. In this respect the vision of Virginia was clearer than that of the nation. Conscious of her guilt and therefore full of suspicion, sleeping on pistols for pillows, startled at every unusual sound, constantly fearing and expecting a repetition of the Nat Turner insurrection, she at once understood the meaning, if not the magnitude of the affair. It was this understanding which caused her to raise the lusty and imploring cry to the Federal government for help, and it was not till he who struck the blow had fully explained his motives and object, that the incredulous nation in any wise comprehended the true spirit of the raid, or of its commander. Fortunate for his memory, fortunate for the brave men associated with him, fortunate for the truth of history, John Brown survived the saber gashes, bayonet wounds and bullet holes, and was able, though covered with blood, to tell his own story and make his own defense. Had he with all his men, as might have been the case, gone down in the shock of battle, the world would have had no true basis for its judgment, and one of the most heroic efforts ever witnessed in behalf of liberty would have been confounded with base and selfish purposes. When, like savages, the Wises, the Vallandinghams,[7] the Washingtons, the Stuarts and others stood around the fallen and bleeding hero, and sought by torturing questions to wring from his supposed dying lips some word by which to soil the sublime undertaking, by implicating Gerrit Smith, Joshua R. Giddings, Dr. S. G. Howe, G. L. Stearns, Edwin Morton, Frank Sanborn, and other prominent Anti-slavery men, the brave old man, not only avowed his object to be the emancipation of the slaves, but serenely and proudly announced himself as solely responsible for all that had happened. Though some thought of his own life might at such a moment have seemed natural and excusable, he showed none, and scornfully rejected the idea that he acted as the agent or instrument of any man or set of men. He admitted that he had friends and sympathizers, but to his own head he invited all the bolts of slave-holding wrath and fury, and welcomed them to do their worst. His manly courage and self-forgetful nobleness were not lost upon the crowd about him, nor upon the country. They drew applause from his bitterest enemies. Said Henry A. Wise, "He is the gamest man I ever met." "He was kind and humane to his prisoners," said Col. Lewis Washington.

To the outward eye of men, John Brown was a criminal, but to their inward eye he was a just man and true. His deeds might be disowned, but the spirit which made those deeds possible was worthy highest honor. It has been often asked, why did not Virginia spare the life of this man? why did she not avail herself of this grand opportunity to add to her other glory that of a lofty magnanimity? Had they spared the good old man's life—had they said to him, "You see we have you in our power, and could easily take your life, but we have no desire to hurt you in any way; you have committed a terrible crime against society; you have invaded us at

7 Vallandighams.

midnight and attacked a sleeping community, but we recognize you as a fanatic, and in some sense instigated by others; and on this ground and others, we release you. Go about your business, and tell those who sent you that we can afford to be magnanimous to our enemies." I say, had Virginia held some such language as this to John Brown, she would have inflicted a heavy blow on the whole Northern abolition movement, one which only the omnipotence of truth and the force of truth could have overcome. I have no doubt Gov. Wise would have done so gladly, but, alas, he was the executive of a State which thought she could not afford such magnanimity. She had that within her bosom which could more safely tolerate the presence of a criminal than a saint, a highway robber than a moral hero. All her hills and valleys were studded with material for a disastrous conflagration, and one spark of the dauntless spirit of Brown might set the whole State in flames. A sense of this appalling liability put an end to every noble consideration. His death was a foregone conclusion, and his trial was simply one of form.

Honor to the brave young Col. Hoyt who hastened from Massachusetts to defend his friend's life at the peril of his own; but there would have been no hope of success had he been allowed to plead the case. He might have surpassed Choate or Webster in power—a thousand physicians might have sworn that Capt. Brown was insane, it would have been all to no purpose; neither eloquence nor testimony could have prevailed. Slavery was the idol of Virginia, and pardon and life to Brown meant condemnation and death to slavery. He had practically illustrated a truth stranger than fiction—a truth higher than Virginia had ever known,—a truth more noble and beautiful than Jefferson ever wrote. He had evinced a conception of the sacredness and value of liberty which transcended in sublimity that of her own Patrick Henry and made even his fire-flashing sentiment of "Liberty or Death" seem dark and tame and selfish. Henry loved liberty for himself, but this man loved liberty for all men, and for those most despised and scorned, as well as for those most esteemed and honored. Just here was the true glory of John Brown's mission. It was not for his own freedom that he was thus ready to lay down his life, for with Paul he could say, "I was born free." No chain had bound his ankle, no yoke had galled his neck. History has no better illustration of pure, disinterested benevolence. It was not Caucasian for Caucasian—white man for white man; not rich man for rich man, but Caucasian for Ethiopian—white man for black man—rich man for poor man—the man admitted and respected, for the man despised and rejected. "I want you to understand, gentlemen," he said to his persecutors, "that I respect the rights of the poorest and weakest of the colored people, oppressed by the slave system, as I do those of the most wealthy and powerful." In this we have the key to the whole life and career of the man. Than in this sentiment humanity has nothing more touching, reason nothing more noble, imagination nothing more sublime; and if we could reduce all the religions of the world to one essence we could find in it nothing more divine. It is much to be regretted that some great artist, in sympathy with the spirit of the occasion, had not been present when these and similar words were spoken. The situation was thrilling. An old man in the center of an excited and angry crowd, far away from home, in an enemy's country—with no friend near—overpowered, defeated, wounded, bleeding—covered with reproaches—his brave companions nearly all dead—his two faithful sons stark and cold by his side—reading his death-warrant in his fast-oozing blood and increasing weakness as in the faces of all around him—yet calm, collected, brave, with a heart for any fate—using his supposed dying moments to explain his course and vindicate his cause; such a subject would have been at once an inspiration and a power for one of the grandest historical pictures ever painted. . . .

With John Brown, as with every other man fit to die for a cause, the hour of his physical weakness was the hour of his moral strength —the hour of his defeat was the hour of his triumph—the moment of his capture was the crowning victory of his life. With the Alleghany mountains for his pulpit, the country for his church and the whole civilized world for his audience, he was a thousand times more effective as a preacher than as a warrior, and the consciousness of this fact was the secret of his amazing complacency. Mighty with the sword of steel, he was mightier with the sword of truth, and with this sword he literally swept the horizon. He was more than a match for all the Wises, Masons, Vallandinghams and Washingtons, who could rise against him. They could kill him, but they could not answer him.

In studying the character and works of a great man, it is always desirable to learn in what he is distinguished from others, and what have been the causes of this difference. Such men as he whom we are now considering, come on to the theater of life only at long intervals. It is not always easy to explain the exact and logical causes that produce them, or the subtle influences which sustain them, at the immense hights where we sometimes find them; but we know that the hour and the man are seldom far apart, and that here, as elsewhere, the demand may in some mysterious way, regulate the supply. A great iniquity, hoary with age, proud and defiant, tainting the whole moral atmosphere of the country, subjecting both church and state to its control, demanded the startling shock which John Brown seemed especially inspired to give it.

Apart from this mission there was nothing very remarkable about him. He was a wool-dealer, and a good judge of wool, as a wool-dealer ought to be. In all visible respects he was a man like unto other men. No outward sign of Kansas or Harper's Ferry was about him. As I knew him, he was an even-tempered man, neither morose, malicious nor misanthropic, but kind, amiable, courteous, and gentle in his intercourse with men. His words were few, well chosen and forcible. He was a good business man, and a good neighbor. A good friend, a good citizen, a good husband and father: a man apparently in every way calculated to make a smooth and pleasant path for himself through the world. He loved society, he loved little children, he liked music, and was fond of animals. To no one was the world more beautiful or life more sweet. How then as I have said shall we explain his apparent indifference to life? I can find but one answer, and that is, his intense hatred to oppression. I have talked with many men, but I remember none, who seemed so deeply excited upon the subject of slavery as he. He would walk the room in agitation at mention of the word. He saw the evil through no mist or haze, but in a light of infinite brightness, which left no line of its ten thousand horrors out of sight. Law, religion, learning, were interposed in its behalf in vain. His law in regard to it was that which Lord Brougham described, as "the law above all the enactments of human codes, the same in all time, the same throughout the world—the law unchangeable and eternal—the law written by the finger of God on the human heart—that law by which property in man is, and ever must remain a wild and guilty phantasy."

Against truth and right, legislative enactments were to his mind mere cobwebs—the pompous emptiness of human pride—the pitiful outbreathings of human nothingness. He used to say "whenever there is a right thing to be done, there is a 'thus saith the Lord' that it shall be done."

It must be admitted that Brown assumed tremendous responsibility in making war upon the peaceful people of Harper's Ferry, but it must be remembered also that in his eye a slave-holding community could not be peaceable, but was, in the nature of the case, in one incessant state of war. To him such a community was not more sacred than a band of robbers: it was the right of any one to assault it by day or night. He saw no hope that slavery would ever be abolished by moral or political means: "he knew," he said, "the proud and hard hearts of the slave-holders, and that they never would consent to give up their slaves, till they felt a big stick about their heads."

It was five years before this event at Harper's Ferry, while the conflict between freedom and slavery was waxing hotter and hotter with every hour, that the blundering statesmanship of the National Government repealed the Missouri Compromise, and thus launched the territory of Kansas as a prize to be battled for between the North and the South. The remarkable part taken in this contest by Brown has been already referred to, and it doubtless helped to prepare him for the final tragedy, and though it did not by any means originate the plan, it confirmed him in it and hastened its execution.

During his four years' service in Kansas it was my good fortune to see him often. On his trips to and from the territory he sometimes stopped several days at my house, and at one time several weeks. It was on this last occasion that liberty had been victorious in Kansas, and he felt that he must hereafter devote himself to what he considered his larger work. It was the theme of all his conversation, filling his nights with dreams and his days with visions. An incident of his boyhood may explain, in some measure, the intense abhorrence he felt to slavery. He had for some reason been sent into the State of Kentucky,[8] where he made the acquaintance of a slave boy, about his own age, of whom he became very fond. For some petty offense this boy was one day subjected to a brutal beating. The blows were dealt with an iron shovel and fell fast and furiously upon his slender body. Born in a free State and unaccustomed to such scenes of cruelty, young Brown's pure and sensitive soul revolted at the shocking spectacle and at that early age he swore eternal hatred to slavery. After years never obliterated the impression, and he found in this early experience an argument against contempt for small things. It is true that the boy is the father of the man. From the acorn comes the oak. The impression of a horse's foot in the sand suggested the art of printing. The fall of an apple intimated the law of gravitation. A word dropped in the woods of

8 Emerson, see p. 297, gives Pennsylvania as the locale. The true locale, assuming that the incident is authentic, has never been determined.

Vincennes, by royal hunters, gave Europe and the world a "William the Silent," and a thirty years' War. The beating of a Hebrew bondsman, by an Egyptian, created a Moses, and the infliction of a similar outrage on a helpless slave boy in our own land may have caused, forty years afterwards, a John Brown and a Harper's Ferry Raid.

Most of us can remember some event or incident which has at some time come to us, and made itself a permanent part of our lives. Such an incident came to me in the year 1847. I had then the honor of spending a day and a night under the roof of a man, whose character and conversation made a very deep impression on my mind and heart; and as the circumstance does not lie entirely out of the range of our present observations, you will pardon for a moment a seeming digression. The name of the person alluded to had been several times mentioned to me, in a tone that made me curious to see him and to make his acquaintance. It was a merchant, and our first meeting was at his store—a substantial brick building, giving evidence of a flourishing business. After a few minutes' detention here, long enough for me to observe the neatness and order of the place, I was conducted by him to his residence where I was kindly received by his family as an expected guest. I was a little disappointed at the appearance of this man's house, for after seeing his fine store, I was prepared to see a fine residence; but this logic was entirely contradicted by the facts. The house was a small, wooden one, on a back street in a neighborhood of laboring men and mechanics, respectable enough, but not just the spot where one would expect to find the home of a successful merchant. Plain as was the outside, the inside was plainer. Its furniture might have pleased a Spartan. It would take longer to tell what was not in it, than what was; no sofas, no cushions, no curtains, no carpets, no easy rocking chairs inviting to enervation or rest or repose. My first meal passed under the misnomer of tea. It was none of your tea and toast sort, but potatoes and cabbage, and beef soup; such a meal as a man might relish after following the plough all day, or after performing a forced march of a dozen miles over rough ground in frosty weather. Innocent of paint, veneering, varnish or tablecloth, the table announced itself unmistakably and honestly pine and of the plainest workmanship. No hired help passed from kitchen to dining room, staring in amazement at the colored man at the white man's table. The mother, daughters and sons did the serving, and did it well. I heard no apology for doing their own work; they went through it as if used to it, untouched by any thought of degradation or impropriety. Supper over, the boys helped to clear the table and wash the dishes. This style of housekeeping struck me as a little odd. I mention it because household management is worthy of thought. A house is more than brick and mortar, wood or paint; this to me at least was. In its plainness it was a truthful reflection of its inmates: no disguises, no illusions, no make-believes here, but stern truth and solid purpose breathed in all its arrangements. I was not long in company with the master of this house before I discovered that he was indeed the master of it, and likely to become mine too, if I staid long with him. He fulfilled St. Paul's idea of the head of the family—his wife believed in him, and his children observed him with reverence. Whenever he spoke, his words commanded earnest attention. His arguments which I ventured at some points to oppose, seemed to convince all, his appeals touched all, and his will impressed all. Certainly I never felt myself in the presence of a stronger religious influence than while in this house. "God and duty, God and duty," run like a thread of gold through all his utterances, and his family supplied a ready "Amen." In person he was lean and sinewy, of the best new England mould, built for times of trouble, fitted to grapple with the flintiest hardships. Clad in plain American woolen, shod in boots of cowhide leather, and wearing a cravat of the same substantial material, under six feet high, less than one hundred and fifty lbs. in weight, aged about fifty, he presented a figure straight and symmetrical as a mountain pine. His bearing was singularly impressive. His head was not large, but compact and high. His hair was coarse, strong, slightly gray and closely trimmed and grew close to his forehead. His face was smoothly shaved and revealed a strong square mouth, supported by a broad and prominent chin. His eyes were clear and grey, and in conversation they alternated with tears and fire. When on the street, he moved with a long springing, race-horse step, absorbed by his own reflections, neither seeking nor shunning observation. Such was the man whose name I heard uttered in whispers—such was the house in which he lived—such were his family and household management—and such was Captain John Brown.

He said to me at this meeting, that he had invited me to his house for the especial purpose of laying before me his plan for the speedy emancipation of my race. He seemed to apprehend opposition on my part as he opened the subject and touched my vanity by saying, that he had observed my course at home and abroad, and wanted my co-operation. He said he had been for the last thirty years looking for colored men to whom he could safely reveal his secret, and had almost despaired, at times, of finding such, but that now he was encouraged for he saw heads rising up in all directions, to whom he thought he could with safety impart his plan. As this plan then lay in his mind it was very simple, and had much to commend it. It did not, as was supposed by many, contemplate a general rising among the slaves, and a general slaughter of the slave masters (an insurrection he thought would only defeat the object), but it did contemplate the creating of an armed force which should act in the very heart of the South. He was not averse to the shedding of blood, and thought the practice of carrying arms would be a good one for the colored people to adopt, as it would give them a sense of manhood. No people he said could have self-respect or be respected who would not fight for their freedom. He called my attention to a large map of the U. States, and pointed out to me the far-reaching Alleghanies, stretching away from the borders of New York into the Southern States. "These mountains," he said, "are the basis of my plan. God has given the strength of these hills to freedom; they were placed here to aid the emancipation of your race; they are full of natural forts, where one man for defense would be equal to a hundred for attack; they are also full of good hiding places where a large number of men could be concealed and baffle and elude pursuit for a long time. I know these mountains well and could take a body of men into them and keep them there in spite of all the efforts of Virginia to dislodge me, and drive me out. I would take at first about twenty-five picked men and begin on a small scale, supply them arms and ammunition, post them in squads of fives on a line of twenty-five miles, these squads to busy themselves for a time in gathering recruits from the surrounding farms, seeking and selecting the most restless and daring." He saw that in this part of the work the utmost care must be used to guard against treachery and disclosure; only the most conscientious and skillful should be sent on this perilous duty. With care and enterprise he thought he could soon gather a force of one hundred hardy men, men who would be content to lead the free and adventurous life to which he proposed to train them. When once properly drilled and each had found the place for which he was best suited, they would begin work in earnest; they would run off the slaves in large numbers, retain the strong and brave ones in the mountains, and send the weak and timid ones to the North by the underground Rail-road; his operations would be enlarged with increasing numbers and would not be confined to one locality. Slave-holders should in some cases be approached at midnight and told to give up their slaves and to let them have their best horses to ride away upon. Slavery was a state of war, he said, to which the slaves were unwilling parties and consequently they had a right to anything necessary to their peace and freedom. He would shed no blood and would avoid a fight except in self-defense, when he would of course do his best. He believed this movement would weaken slavery in two ways—first by making slave property insecure, it would become undesirable; and secondly it would keep the anti-slavery agitation alive and public attention fixed upon it, and thus lead to the adoption of measures to abolish the evil altogether. He held that there was need of something startling to prevent the agitation of the question from dying out; that slavery had come near being abolished in Virginia by the Nat. Turner insurrection, and he thought his method would speedily put an end to it, both in Maryland and Virginia. The trouble was to get the right men to start with and money to equip them. He had adopted the simple and economical mode of living to which I have referred with a view to save money for this purpose. This was said in no boastful tone, for he felt that he had delayed already too long and had no room to boast either his zeal or his self-denial.

From 8 o'clock in the evening till 3 in the morning, Capt. Brown and I sat fact to face, he arguing in favor of his plan, and I finding all the objections I could against it. Now mark! this meeting of ours was full twelve years before the strike at Harper's Ferry. He had been watching and waiting all that time for suitable heads to rise or "pop up" as he said among the sable millions in whom he could confide; hence forty years had passed between his thought and his act. Forty years, though not a long time in the life of a nation, is a long time in the life of a man; and here forty long years, this man was struggling with this one idea; like Moses he was forty years in the wilderness. Youth, manhood, middle age had come and gone; two marriages had been consummated, twenty children had called him father; and through all the storms and vicissitudes of busy life, this one thought, like the angel in the burning bush, had confronted him with its blazing light, bidding him on to his work. Like Moses he had made excuses, and as with Moses his excuses were overruled. Nothing should postpone further what was to him a divine command, the performance of which seemed to him his only apology for existence. He often said to me, though life was sweet to him, he would willingly lay it down for the freedom of my people; and on one occasion he added, that he had already lived about as long as most men, since he had slept less, and if he should now lay down his life the loss would not be great, for in fact he knew no better use for it. During his last visit to us in Rochester there appeared in the newspapers a touching story connected with the horrors of the Sepoy War in British India. A Scotch missionary and his family were in the hands of the enemy, and were to be massacred the next morning. During the night, when they had given up every hope of rescue, suddenly the wife insisted that relief would come. Placing her ear close to the ground she declared she heard the Slogan—the Scotch war song. For long hours in the night no member of the family could hear the advancing music but herself. " Dinna ye hear it? Dinna ye hear it? " she would say, but they could not hear it. As the morning slowly dawned a Scotch regiment was found encamped indeed about them, and they were saved from the threatened slaughter. This circumstance, coming at such a time, gave Capt. Brown a new word of cheer. He would come to the table in the morning his countenance fairly illuminated, saying that he had heard the Slogan, and he would add, " Dinna ye hear it? " " *Dinna* ye hear it? " Alas! like the Scotch missionary I was obliged to say " No." Two weeks prior to the meditated attack, Capt. Brown summoned me to meet him in an old stone quarry on the Conecochequi[9] river, near the town of Chambersburg, Penn.[10] His arms and ammunition were stored in that town and were to be moved on to Harper's Ferry. In company with Shields Green I obeyed the summons, and prompt to the hour we met the dear old man, with Kagi, his secretary, at the appointed place. Our meeting was in some sense a council of war. We spent the Saturday and succeeding Sunday in conference on the question, whether the desperate step should then be taken, or the old plan as already described should be carried out. He was for boldly striking Harper's Ferry at once and running the risk of getting into the mountains afterwards. I was for avoiding Harper's Ferry altogether. Shields Green and Mr. Kagi remained silent listeners throughout. It is needless to repeat here what was said, after what has happened. Suffice it, that after all I could say, I saw that my old friend had resolved on his course and that it was idle to parley. I told him finally that it was impossible

9 Conococheague.
10 Frederick Douglass and Shields Green met Henry Watson, a barber in Chambersburg, who directed them to the old rock quarry. They were particularly cautious in approaching the place because Brown and his party were heavily armed. Douglass made a speech at Chambersburg while there on this occasion. See *Life and Times of Frederick Douglass.* Written by Himself (New York: Pathway Press, 1941), p. 351.

for me to join him. I could see Harper's Ferry only as a trap of steel, and ourselves in the wrong side of it. He regretted my decision and we parted.

Thus far, I have spoken exclusively of Capt. Brown. Let me say a word or two of his brave and devoted men, and first of Shields Green. He was a fugitive slave from Charleston, South Carolina, and had attested his love of liberty by escaping from slavery and making his way through many dangers to Rochester, where he had lived in my family, and where he met the man with whom he went to the scaffold. I said to him, as I was about to leave, "Now Shields, you have heard our discussion. If in view of it, you do not wish to stay, you have but to say so, and you can go back with me." He answered, "I b'l'eve I'll go wid de old man;" and go with him he did, into the fight, and to the gallows, and bore himself as grandly as any of the number. At the moment when Capt. Brown was surrounded, and all chance of escape was cut off, Green was in the mountains and could have made his escape as Osborne Anderson did, but when asked to do so, he made the same answer he did at Chamberburg, "I b'l'eve I'll go down wid de ole man." When in prison at Charlestown, and he was not allowed to see his old friend, his fidelity to him was in no wise weakened, and no complaint against Brown could be extorted from him by those who talked with him.

If a monument should be erected to the memory of John Brown, as there ought to be, the form and name of Shields Green should have a conspicuous place upon it. It is a remarkable fact, that in this small company of men, but one showed any sign of weakness or regret for what he did or attempted to do. Poor Cook broke down and sought to save his life by representing that he had been deceived, and allured by false promises. But Stephens, Hazlett and Green went to their doom like the heroes they were, without a murmur, without a regret, believing alike in their captain and their cause.

For the disastrous termination of this invasion, several causes have been assigned. It has been said that Capt. Brown found it necessary to strike before he was ready; that men had promised to join him from the North who failed to arrive; that the cowardly negroes did not rally to his support as he expected, but the true cause as stated by himself, contradicts all these theories, and from his statement there is no appeal. Among the questions put to him by Mr. Vallandingham after his capture were the following: "Did you expect a general uprising of the slaves in case of your success?" To this he answered, "No, sir, nor did I wish it. I expected to gather strength from time to time and then to set them free." "Did you expect to hold possession here until then?" Answer, "Well, probably I had quite a different idea. I do not know as I ought to reveal my plans. I am here wounded and a prisoner because I foolishly permitted myself to be so. You overstate your strength when you suppose I could have been taken if I had not allowed it. I was too tardy after commencing the open attack in delaying my movements through Monday night and up to the time of the arrival of government troops. It was all because of my desire to spare the feelings of my prisoners and their families."

But the question is, Did John Brown fail? He certainly did fail to get out of Harper's Ferry before being beaten down by United States soldiers; he did fail to save his own life, and to lead a liberating army into the mountains of Virginia. But he did not go to Harper's Ferry to save his life. The true question is, Did John Brown draw his sword against slavery and thereby lose his life in vain? and to this I answer ten thousand times, No! No man fails, or can fail who so grandly gives himself and all he has to a righteous cause. No man, who in his hour of extremest need, when on his way to meet an ignominious death, could so forget himself as to stop and kiss a little child, one of the hated race for whom he was about to die, could by any possibility fail. Did John Brown fail? Ask Henry A. Wise in whose house less than two years after, a school for the emancipated slaves was taught. Did John Brown fail? Ask James M. Mason, the author of the inhuman fugitive slave bill, who was cooped up in Fort Warren, as a traitor less than two years from the time that he stood over the prostrate body of John Brown. Did John Brown fail? Ask Clement C. Vallandingham, one other of the inquisitorial party; for he too went down in the tremendous whirlpool created by the powerful hand of this bold invader. If John Brown did not end the war that ended slavery, he did at least begin the war that ended slavery. If we look over the dates, places and men, for which this honor is claimed, we shall find that not Carolina, but Virginia—not Fort Sumpter [Sumter], but Harper's Ferry and the arsenal—not Col. Anderson, but John Brown, began the war that ended American slavery and made this a free Republic. Until this blow was struck, the prospect for freedom was dim, shadowy and uncertain. The irrepressible conflict was one of words, votes and compromises. When John Brown stretched forth his arm the sky was cleared. The time for compromises was gone—the armed hosts of freedom stood face to face over the chasm of a broken Union—and the clash of arms was at hand. The South staked all upon getting possession of the Federal Government, and failing to do that, drew the sword of rebellion and thus made her own, and not Brown's, the lost cause of the century.

GUIDE TO PART ONE

THE LETTERS AND OTHER WRITINGS
OF JOHN BROWN

To *Henry L. Stearns, July 15, 1857*. From a photostat of the original letter provided by Mrs. Charles L. Stover, of Ardsley-on-Hudson, New York.

To *Dear Father, August 11, 1832, Randolph, Pa*. From a copy owned by Dr. Clarence S. Gee, of Lockport, New York.

To *Dear Brother, November 21, 1834, Randolph, Pa*. From Franklin B. Sanborn, *The Life and Letters of John Brown*, London: 1885, pp. 40-41.

To *Dear Wife and Children, December 5, 1838, New York*. From the original, owned by Mr. Boyd B. Stutler, Charleston, West Virginia.

To *My Dear Wife and Children, June 12, 1839, New Hartford*. From a copy in the Sanborn Folder, Houghton Library, Harvard University.

To *My Dear Wife and Children, June 19, 1839, Winchester, Conn*. From a copy in the Sanborn Folder, Houghton Library, Harvard University.

To *George Kellogg, Esqr., August 27, 1839, Franklin Mills*. From a photostat in the Library of Congress.

To *My Dear Wife & Children, April 27, 1840, Tyler Co., Virginia*. From the original, owned by the Henry E. Huntington Library, San Marino, California, with whose permission it is reproduced.

To *Dear Son John, January 18, 1841, Hudson*. From the original, owned by the Ohio Historical Society.

Agreement with George Kellogg, October 17, 1842, Richfield. From Franklin B. Sanborn, *The Life and Letters of John Brown*, Boston: Roberts Brothers, 1885, pp. 55-56.

To *George Kellogg, Esq., October 17, 1842, Richfield, Summit County, Ohio*. From Sanborn, *John Brown*, p. 56.

Agreement with Heman Oviatt, October 29, 1842, Richfield. From the original, owned by the Western Reserve Historical Society, Cleveland, Ohio.

To *Dear Son, September 25, 1843, Richfield*. From the original, owned by the Illinois State Historical Society, Springfield.

Agreement—John Brown & Simon Perkins, January 9, 1844. From a copy in the Sanborn Folder, Houghton Library, Harvard University.

To *Dear Son, January 11, 1844, Richfield*. From the original, owned by the Ohio Historical Society.

To *Dear Son John, May 23, 1845, Akron*. From the original, owned by the Massachusetts Historical Society.

To *Friend Perkins, July 23, 1846, Springfield, Mass*. From the original, owned by the Yale University Library, New Haven, Connecticut.

To *My Dear Afflicted Wife & Children, November 8, 1846, Springfield*. From Oswald Garrison Villard, *John Brown, 1800-1859: A Biography Fifty Years After*, New York: Alfred A. Knopf, 1943, pp. 35-36.

To *Dear Mary, November 29, 1846, Springfield.* From the original, owned by Mr. Boyd B. Stutler. The letter printed in part in Sanborn, *John Brown,* p. 142, is erroneously dated.

To *Dear Daughter Ruth, January 5, 1847, Springfield, Mass.* From a copy in the Oswald Garrison Villard Collection of John Brown materials, Columbia University Library, New York City.

To *My Dear Mary, March 7, 1847, Springfield, Mass.* From the original, owned by Mr. Boyd B. Stutler.

To *Dear Father, April 2, 1847, Springfield, Mass.* From the original, owned by Mr. Boyd B. Stutler. The signature is clipped from the original.

Sambo's Mistakes. From the original, owned by the Maryland Historical Society, Baltimore, Maryland.

To *Dear Father, January 16, 1848, Springfield, Mass.* From Sanborn, *John Brown,* pp. 24-25.

To *Hon. J. R. Giddings, June 22, 1848, Springfield, Mass.* From a copy in the Villard Collection, Columbia University Library. The original is owned by Mr. Ned Williams, Ashtabula, Ohio.

To *Hon. Joshua R. Giddings, September 7, 1848, Springfield, Mass.* From a copy in the Villard Collection, Columbia University Library.

To *Dear Father, January 10, 1849, Springfield, Mass.* From the original, owned by the Kansas State Historical Society, Topeka, Kansas.

To *Friend Perkins, May 24, 1849, Springfield, Mass.* From the original, owned by Mr. Boyd B. Stutler.

To *Simon Perkins Esqr., August 15, 1849, Boston.* From the original, owned by the Rush Rhees Library, University of Rochester, New York.

To *Dear Son John, August 29, 1849, London.* From Sanborn, *John Brown,* p. 72.

To *Simon Perkins Esqr., October 1849, London.* From the original, owned by the Yale University Library.

To *Dear Son John and Wife, April 12, 1850, Burgettstown, Penn.* From Sanborn, *John Brown,* p. 74.

To *Dear Wife, November 28, 1850, Springfield, Mass.* From a copy in the Sanborn Folder, Houghton Library, Harvard University.

To *Dear Sons John, Jason & Frederick, & Daughters, December 4, 1850, Springfield, Mass.* From the original, owned by the Ohio Historical Society.

To *Dear Wife, January 17, 1851, Springfield, Mass.* From Sanborn, *John Brown,* p. 132.

Words of Advice. Branch of the United States League of Gileadites. Adopted Jan. 15, 1851, as written and recommended by John Brown. From Sanborn, *John Brown,* pp. 124-126. It is also printed, with slight variations, in Wm. Wells Brown, "John Brown and the Fugitive Slave Law," *The New York Independent,* March 10, 1870, p. 6.

To *Dear Mary, December 22, 1851, Boston, Mass.* From a copy in the Sanborn Folder, Houghton Library, Harvard University.

To *Dear Children, January 23, 1852, Troy, N.Y.* From the original, owned by the Chicago Historical Society, Chicago, Illinois.

To *Dear Children, June 30, 1853, Akron, Ohio.* From Sanborn, *John Brown,* pp. 109-110.

To *Dear Son John, August 26, 1853, Akron, Ohio.* From Sanborn, *John Brown,* pp. 45-51. The original is owned by Mr. Boyd B. Stutler.

To *F. Douglass, Esqr., Dear Sir: January 9, 1854, Akron, O.* From *Frederick Douglass' Paper* (Rochester, N.Y.), January 27, 1854, p. 3. I am indebted to Mr. Stutler for a photostat of the essay.

To *John Brown, Jr., August 21, 1854, Akron.* From Sanborn, *John Brown,* p. 191. (Sanborn does not indicate if this portion is from the beginning or the end of the letter.)

To *Dear Children, September 30, 1854, Akron, Ohio.* From the original, owned by the Western Reserve Historical Society, Cleveland, Ohio.

To *Dear Children, November 2, 1854, Akron.* From Sanborn, *John Brown,* pp. 110-111.

To *Dear Father, October 19, 1855, Brownsville, Kansas Territory.* From the original, owned by Dr. Clarence S. Gee.

To *Editor of Summit Beacon, December 20, 1855, Osawatomie, Kansas Territory.* Published in the *Summit Beacon,* Akron, Ohio (now Akron *Beacon-Journal*), in early 1856, exact date not known. This letter was later reprinted in *Peterson Magazine,* in an essay by Will M. Clemens, " John Brown, American Reformer," VIII (March, 1898), 216-218. I am indebted to Mr. Boyd B. Stutler for this information and for a photostat of the letter as it appeared in *Peterson Magazine.*

To *Dear Wife & Children every one, February 1, 1856, Osawatomie, Kansas Territory.* From the original, owned by the Kansas State Historical Society.

To *Dear Wife and Children, every one, June, 1856, Near Brown's Station, K. T.* From Sanborn, *John Brown,* pp. 236-241.

To *Dear Wife & Children, every one, July 4, 1856, Topeka, Kansas Ter.* From the original, owned by the Illinois State Historical Society.

To *Dear Wife & Children every one, September 7, 1856, Lawrence, K. T.* From the original, owned by the Kansas State Historical Society.

Speech delivered in Lawrence, on September 13, 1856. From Sanborn, *John Brown,* p. 335.

To *Dear Wife & Children every one, October 11, 1856, Tabor, Iowa.* From the original, owned by Mr. Boyd B. Stutler.

Part of a speech. Begins, " I am trying to raise . . ." From Sanborn, *John Brown,* p. 379.

To the Friends of Freedom, from the New York *Tribune,* March 4, 1857.

To *Dear Wife, March 31, 1857, Springfield, Mass.* From the original, owned by Mr. Boyd B. Stutler.

Inscription in Bible given to his daughter, Ellen. From Thomas Wentworth Higginson, *Contemporaries,* Boston and New York: Houghton Mifflin Company, 1899, p. 237.

To *Wm Barnes Esqr, April 3, 1857, Boston, Mass.* From a copy in the Villard Collection, Columbia University Library.

To *Dear Son John, April 15, 1857, West Newton, Mass.* From the original, owned by Mr. Boyd B. Stutler.

Old Browns Farewell to the Plymouth Rocks . . . ., Boston, April, 1857. From the original, owned by the Kansas State Historical Society. Other copies in John Brown's hand are owned by the Chicago Historical Society and Mr. Boyd B. Stutler.

To *Dear Wife and Children every one, May 27, 1857, Hudson, Ohio*. From Sanborn, *John Brown*, pp. 410-411.

To *Franklin B. Sanborn, August 13, 1857, Tabor, Fremont County, Iowa*. From Sanborn, *John Brown*, pp. 412-414.

To *My Dear Wife and Children, every one, January 30, 1858, Rochester, N. Y.* From Sanborn, *John Brown*, pp. 440-441.

To *My Dear Sir* (Thomas Wentworth Higginson), *February 12, 1858, Rochester, N. Y.* From Thomas Wentworth Higginson, *Cheerful Yesterdays*, Boston and New York: Houghton Mifflin Company, 1898, p. 218.

Provisional Constitution and Ordinances for the People of the United States. From the *Mason Report*, Report of the Select Committee on Harper's Ferry Invasion, U. S. Senate, Rep. Com. No. 278, 36th Congress, 1st Session, "Testimony," pp. 48-59.

Old Brown's Parallels. Correspondence of the *N. Y. Tribune.* January, 1859, Trading Post, Kansas. From the New York Daily *Tribune*, January 22, 1859.

To *My Dear Daughter Ellen, May 13, 1859, Boston, Mass.* From the original, owned by Mr. Boyd B. Stutler.

To *Dear Wife & Children All, September, 1859, Chambersburg, Pa.* From the original, owned by Mr. Boyd B. Stutler.

Interview of Brown after his capture. The original text of this interview appeared in the New York *Herald*, on October 21, 1859, and was reprinted with the omission of the first two paragraphs and additional minor omissions by Sanborn, *John Brown*, pp. 562-569. The text used in this book consists of the first two paragraphs from the *Herald* and the remainder from Sanborn.

John Brown's last speech to the Court, November 2, 1859. From *Old South Leaflets*, Boston, Directors of the Old South Work, IV (No. 84), 16-17.

To *Hon. Thos. Russell, October 21, 1859, Charlestown, Jefferson County, Va.* From the original, owned by the Kansas State Historical Society.

To *My dear Wife, and Children every one, October 31, 1859.* From the original owned by Mr. Boyd B. Stutler.

To *My Dear Friend E. B. of R. I., November 1, 1859.* From Sanborn, *John Brown*, pp. 582-583.

To *Rev. T. W. Higginson, November 4, 1859.* From a photograph owned by Mr. Boyd B. Stutler. The photograph was made by Sanborn and presented to William E. Connelley, April 6, 1913. The location of the original letter is unknown.

To *Mrs. L. Maria Child, November 4, 1859.* From the original, owned by Mr. Boyd B. Stutler.

To *Dear Wife and Children every one, November 8, 1859.* From Sanborn, *John Brown*, pp. 585-587.

To *Dear Brother Jeremiah, November 12, 1859.* From Sanborn, *John Brown*, p. 588.

To *Rev. H. L. Vaill, November 15, 1859.* From the original, owned by Mr. Dudley L. Vaill, Jr., of Albany, New York.

To *My Dear Wife, November 16, 1859.* From a copy in the Villard Collection, Columbia University Library.

To *J. B. Musgrave, Esqr., November 17, 1859.* From the original, owned by Mrs. Henry M. Sage, of Albany, New York.

To *Rev. Luther Humphrey, November 19, 1859*. From the original, owned by Storer College, Harpers Ferry, West Virginia.

To *My Dear Wife, November 21, 1859*. From Sanborn, *John Brown*, pp. 295-296.

To *Dear Children, All, November 22, 1859*. From Sanborn, *John Brown*, pp. 596-597.

To *Dear Children, November 22, 1859*. From Sanborn, *John Brown*, pp. 597-598.

To *Dear Sir* (Andrew Hunter, Esq.), *November 22, 1859*. From *Mason Report*, Report of the Select Committee of the Senate appointed to inquire into the late invasion and seizure of the public property at Harper's Ferry. Report Com. No. 278, 36th Congress, 1st Session, "Testimony," pp. 67-68.

To *Rev. T. W. Higginson, November 22, 1859*. From the original, in the Boston Public Library. Courtesy of the Trustees of the Boston Public Library.

To *Rev. McFarland, November 23, 1859*. From James Redpath, *The Public Life of Capt. John Brown*, Boston : Thayer and Eldridge, 1860, p. 359.

To *My Dear Mrs. Spring, November 24, 1859*. From Sanborn, *John Brown*, pp. 599-601.

To *Rev. Heman Humphrey, D.D., November 25, 1859*. From Sanborn, *John Brown*, pp. 603-605.

To *My dear Wife, November 26, 1859*. From a copy in the Villard Collection, Columbia University Library.

To *My dearly beloved Sisters Mary A. & Martha, November 27, 1859*. From the original, owned by the Chicago Historical Society.

To *Hon. D. R. Tilden, November 28, 1859*. From Redpath, *The Public Life of Capt. John Brown*, pp. 363-364.

To *Mrs. George L. Stearns, November 29, 1859*. From Villard, *John Brown*, p. 551.

To *S. E. Sewall, November 29, 1859*. From Redpath, *The Public Life of Capt. John Brown*, p. 364.

To *My Dearly beloved Wife, Sons: & Daughters, every one, November 30, 1859*. From the original, owned by the Historical Society of Pennsylvania, Philadelphia.

To *My Dear Sir* (Mr. Lora Case), *December 2, 1859*. From the original, in the Henry W. and Albert A. Berg Collection of the New York Public Library.

Statement. "I John Brown am now. . . ." *December 2, 1859*. From the original, owned by Chicago Historical Society.

GUIDE TO PART TWO

THE WORDS OF THOSE WHO KNEW HIM

James Foreman to James Redpath, December 28, 1859, Youngsville, Warren Co., Pa. From the original, owned by the Kansas State Historical Society. A portion of an address by George B. Delamater, delivered at Meadville, Pa. The date of this address is unknown. A copy was given the writer by Mr. Boyd B. Stutler, from a copy made by Miss Katherine Mayo, assistant and secretary to Oswald Garrison Villard. Miss Mayo's copy, which is in the Villard Collection at Columbia University, was made in 1908 from a copy in the possession of Mrs. Ruth Brown Thompson, John Brown's daughter, of Pasadena, California. A second speech by Mr. Delamater appeared in the *Tribune Republican*, of Meadville, Pa., on May 11, 1888.

The reminiscences of John Brown, Jr. From Franklin B. Sanborn, *The Life and Letters of John Brown*, Boston: Roberts Brothers, 1885, pp. 91-93.

The reminiscences of Ruth Brown Thompson. From Sanborn, *John Brown*, pp. 93-95, 37, and 37-38, respectively.

The reminiscence of The Rev. Edward Brown, concerning John Brown's anti-slavery vow at a public meeting in Hudson, Ohio, in November, 1837. From *The Nation*, XCVIII (February 12, 1914), 157.

John Brown, Jr. writes of his father's opposition to racial segregation in church. From Sanborn, *John Brown*, pp. 52-53.

Salmon Brown, " My Father, John Brown." From *The Outlook*, CIII (January 25, 1913), 212-217.

Salmon Brown, "John Brown and Sons in Kansas Territory." From the Indiana Magazine of History, XXXI (June, 1935), 142-150.

James Townsley gives his view of the Pottawatomie killings. From the Lawrence (Kansas) *Daily Journal*, December 10, 1879. The editorial explanation accompanied the original article.

An interview with Geo. W. Grant and H. C. Grant, concerning the Pottawatomie killings. From the Lawrence *Daily Journal* of December 5, 1879.

W. A. Phillips, "Three Interviews with Old John Brown," *Atlantic Monthly*, XLIV (December, 1879), 738-744

Thomas Wentworth Higginson, "A Visit to John Brown's Household in 1859." In James Redpath, *The Public Life of Capt. John Brown*, pp. 60-72; reprinted in T. W. Higginson, *Contemporaries*, Boston and New York: Houghton Mifflin Company, 1899, pp. 219-243.

George B. Gill to Richard J. Hinton. Letter dated July 7, 1893, Milan, Sumner Co., Kansas. From the original owned by the Kansas State Historical Society.

Miss Katherine Mayo interviews Mrs. Thomas Russell. From the New York *Evening Post*, October 23, 1909. Title, "Brown in Hiding and in Jail."

Osborn Perry Anderson, *A Voice from Harper's Ferry*, Boston, 1861, pp. 23-24, 24-25, 28-29.

John G. Rosengarten, "John Brown's Raid: How I Got into It, and How I Got out of It," *Atlantic Monthly*, XV (June, 1865), 711-717.

Letter from Theodore Parker to Francis Jackson, Rome, November 24, 1859. From *The Collected Works of Theodore Parker*, Frances Power Cobbe, Ed., London: Trubnepy Co., XII, 164-177.

Wendell Phillips, "Burial of John Brown." From *Speeches and Lectures*, Boston: Lee and Shepard, 1863, First Series, pp. 289-293.

Ralph Waldo Emerson, "John Brown." From *Emerson's Complete Works*, Boston and New York: Houghton Mifflin Company, 1878 and 1883, XI, 257-263.

Henry David Thoreau, "The Last Days of John Brown." From *The Writings of Henry David Thoreau*, Boston and New York: 1894, X, 237-248.

"John Brown," as transcribed by Fanny Marshall in 1862. Poem by Rev. William W. Patton. From the New York *Independent*, LXIX (July 21, 1910), 116.

Oliver Wendell Holmes. A selection from "Two Poems to Harriet Beecher Stowe," on her Seventieth Birthday, June 14, 1882, in *Complete Poetical Works*, Boston: Houghton Mifflin Company, 1900, III, 129.

Frederick Douglass, "John Brown." From a pamphlet entitled *John Brown*. An address by Frederick Douglass, at the fourteenth anniversary of Storer College, Harper's Ferry, West Virginia, May 30, 1881. Dover, N. H.: Morning Star Job Printing House, 1881, 28 pp.

INDEX

INDEX

313